Real U Case Files

List Of True Crime Mysterious Stories

RACHEL HUDSON

Real Unsolved Case Files

Copyright © 2020 Rachel Hudson.

All rights reserved.

ISBN: 9798690143367

As time goes on, these cases get colder and colder and the shroud of mystery thicker.

Real Unsolved Case Files

CONTENTS

1 The Killing of FBI Informant Susan Daniels Smith   1
2 Accident or Murder   30
3 Double Murder on Robins Air Force Base   52
4 The Murder of Cheryl Fergeson   74
5 The Murder of Katie Autry   103
6 Mark Barton The Spree Killer   132
7 Boney & Claude   150
8 The Novack Murders   178
ABOUT THE AUTHOR   235

Real Unsolved Case Files

1 THE KILLING OF FBI INFORMANT SUSAN DANIELS SMITH

In 1987, an ambitious new FBI agent was assigned to his first field office in Pikeville, Kentucky. Pikeville is a small town in a holler next to the poverty stricken Hills for almost everyone was on welfare. Meth was rampant and the teen pregnancy rate was among the highest in the country. The post was pretty dismal and Mark Putnam was disappointed.

But determined to make a name for himself and do a good job. He brought his wife, Kathy and his young daughter with him, drugs, political crime option, and even bank robberies plagued the area. An agent could sit and cool his Hills waiting for his next post, or he could roll up the sleeves and make the best of it.

Mark made the best of it. He was soon introduced to an FBI informant in the area. A mountain girl named Susan Daniel Smith. Susan had the reputation of a drug addict with a big mouth, but she had come through for the FBI before she could be a pain in the ass, but she had good information on the criminal activity in the area.

Susan also got really close to Mark's wife, Kathy, who also made herself an extremely valuable asset to Mark during their time in Kentucky. She practically worked for the FBI without pay and

Susan and Mark worked well together. A little too well. She developed a sexual obsession with a handsome young FBI agent.

Neither of them could have guessed the deadly collision course their lives were set on in those lonely desolate Hills.

Pikeville a small town in Eastern Kentucky, at least in the 1980s, when our story takes place was as grim as I described in the opening nestled in a Valley in the Appalachian mountains between two rivers, the Lavasa fork and tug fork, the beautiful landscape had first been pillaged of its majestic hardwood forest after the civil war by timber barons.

But the land was also rich with minerals and other natural resources. So not long after the temper barons came, the coal barons, coal mining strip, the bleak mountains, even more broken trees, chunks of coal and rock littered. The Hills surrounding Pikeville, soon, Appalachian people and Kentucky and all over the South were exploited for cheap labor poverty became ubiquitous with coal mining and the divide between the people of the area was evident.

The rich lived in small towns while the poor lived in the Hills. It's where we get the term hillbilly. The small town of Pikeville had 4,500 residents in 1987 and they were proud of people. Maybe it's because this is McCoy country. As in the Hatfields and McCoys, I'm sure American listeners know exactly who I'm referring to, but just in case, I'll give you a quick rundown.

The two families lived in and around tug fork, a tributary where Kentucky, Virginia, and West Virginia meet. The McCoys were on the Kentucky side and the Hatfield's we're on the West Virginia side, the patriarchs of these clans were William Anderson, Hatfield, better known as devil ants and Randolph McCoy known as old Randall.

Both families fought for the Confederacy in the civil war, except for one McCoy who fought for the union and was murdered on his way home. There was no proof, but the McCoys were certain that a Hatfield had a hand in it. Early feuds won over ownership of a pig. Turn the families into bitter rivals. There was a Romeo and Juliet romance between Johnsy Hatfield and Rosanna McCoy that caused further bloodshed after Johnsy abandoned the pregnant Rosanna, marrying her cousin over a dozen people from both families were killed between 1880 and 1891.

But the culmination of the war between the families was the new year's night massacre in 1888. Members of the Hatfield clan, surrounded Randolph McCoy's cabin. They opened fire on the sleeping family and then said the cabin of flame, trying to flush out all Randall, the Hatfield and McCoy war lasted into the early 20th century.

In 2003, unofficial truce was written up between the families with more than 60 to send it, signing it. They even have Hatfield and McCoy reunion festivals annually, June. But to this day, the name Hatfield and McCoy evoke clannish gun, toting, hillbillies hell bent on keeping their better grudges. I don't just mention the Hatfields and McCoys for the interesting history of Pikeville.

Susan Daniel Smith was a coal miner's daughter. She was born in 1961 and Mattawan West Virginia and her mother Tracy was a direct descendant. Of the McCoy's her father said Daniels homeowner, but according to author Joe Sharkey, he was chronically unemployed and a heavy drinker. Susan's family lived in a small house up in the Baron.

She hollow a Freeborn Kentucky. It was a dingy area that locals called lonesome holler. Joe Sharkey read the definitive book on this case above suspicion, but when he first released it, 25 years ago, it was titled the girl from lonesome holler, Susan. The fifth of nine children was known as a smart girl in the seventh grade, she was on the drill team.

And that was the pinnacle of her school career. Like so many holler teens. She quit school before making it to high school. She said she had better things to do. A former neighbor told Joe Sharkey that Susan was like a stray kitten with a temper Susan's fiery temper would be part of her calling card as an adult as well.

She met Kenneth Smith when she was just 15 years old and he was 24. Kenneth's claim to fame was being one of the premier meth dealers in the tri corner area. When Susan was 19, Kenneth finally proposed the couple had two kids, Miranda and Brady, but divorced shortly after their son, Brady was born. It said that this divorce was for practical reasons.

As the couple kept living together. Now they could collect two welfare checks, but as the years went by, Kenneth became very abusive as Susan. As well as cheating on her and taking whatever money she had. She left Kenneth for awhile and stayed with her sister in West Virginia. When she was about 24, she was very unhappy and soon returned to Kenneth.

Like she always did this time. Susan stayed with him, maybe not seeing much of a way out the two managed to buy a tiny shack, close to a railroad. They still live there together. When Mark Putnam rolled into town, Mark was a rookie agent with the FBI. He was 27 years old and just a week out of the Academy, when he was sent to Pikeville, as I said, it was a dismal location and not what Mark wanted, but the criminal activity in the area could keep a good agent busy.

I can make a name for a great agent Mark and his wife, Kathy also 27 at the time had grown up in Connecticut. He grew up fairly poor. Walter Putnam usually had a couple of part time jobs to supplement his full time salary, driving a truck for Sears. His mother Barbara stressed the importance of a good education to Mark and his brother and sister Mark was a jock and was offered a scholarship to a prestigious school in Pomfret Connecticut.

He wasn't really the academic in his family. That was his brother, but as a star soccer player in high school, the teachers padded his grades. Mark already knew he wanted to be an FBI agent and he knew he needed a college degree to get into the Academy, even with a scholarship. Mark's parents paid around a thousand dollars a year to send him to college.

That would be around 4,000 now and a very tight pinch for the Putnam family, but they made it work. Mark was a good student and again, a star athlete, but he lost his dad to lung cancer. His sophomore year, it only made him more serious and more ambitious. Kathy had come from a different, more dark background.

Though she was from a good family. She rebelled and met a lot of bad choices. When she was young. She dropped out of high school and took a job bartending. She impetuously married around age 22, a man, 10 years, her senior who beat her, she quickly left him, but was determined to make it on her own. She naively took a job at a massage parlor, not knowing the details of a happy ending.

When she refused the advances of one customer, he tracked her down at her apartment and raped her. She went to the police, but they considered it a matter of, he said, she said, It wasn't until he broke into and trashed her apartment that he was arrested and it was not for Kathy's. Right. The cops were more interested in busting the massage parlor, but Cathy got her GED and even an associates degree and moved on with her life.

She was blossoming in a career as an apartment manager when she was introduced to Mark. She happened to meet Mark's mother at a restaurant one night in 1982, and then overheard Barbara calling her or son to tell him that he just had to meet them girl. She was gorgeous and they were perfect for each other.

Kathy laughed and then picked up phone and exchange numbers with Mark. They started dating and eloped on Easter weekend in 1984. On a cold day in February, 1987, the couple were looking at the bleak landscape as they wound their way through the mountain roads to Pikeville, to Mark's first FBI posting, the couple was trepidatious, but still excited about Mark's first posting Mark almost didn't make it into the Academy due to an old shoulder injury from soccer with Kathy's help.

He tenaciously kept applying until they did him, but his posting in Pikeville, was it by accident? That office was plagued with administrative problems. They really needed a clerk, not a rookie gung-ho FBI agent. Before Mark was finally accepted into the Academy to become a special agent. He worked as a clerk at the new Haven Connecticut field office.

He learned everything he could from the agents around him, and it didn't deter his passion and Pikeville was his first post, no matter how Backwoods Mark plan to Excel. He quickly endeared himself to local cops by not acting above them. There has always been a divide between G-Man and local police. They both looked down on each other and rarely worked well together, but Mark was different.

He knew that in order to do his job well, he had to learn his jurisdiction. And the best way to do that was to be friendly with the local cops. And he couldn't help, but laugh that the cops he met had the last names of our country's most famous feuding families. Paul Hatfield, Bert Hatfield and Fred McCoy, all with the pike County Sheriff's department.

Let Mark right along with him and introduced him to the locals. And it wasn't long before he heard about a local informant named Susan Smith. Mark was naturally wary of her. At first. Susan did come with quite the reputation, but she claimed to have a connection to a local bank robber, a fellow who went by the name of cat eyes who had recently left prison.

And then a slew of bank robberies and his exact style started popping up in his old stomping grounds and Eastern Kentucky and West Virginia back then local banks were just that local. They were not connected to national banks and therefore not afforded the same protections. They serve the people of their area, meaning they cashed welfare and social security checks.

They also handled the coal miners union pensions, and they accepted cash deposits. Without many questions, cat eyes, real name Carl Edward Lockhart got his nickname reportedly for his beautiful green eyes and good looks. But even after a hundred thousand dollar hall, he would rather couch surf in the holler and smoke meth with his friends than run a motel room.

He landed on the couch of Susan and Kenneth Smith. Susan liked cat eyes, and he did a lot of talking in front of her, but Susan was smart and always upwardly mobile. She knew this information was leveraged and she did not feel any or enough allegiance to mr.to stop her from informing on him. Susan made decent money as an informant, despite her infamous big mouth, she was born in the holler and she knew every family and criminal in her area.

And she was charming. Even when her friends suspected her of informing on them. It was Bert Hatfield who suggested Mark meet Susan Smith. When he found out was sleeping on her couch. He had known Susan all her life. Yeah. She had a big mouth, but this suspected bank robber was literally living on her couch.

Chances are, she would have good information on him. Mark and Bert met Susan and Kenneth at a restaurant. Susan Daniel Smith was then 25 years old and a beautiful young woman by any standard. She was brunette with a lovely smile, stood five feet, five inches tall. And wait around 125 pounds, Susan prided herself on her trim figure and love to wear skimpy and tight clothes to show it off.

There are lots of pretty girls and lots of hollers, but Susan also had the charisma and the nerve to play both sides. Kenneth tried to dominate the conversation that first day, but bird Hatfield had warned Mark that Kenneth didn't really know anything. He needed to talk to Susan. Mark told the table that he would like to talk to Susan alone and the two of them headed out to chat and Bart's car as Kenneth glowered.

Susan played coy in this first meeting. Mark was well aware that informants funny, a lot of Cokes. She strangely asked him what his wife looked like. He said she was pretty. And then Susan asked if she had a good body. Mark said, Yes. She kept herself in really good shape. At the time she was evading answering his questions about cat eyes or Mark.

Might've been more wary of her personal questions, but she did agree to meet Mark again at his office in Pikeville. Soon. She was in his office two or three times a week. Mark had a $5,000 budget for informants, but he was nervous about giving Susan money because he still thought she was playing games.

Susan knew that she could earn thousands band forming for the FBI. This was big time. This wasn't the little pike County Sheriff's department, but she was nervous. Her first payment for Mark was $500 and then it was done. She was an FBI informant. Susan's first useful tip to Mark was in September of 1987.

She had seen cat eyes come home with a big bag of sawed off shotguns and ski masks. She paid attention and found out he planned to hit the first national bank and ferals Creek, just 15 miles South of Pikeville. Cat has followed through on his plan. Susan's Intel was good. But when he was apprehended, Mark was out of town serving a fugitive warrant.

Susan was furious that another agent was named in the papers. When she went to see Mark, he gave her $1,500 for the tip. She tried to give it back to him, still angry that he didn't get the credit for cat eyes, even though it was his case. Mark told her he couldn't take the money back and she angrily dropped it on his desk and stomped out the door.

Mark called a supervisor at the Covington office who told him to write up a memo, explaining what happened and put the money back in the safe Mark was treading carefully because he still needed Susan to testify against cat eyes. When he asked her about testifying, she said she needed money to move her and her kids out of the area.

But ironically, Susan was bragging to anyone who would listen that she was working for the FBI as dangerous as informing was. She couldn't help, but revel in the glamour of it. In the fall of 1987, Susan became friendly with Mark's wife, Cathy simply by calling their house. Kathy was warm and a good listener.

She was also very accustomed to take a messages for her husband who was often out in the field rather than out his desk. She even took to typing up his reports for him. They really made a great team. And Kathy, didn't just feel sorry for Susan. She felt a sort of kinship. She understood her ambition and her loneliness.

Kathy had lived through some rough times herself. Soon as she and Susan talked all the time. Susan quizzed, Kathy for makeup and hair tips. She asked a lot of personal questions about Mark Kathy wasn't naive. She knew Susan was enamored with her husband, but it really didn't worry. Her Mark was a consummate professional.

Susan started trying to clean up her language and grammar. And when she found out that Kathy had cut her long dark hair, She also cut her hair short. She even asked Mark if it looked like Kathy's Mark was professional, but he was also wary. He warned Kathy to be careful around Susan, but the women talked practically every night.

Kathy even told Susan about her rape. Meanwhile, Mark was working another big case with another informant named Charlie Trotter. Charlie told him about a big truck stealing and shop, shop operation. Mark was very interested in busting a huge criminal conspiracy like this and his background as a clerk would serve him.

Well, there would be thousands of pieces of evidence to catalog. Charlie was in on a job, uh, three hijacked trucks that fall of 1987. The case was going well. And Mark was excited. Kathy was preparing for the birth of their second child. She had gotten pregnant a month after they moved to Pikeville. In late October, she planned to take their daughter Danielle and stay with her parents in Connecticut, waiting for Mark to join them in December and time for the baby's birth.

The FBI's right on the chop shop was scheduled for the end of October, around when Kathy would be leaving. Mark was very happy with the timing. It would give him weeks to catalog all the evidence before he took time off for the birth of their son. But there was a problem. Kathy was set to fly out of Lexington with Danielle.

So the Putnam's drove there the night before Kathy's flight, he found out while he was still at the hotel, that there had been a problem with the search warrants and the FBI had to move the next day when Mark wouldn't be there, Mark raced to the site after he dropped Kathy and Danielle off the next morning.

But it was too late. The owner of this operation had been warned. There were no arrests, no one was even there to arrest, but two old dogs. But Mark still had the huge task of cataloging, all the stolen items. It was still a big deal for Mark and the FBI, despite not being able to make immediate arrest.

Mark estimated, they recovered over $2 million in stolen equipment. The local papers reported 6 million either way. It was the biggest bust for stolen parts in recent history. On December 9th, Mark's son was born and he did make it a time to be with Kathy for the birth. They named him Mark Putnam, jr. When Mark and Kathy returned to Pikeville with their small family, right after Christmas, Susan surprised Mark at the office.

She kissed him on the lifts without warning. And then she said she had gifts for him. It was running shoes and a Nike t-shirt he, again, tried to decline the gifts unsettled by her overly familiar kiss. But Susan said it would hurt her feelings. Mark had been good to her and she was just trying to show her appreciation.

He said, okay. And kept the items when she left. He wrote yet another memo. Putting this stuff in the safe, despite Susan's behavior, he was trying to remain as professional as he could. He still needed her to testify. He couldn't risk pissing her off before he left for Connecticut for the birth of his son.

He had a final meeting with Susan where she had propositioned him for a flame. He definitively said, no. And pointed out that Kathy was her friend. Susan told him, Kathy didn't have to know. She seemed to take the rejection and stride though. And Mark was now more alert to how intense her feelings were about him.

But Susan came through in spades for him at cat eyes trial at a great risk to herself, but she held her head up high and was a great witness. After the trial. Mark's regular partner in Pikeville, transferred out. They hadn't exactly got on. Great. Some Ark was looking forward to his replacement. He was very disappointed when special agent Ronald Poole showed up the portly 37 year old agent seemed to lazy to Mark it.

Wasn't just pulls looks, but Mark did have strong feelings on how physically fit an FBI agent should be after all. He almost didn't make it into the Academy of her, an old injury. He jogged every day. He didn't smoke and rarely drank. For his part, Ronald Poole didn't particularly care to be paired with a rookie Yankee, but Ronald Poole had worked undercover narcotics in Chicago.

And even Mark had to admit that his looks probably didn't raise any flags and helped him in his undercover work and pull did come with a good reputation and to Mark's relief. The tip Susan had been passing to him recently. We're all drug-related. So he saw the opportunity to pass Susan off as an informant to pull.

Kathy invited Mark's new partner to dinner and pull gave Mark further reason to dislike him when he kept openly leering at Kathy. And then he soon joined Susan, Charlie Trotter, and other nighttime callers that Kathy was willing to talk to. She was repulsed by Ronald pole, but savvy enough to know that she needed to remain cordial Bert Hatfield Mark's buddy, and the pike County Sheriff's department told author Joe Sharkey quote.

Pull that boy was just a pussy hound first and foremost, and an FBI agent, maybe second bird Hatfield was right about pole. He quickly had designs on Susan Smith who liked Kathy found Ronald pool. Disgusting. And Susan was no fool. She knew Mark was trying to pass her off to pool. Her calls to Kathy became more emotional and urgent.

She admitted she was taking a lot of pills and drinking. Kathy tried to be supportive, but it wasn't easy. She was growing tired of all of this. Kathy was sick of Pikeville and who could blame her? Most postings lasted for a minimum of two years. And Mark still meant to make the best of it. In August of 1988, Kathy insisted on a vacation.

So they had a blissful 10 days at Myrtle beach together with their kids, but they still had to come back to Pikeville. And as soon as they returned, Kathy got an anonymous caller who said, Your old man is fooling around with a girl named Susan Smith. Kathy tried to talk to Mark, but he told her not to be ridiculous.

He had done nothing wrong, but failed to see that he really needed to talk to his wife about it. Kathy sunk into a depression and Mark buried himself with work. Susan was canny enough to know that she had to keep bringing him good tips, not just the drug stuff. She warned him about a bank robbery and sure enough, it happened, but he still passed it off to pool.

Susan was becoming more and more desperate. Her friends and family knew that she was an informant and many had stopped talking to her, but she kept running her mouth around Pikeville. Now she bragged that she was having an affair with Mark Putnam, but nothing was happening between them yet. If anything, Mark avoided her with Kathy pressuring him.

He officially requested a transfer after the chop shop raid scary things had been happening. Mark walked outside one morning fund all his tires slashed. There are a lot of hangup calls, heavy breathers, and even some outright threats. None of this was helping Kathy's anxiety about Pikeville in November of 1988.

Kathy's sister, Chris came to visit for the first time since they moved to Pikeville, Kathy and Mark had a babysitter, they went to dinner and then went for some drinks at a cocktail lounge in the landmark hotel and Pikeville. They ran into a local politician. He was a guy Mark was interested in a couple of months earlier.

Susan had barged into his office with a huge bag of black and red pills. She said that this politician was handing them out and exchange for votes. Mark, didn't take her word for this. She was becoming increasingly unreliable. He reluctantly flushed the pills down the toilet. But he was very interested in busting a corrupt politician and despite houses and got those pills.

She could be right about this guy. Turns out she was Mark introduced Kathy to the politician who immediately leered at her. He sat down with him at the table and Mark watched amused as the politician kept inching closer to Kathy. Kathy was throwing her husband looks. I can handle, this is what those look said and sure enough, she was grinning and flirting back.

Mark got up to talk to someone he saw at the bar and Cathy and the politicians conversation turned dirty. She told author Joe Sharkey that the politician said to her quote, Honey, your husband doesn't know what he's got. Does he? You're a hot little bitch. Ain't you? Kathy continued to play alone and turn the conversation smoothly.

And to having sex on cocaine, the politician didn't believe her at first saying, hell you ain't never touched no Coke. She said she shared it back East before she was an agent's wife. He got up to go to the bathroom. And when he came back, the Letcher County politician passed her two grams of cocaine.

Mark's reaction was a mixture of being horrified and electrified at his wife's bold game. When she told him how the politician said, there was plenty more where that came from, they rushed over to the Pikeville office and Mark called a supervisor in Covington to tell them exactly what happened. The supervisor told him to get pulled to the office, to witness him taking possession of the cocaine.

He offered to have Kathy go get a blood and urine test to prove she had not taken any of the Coke or any other drugs. His supervisor said that wasn't necessary. They just needed to log the cocaine officially and lock it in the safe. Both Kathy and Mark left for home that night with new hope. Mark now wanted to go after the politician.

Susan had been right, and Kathy's instincts and incredible acting skills had paid off. Kathy felt so much better for just having done something herself. She wanted out of this godforsaken place and of helping Mark with a drug, staying on a local politician would get him another leg up. She was happy to help.

She got set up with a phone call with a politician that was recorded, but he didn't take the bait. He was too smart to talk over the phone, reenergized and happy. Kathy looked forward to

Thanksgiving. She even asked Mark if he wanted to invite Susan and her kids for dinner, she still felt sorry for Susan.

Mark blew up at her. He didn't want an informant in his house, especially not on Thanksgiving when he wanted to be with his family, but honestly never. He didn't want Susan Charlie Trotter or any criminal informants he worked with coming to his home on Thanksgiving night, Susan called the house to chat with Kathy.

She knew all about her little drug sting with the politician and the plans they were making. Kathy was shocked that Susan knew and asked her how Ron Poole had told her. Kathy was furious. And without saying anything to Mark, she called Paul demanding to know why he was running his mouth about such sensitive information to an informant.

Ron Poole blew his top. He denied telling Susan and shouted at her. Your fucking husband probably told her, but Kathy knew Mark Hatton. She was shaken up, but determined to continue plans to entrap the politician, went up the chain. But when they informed FBI headquarters and the DEA, they were shut down immediately.

This was unheard of. Kathy was an agent's wife, a civilian, a criminal informant is one thing, but this was absurd. Mark was relieved. Kathy had been so enthusiastic about helping, but he had been worried. So things went on. Mark was still waiting for word on a transfer and he was still burying himself in work.

A couple of weeks later, Susan called. She had Intel on another drug dealer. This one was a cop Mark was paying attention, but he still wanted to pass it on the pool after all it wasn't just to avoid working with Susan pull did have experience with narcotics work. The problem was Susan was adamant that she wasn't going to work with Ron pool, pulled it and take this well either.

He was already pissed that he hadn't convinced Susan to sleep with him. Mark was sick of all of them. But a week before Christmas, he picked Susan up and took her for a ride. It was more or less to placate her Susan needed attention, or she would stir the shit. It would be a huge mistake. According to what Mark Putnam told author, Joe Sharkey, Susan was all soft voiced and expressed concern for him.

He looked stressed and she knew that he was unhappy at home because Kathy had told her. So, and Mark was unhappy. His sex life with Kathy had been sporadic at best. In the last several months after the drug sting was called off, Kathy had some back into an angry depression. She was either morose or actively irritated with him.

When he came home at night, he admitted to Joe Sharkey that despite how much Susan could get on his nerves, he did not hate her. He felt sorry for her. And in a way responsible for her during this meeting, according to Mark, Susan seized the opportunity of his mood. Telling him, anytime you need a release I'm around.

And then she kissed him and he didn't push her off. According to Mark Putnam, they had sex in his car for the first time. Then he would later insist that hand. Susan had sex five times over a two week period, always an only in his car. There were no seedy motels. They just drove out to a secluded spot, but it was done.

Whatever else happened. He had to get the hell out of Pikeville before Susan Smith ruined his life.

Despite her misgivings, Kathy insisted that she never really suspected Mark was sleeping with Susan. And it makes sense because she kept talking to her even after she was warned on that anonymous call. But in hindsight, she later told author Joe Sharkey, that she did notice a change in Susan's demeanor around Christmas of that year.

She didn't call us much. And when she did, she was unusually upbeat. Kathy said it was like she was on top of the world and cats. He honestly just felt happy about Susan's new behavior. She had often counseled her to take responsibility for her life and her own happiness to work on herself esteem. It seemed to her that maybe Susan was doing just that sadly, no.

Susan had just finally gotten what she wanted. And then

Kenneth called the Putnam house at Dawn one morning in January with Susan screaming and crying in the background. He informed Kathy that his wife was sleeping with her husband. Susan had told Kenneth that she had miscarried Mark's baby Susan screened that it wasn't true, but for the first time, Kathy was really rattled.

She went to Mark who brushed her off yet again, saying Sue, as an only told the truth about a 10th of the time and it wasn't worth discussing, but he was angry. The seed had been sown with Kathy and Susan kept calling Kathy offhand remarks about Mark too intimate. She wants Steven said, Oh, got to go March, hold up.

Kathy furious called the Pikeville FBI office. Mark answered the phone immediately. Susan was bullshitting Kathy. Once again felt foolish for doubting her husband in February. The indictments for the chop shop operation had come through and the Putnam's started receiving threats. Again. Mark went before the magistrate to request no bill for the chop shop crew on the grounds that he felt they were making felt threats to his family.

And he honestly thought they meant him harm. But this local judge still allowed bell just admonishing these hardened criminals to stay away from the Putnam family. Well, that was enough for Mark's supervisor. He had already been sympathetic to Mark and Kathy's misery and Pikeville. He started petitioning his own supervisor for Mark's transfer in a followup memo.

He even said that it should be an agent with law enforcement experience that should replace Mark because quote. Individuals groups and entire families except violence as a way of life routinely carry firearms and have little regard for law and order. The official transfer came just days later to Kathy's delight.

She couldn't believe the nightmare was over. Mark was being transferred to Miami. The FBI sent movers for Kathy and the kids. Walmart stayed behind to put the house up for sale. It was really happening and so quickly the move was set for the middle of April, 1989. Mark just spent a week in Pikeville after Cathy and the kids left and he kept to himself determined to keep his head down until he got out of this hell hole.

As soon as Mark was in Miami, Ron pool kept calling to complain about Susan. She was uncooperative, she was a pain in the ass, but in reality, he was still trying to get in her pants in early may. Susan filed charges against Kenneth for domestic abuse. He retaliated by reporting her to the West Virginia welfare office for claiming benefits and to States.

So Susan lost half of her welfare. She was down to only $250 a month and she was as addicted to pills as ever. And now she had added cocaine into the mix. Desperate for money. Susan started renting a motel room in Pikeville once a week, a clerk who worked nights later identified her and said she was a sex worker.

It was pretty obvious what she was doing. Making matters worse. Susan behave like an ass to the motel staff. So they remembered her clearly in April, Susan called Mark in Miami and told him she was pregnant. She wanted to know what he planned to do about it. Mark asked if she was sure. And she said she was, he told her he would be back in Pikeville soon to wrap up the chop shop trial.

They would talk. Then, then in may she ran into cat Oz girlfriend. The bank robbery. She had testified against the woman beat Susan up pretty badly and threatened to kill her all while Kenneth Susan's brother and his girlfriend watched. Is it any wonder Susan was coming on so hard to the only normal man who had ever paid her any attention.

She came from a hard life, a life of poverty, drugs, violence, and misery. It's easy to see how she became fixated on Mark Putnam, and even Kathy, to a certain extent. Kathy was the only respectable female friend she had ever had. But with Mark and Kathy in Florida, Susan was now spiraling out of control.

Mark did plan to trips to Pikeville in late may and early June for pretrial hearings. He managed to avoid Susan on the first trip, but Ron pool ever jealous and vindictive, I made sure to call Susan and let her know that Mark would be back in town. On June 5th, Mark flew into Huntington West Virginia, which was the closest commercial airport to Pikeville.

And then he rented a car and headed South. He was ready for the 18 months, stress of the chop shop job to be over. He knew he had to go face what he had done with Susan. He was heart sick, a lot. It's been made of the fact that he rented a car instead of using an official vehicle. But if he was doing it to enter pipe, we'll secretly.

He did it wrong. He rented the car in his own name and from everything I read, he turned over the trip expenses. It's not that unusual. Meanwhile, Susan had been to see a doctor at the public health center in Pikeville. She had gotten a written report saying that her baby was due November 19, which would put conception at the end of February.

Mark Putnam has always maintained that his two weeks of car sex with Susan. Happened at the end of December, the doctor did note that Susan had suffered a miscarriage and had a DNC on January 2nd. Even if she had been carrying March child, this pregnancy better fits the timeline. And I understand we only have Mark Putnam's word for it.

We do also have Kathy's word for when Kenneth called about the miscarriage that was in January and Mark had been consumed with a chop shop indictments in February. He maintains to this day that any sexual contact with Susan had ended before January of 1989. And I'm sorry to point this out. I am not in any way shaming her, but Susan was spotted several times by motel staff in Pikeville, working as a prostitute and the months leading up to her death.

She was on pills and cocaine and still drinking heavily. I think it's entirely possible that she convinced herself it was Mark's child. She had made no bones about her obsession with him. She wanted it to be his baby. And in that state of mind on that many substances, maybe she really did believe it was his, but we'll never know for sure.

Self had doubts. He told author Joe Sharkey, that when he got to Susan had left a form on his desk that she had had to sign about her pregnancy. It said results positive. It didn't have a due date. That was on the other paper the doctor had given Susan, which he never saw. He said he felt horribly guilty.

He thought Susan. Yeah. And her own way would have been faithful to him in her mind. It was a relationship. And he felt that if she had been sleeping with someone else, when they had been having sex, then she would have told him to talk to him. He checked into landmarks motel and was startled. When Susan called him, she informed him that she was in the same motel.

And that Ron Poole had put it on his American express card for her Mark declined to see her that night. He had to be up early to drive to Lexington for court. The next day, that night he got home. And as soon as he was out of the shower, Susan was at his door. He said that she yelled at him that he, he was avoiding her and then turned despondent.

He could tell that she was high. He offered to take her to get something to eat. They drove to him McDonald's and talked in the car. Susan was hurting. She told him all about the beatings from Kenneth and his girlfriend. She had no money and Kenneth wouldn't let her see her kids. And Mark had gotten her pregnant and deserted her.

He asked her if she would consider an abortion that brought Susan's famous temper back, she most certainly would not. She told him she planned to be a thorn in his ass. She would come to Florida to make sure he didn't forget her. Mark said he drove back to the motel and couldn't help, but think, looking at her that it it was his child, she would have to be at least five months pregnant.

The last time they had sex was before January, he thought she wasn't showing at all. And then he felt guilty. It wasn't fair to judge her based on her appearance. On June 8th, Mark said he got up. Wearily deeply worried about the mess he was in and feeling deep shame as well. He told author Joe Sharkey. He hated cops who kept framed pictures of their wives on their desks while sleeping with anyone who didn't resist.

That wasn't him. That had never been him. Not once in his life had Mark Putnam even been in trouble. He had always been a straight arrow. His marriage and career meant everything to him. And with the incredibly stupid choice of sleeping with Susan Smith, he had jeopardized both. He said that by the time he got out of the shower, she was banging on his door.

He had to be in Lexington again for court. And he tried to get rid of her, but she needed to use his phone and she needed to borrow some clothes. She would not let it go. He left her in his room and headed for Lexington. When he got back that evening, Susan was waiting at a store. He said that she was high again and ready for a loud public fight.

He said she screamed, my life has been fucked up. Ever since I met you. She yelled that she wasn't having an abortion. Mark said he understood. And if it was his baby, he and Kathy would raise it. He instantly realized his mistake and the hurt that call Susan. She was screaming and crying now that she was a good mother and insisting that it was his baby.

He finally suggested that they take a ride. He was worried about his motel neighbors, hearing all of this, and that's what they did. Right. They went for rides. Citizens seemed to temporarily mollified. He drove them out of Pikeville and up the mountain road. As they drove. He said that she continued to parade him.

She threatened to call the FBI, Cathy, who she kept calling a whore. He kept driving. And when they were nearing barren, she Holly and the town of Freebird Susan's hometown, Mark claims. She lunged at him. He said with difficulty, he managed to keep the car on the road until he could pull over. They were at the crest of Peter mountain.

And now Mark says she was slapping at him, scratching and screaming her head off. She was completely hysterical and he was trying to fight her off. He tried talking to her and she says she planned to name the baby Mark jr. And go quote, put the little bastard right into your precious daughter's arms.

Mark said he rarely asked what exactly she wanted from him. Well, Susan wanted him to divorce Kathy and marry her. He said he tried to reason with her and remind her that Kathy had been so good to her. Susan just screamed. Fuck you. And your whore wife. Then Mark said he tried to course correct. He had tried negotiating.

Now. He was going to tell her what would happen if she wouldn't have an abortion. Then after the baby was born, he would make her get a paternity test. Again, saying that if the child was his, he and Kathy would raise it. And then he cruelly pointed out something that he had found out since he got back to Pikeville.

Her sister had thrown her out of her house. And Susan had signed custody of her children over willingly to Kenneth. He said, he told her quote, I'll be damned if I'd let any kid of mine grow up here, the slut like you. And that was it. Susan started flailing, slapping, punching, and scratching. She hit him in the eye with her fingernail enraged.

Mark said he tried to punch her, but he ducked and he hit the dashboard instead. He said she kept screaming. I own you, you used me. You owe me, fuck you to hell. And all he wanted her to do was be quiet. Some art said he put his hands around her throat and squeezed saying, relax, Susan, relax. He claims, he thought he had just subdued her until she slumped over in the seat.

And he realized she wasn't breathing. He claims that he tried to revive her, but it was too late. I want to be really clear again, this is Mark's story. There is no proof that it happened this way, but there is also no proof that it was premeditated. Mark was in Pikeville on legitimate FBI business. He was staying there to tie things up at that office and traveling to Lexington for the chop shop trial hearings, dealing with Susan was something he was forced to face because he was in town.

It's a matter of opinion on whether or not you believe his story. I will say once he told this story, it has never changed that back to the timeline. At this point, Mark said he was spinning out. He considered calling his friend, Burt, Hatfield and confessing, not for special treatment, but as a courtesy.

And he knew Burt would be kind. He also said he considered suicide, but he said he thought of his family. And while he felt horrible for taking Susan's life, he couldn't stand the thought of ruining theirs. In the end, he pulled her body out of the car and put it in his trunk. And he went back to the motel to think he went to bed and then went back to Lexington the next morning with Susan's body, still in his trunk.

He was surprised when he came out that afternoon and there was no smell. Finally, around 7:00 PM. He drove into the mountains again. He turned onto Harman branch road where he knew there were many deserted minds. He took the first mine road he came to and drove up until he was close to a Ridge with a ravine and small Creek below.

He didn't throw her body into the ravine. He climbed down the Ridge and hit it in some brush, just out of view of the road that night, a local reporter told him that she needed to talk to him. Susan had been spreading it everywhere that she was pregnant and that it was his child. He denied it and the reporter believed him again.

Susan Smith had a reputation for lying. Three days after Mark had Susan's body, he called her sister and Freeborn and asked if she had heard from Susan, he was trying to cover up his car crime. There's no denying it. And Shelby ward Susan's sister was worried. She hadn't heard from her, but she knew what her sister had been saying about Mark Putnam.

He advised her to file a missing persons report. Then he called the state police office in Pikeville and said he was worried about his informant. He hadn't heard from her. He mentioned that when they talked last, she said she was going to talk to some drug contacts. Shelby ward also called the state police involved, a missing persons report.

Detective Richard Ray called the case. Detective Ray traveled to Freeborn and questioned witnesses. He found out about Susan sorted past. You also heard about her pregnancy test to the health department and the accusation. She had been spreading around town that FBI agent Mark Putnam was the father. Ray knew Mark Putnam, but only in passing.

He hung around the Lexington courthouse until he bumped into him. Mark was still in the area for the chop shop trial. He showed them the report on Susan and noted that Mark was cooperative, but nervous. He told detective rail about. Her dependence on him and Kathy and all of her personal problems. Ray, let things alone for awhile.

As a detective for the state, he was a busy man, but he had a feeling about Mark back in Florida. Kathy was settling in with the kids in a condo in sunrise, Florida, a 45 minute commute to Mark's new office in North Miami beach. When Susan stopped calling Kathy in June, she was relieved. When she found out she had gone missing, she felt sorry for her.

But she wrote her off. She had done everything she could to help Susan Smith. And while she thought it was sad, she was frankly, ready to be done with everything to do with Pikeville. She just wanted to forget the whole experience. Mark said that he felt horrible guilt and also anxiety and dread. He was a cop.

He knew it was a matter of time before he was caught. He had chronic diarrhea. He wasn't sleeping and Kathy was worried for him. He even told his new supervisor in Florida about Susan's allegations and her disappearance, his supervisor said it was a matter for the state police. The Kentucky rumors had already filtered down to him and he had Susan Smith checked out.

Unfortunately, she had the kind of background that made cops shrug. She consorted with dangerous people. She was a drug user and an informant, and he thought Mark was young and naive. He didn't think he was a murderer. The matter was dropped, but as the months passed, even Susan mother who had little to do with her daughter admitted that Susan had never missed a birthday Christmas before without sending a card.

Detective Ray ran down every time, but he kept coming back to Mark. Those were the rumors that kept surfacing no matter who he spoke with by January, 1990, he was ready to lean on Mark Putnam and the FBI about the Susan Smith case. He would have been surprised to learn that Mark himself was asking his bosses for an internal investigation.

They kept refusing. They pointed out that there was no evidence of foul play, except that Susan was gone. And Mark had a stellar reputation outside of the Kentucky rumors. This pissed detective Ray off Susan was an informant for the FBI. She had worked for them and they didn't care. They refused to cooperate.

He went to the Commonwealth attorney, the same thing as a district attorney in other States. And this man wasn't afraid to yell at some FBI guys. He called the justice department saying that the FBI had thrown one of their informants to the wolves. And if they didn't start an investigation, he would call the press that did it.

The main FBI office in Kentucky opened an investigation, supervisory special agent. Jim Huggins caught the case. On May 1st, he met with agents at the Lexington office to talk about what went down in Pikeville. When Mark was posted there, he then assembled a team of five agents, not from Pikeville to assist in the investigation.

Ironically, now the Pikeville police, including detective Ray, were pissy that the FBI were barging into their case. They now had to show them around town, let them go through their files. It was the classic divide, often seen. Between federal and local cops. And hadn't detective Ray asked for this and whether he liked them or not, the FBI were doing their jobs the way they saw it.

Kenneth Smith was the most likely suspect. He had a record of beating Susan and they felt he had a motive because of the rumors about Mark Putnam, but they also decided they need to rule out March 1st. They were not giving him a pass. And Martin knew about the Pikeville investigation. Thanks to Ron Poole and other contacts who were still calling him.

He went to see his supervisor in Florida, yet again, to request an internal investigation from the office of professional responsibility to look into, to the allegations against him. His boss was still adamant. He said no way, but then he asked if the Kentucky state police asked for a polygraph, would Mark do it?

Mark immediately said, yes, that was enough for his boss. Though he intended to cooperate with the Kentucky investigators. Mark had his first meeting with special agent Jim Huggins a month before the first anniversary of Susan's. He went day by day through the week he spent in Pikeville when she went missing.

His first slip was when they asked how old Susan was and he answered, she was 28. The past tense sent up major red flags. These meetings turned into days and still Mark refused an attorney. Kathy ever the mama bear watch the toll it was taking on her husband. And marched down to that office and read the investigators, the riot act.

She reminded them all that she had personally done for the FBI and demanded to be interviewed after all. Was she a witness? She knew Susan too instigators were surprised, but sympathetic, they assured Kathy everything would be fine. They just needed to clear it all up that Kathy needed to be heard and they let her, she let loose all of her grievances.

Pikeville had almost destroyed her family. And she was convinced that a rumor campaign led by Ron pool was selling her husband's good name. She then gave them a rundown on pool's behavior, including the sharing of sensitive information with an informant. They asked her if she thought that pool killed Susan.

And she said, no, she didn't even believe Susan was dead. In her opinion. Susan had run her mouth about the wrong person was threatened and was laying low. Bye now, Mark wanted to take the polygraph. He told author Joe Sharkey. He didn't think he could really pass it, but this might be his breaking point. He was right.

A couple of questions into the test. The examiner took Jim Huggins out of the room and said, we have a problem. Special agent Huggins decided to sit Mark down and confront him about the deception on the test. Mark told him, Jim, I want to get this over with, but before we do anything, can I call Kathy? He called her and told her it was going badly.

And she savvy FBI wife said, you're not under arrest. Justin just come home. And that's what Mark did. He said he would be back to tell them everything, but he had to talk to his wife first and he told her everything, despite her fears and suspicions, it was a gut punch and she smacked her husband across the face.

But by the end of the evening, she was blaming herself. She told author Joe Sharkey that she could have stopped it. If she was paying attention. I swear, Kathy Putnam is truly one of the most amazing women I've ever heard of this. Wasn't some stand by your man. Bullshit. She honestly felt that she and Mark were a team.

She knew she was actually closer to Susan than he was. And she knew that Susan was obsessed with Mark. She thought she hadn't protected him or Susan for that matter. Don't get me wrong. She was angry at her husband, but she insisted on taking responsibility to Mark got a defense attorney named Bruce Zimmet.

He was a former assistant us attorney. And the first thing he did was called the Pikeville FBI team. And say, you guys know you don't have a case without a body. There might be circumstantial evidence and the polygraph didn't look good, but that's an admissible. But Mark Putnam was now determined to confess.

He wanted a deal. He wanted Kathy to divorce him and move on with her life. He anticipated decades in prison, but Bruce Zimmet brokered a deal for first degree manslaughter. It will be 16 years in prison. Maximum Mark took it. He pled guilty on June 12th, 1990, just days after the first anniversary of Susan's death.

He made a full confession to investigators and then led them to Susan Smith's body. She still lay just 50 feet from the road. The, her remains were nothing but bone and the small ones had scattered down the lonely Kentucky mountain side, Shelby ward, Susan sister was notified of Mark's confession and the plea deal.

And she was enraged. She said it was cold blooded murder to any reporter who had talked to her. But even Shelby told reporters that her sister had been obsessed with Mark Putnam. On the day Shelby went to court to watch Mark's plea. She was caught with a gun in her purse. Many people thought it was for more publicity.

Although local cops thought it wasn't all that unusual for a woman in that area to carry a gun in her purse. When she went to court for her own charge of carrying a concealed weapon, she diplomatically said she didn't believe Mark meant to kill Susan. She did think he just panicked. She swore she had no intention of shooting Mark Putnam that day in court and apologized for causing any trouble.

And then the charge against her was dropped practically on the steps of the courthouse. She took back the apology and told the press, she didn't mean a word of it, but her publicity stunt worked. Prosecutors had been happy with a plea deal, and now they were crucified in the press in may of 1991, Shelby and other friends, family members felt a wrongful death suit against Mark Putnam.

I got a court order to exume Susan's body for a second all time. They're the second autopsy. She found nothing new. They want a $500,000 judgment against Mark Putnam though. He had no assets and they were never able to collect the money. Mark was sent to a federal prison in Rochester, Minnesota. Kathy sold their Florida condo and moved the kids to Minnesota to be closer to him.

But after a year, she moved to Connecticut to be closer to her parents for help. Kathy was the one now living on welfare and she told author Joe Sharkey that while she loved and stood by her husband, she still blamed herself and was haunted by Susan. She said she rarely slept more than three hours a night.

Some nights. I actually wake up with a phone in my hand. Thinking I'm talking to her. And Kathy being Kathy reached out to Susan's sister, Shelby ward, despite everything Shelby had said about her husband and the press, they struck up a friendship similar to Cathy and Susan's they talked on the phone all the time,

February 5th, 1998, 13 year old, Daniel Putnam found her mother dead and their Manchester home.

The press said it was an apparent heart attack. The medical examiner's office ruled that she had died of a combination of pancreatitis and liver disease. Both conditions had been caused by heavy drinking. She was only 38 years old, as you can imagine, Mark was devastated by Kathy's death. He already felt as though he had destroyed his family and Kathy's death was just the culmination.

He told author Joe Sharkey that Kathy's suffered from crippling depression and coped by drinking. And even worse, his children had lived with her suffering and then lost her altogether. Mark was released in the year, 2002 years after Kathy's death. He had served about half of the 16 year sentence. He had been a model prisoner spending his time working in the prison, chapel, the shop and the commissary.

He reunited with his children remarried and now works as a personal trainer in Georgia. Ronald Poole passed away in the year 2000 at the age of 50, despite his Pikeville transgressions, he kept his job with the FBI. Ultimately his time as a narcotics agent out shown his time in Pikeville. Sadly Brady Smith Susan's son died of an overdose of methadone and Xanax.

Miranda is married with a child of her own and declines interviews. Kenneth is quiet too. These days. Living not far from Miranda and Kentucky as my regular listeners know, well, I rarely believe in the heat of passion snapped defense. I do believe that even 30 seconds is enough of a cooling off period and murder as a choice.

But for some reason I believe Mark, or maybe it's that I believe Kathy, I don't believe it was the blind love for her husband that caused her unwavering support. They were truly partners and she felt as responsible for Susan as he did. Kathy Putnam drank herself to death from the guilt of what her husband did to Susan and her traumatic experience in Kentucky and Mark Putnam served his time and he served it honorably.

He lost his beloved wife. He lost the career. He had dreamed of his whole life and he lost himself. He lost who he thought he was in Pikeville. I think he deserves his new life, but that does not diminish the pain. I feel for Susan Smith, she was just a mountain girl trying to make her life better. She didn't have a lot of choices and she did the best she could with what she had.

She was born on welfare and she never got off of it. She lived a hard life and squalor, poverty and violence, and the hollers around Pikeville. I don't think that poor girl ever had a chance and I admire her gumption. It takes a lot of courage to get up in court and testify against a local criminal, exposing herself to her friends, family, neighbors, and enemies, and she never experienced real love.

I think that is the saddest part of Susan's story. As Kathy Putnam said, quote, she never woke up in the morning, opened her eyes and felt that she meant something to someone. Was it so wrong for her to want him for herself? To me, Susan and Kathy are equally tragic figures in the side tail Mark Putnam deluded himself into believing that he just did his job.

He would make it out of Pikeville unscathed. But in the end, none of them did the main Hills of Kentucky swallowed them all home.

2 ACCIDENT OR MURDER

On a hot Sunday in September of 2016, Tex and Diane McGyver played golf in the searing Georgia sun for four hours. You picked up Diane's best friend, Danny, Joe Carter from their Putnam County ranch, where she had been riding horses before they all headed back to Atlanta. Stopping for dinner and Conyers.

The MacGyvers had been drinking. So after dinner, Danny drove the rest of the way home with Diane in the front seat and Tex behind her in the backseat at around 10:00 PM. That Sunday night Atlanta traffic was at a stand still on the downtown connector. Diane told Danny Jo to get off at Edgewood Avenue.

Texed fallen asleep in the backseat and his wife busted him to wake up. So he'd be, are you able to sleep that night? When he looked around and saw the area they were in, he said, girls, this was a bad idea. This is a bad area. And then he said, darlin, hand me my gun, Diane McGyver, then handed her husband the gun that would kill her in a PD charged MacGyver with involuntary manslaughter, but the da disagreed and charge Tex MacGyver with malice murder.

But detects MacGyver really mean to kill his wife.

Atlanta, Georgia is one of the most famous U S Southern cities in the world. During the American civil war, the burning of Atlanta was crucial and general Sherman's March to the sea. It crippled the Confederacy and was the beginning of the end of the civil war. The city fell in September of 1864 and the war ended in April, 1865.

The fall of Atlanta was extensively covered by Northern newspapers. And I gave a huge boost in Northern morale, as well as president Lincoln's political standing, as he won the election that November by significant margin. Sadly Lincoln was assassinated just five days after Confederate general. Robert E.

Lee surrendered in Appomattox, Virginia. Today, modern Atlanta is known for its eclectic diverse culture. It has been a Mecca for African American political power, education and culture. There has been a black mayor in office in Atlanta since 1974 during the civil rights movement in the sixties. A popular Atlanta slogan was, it was a city too busy to hate a slogan that would continue into the nineties.

And in comparison to other large cities in the deep South, the progressive politics and diversity would make that slogan ring true. But in reality, the people of Atlanta are still dealing with racial disparity, tensions and the economic effects of gentrification. In 2016, when Diane McGyver was killed Atlanta, wasn't an exciting transitional phase.

Real estate prices that had lagged since the recession finally saw an uptick, new ground was broken for retail and office spaces. The Braves left Turner filled for SunTrust park, a new entertainment complex within walking distance of bars, shopping and residential areas. In popular culture, the critically acclaimed show, Atlanta premiered as well as stranger things.

The Netflix hit that while set in Indiana had been filmed in Atlanta and surrounding areas. Giving another boost to the local economy on April 14th, Prince played his final show@thefoxtheaterandwhatpatch.com called an intimate stripped down performance just a week before his death that may Atlanta was chosen to host the 2019 super bowl.

Making way for a new one point $4 billion stadium that would host the Atlanta Falcons and the new Atlanta soccer club 2016 was also the third year of the black lives matter movement in July. Hundreds had marched in downtown Atlanta to protest police shootings. The day before a young black man had been found hanging in Piedmont park, the AJC reported that the protest was in part a reaction to what many believed was a modern day lynching.

However, the young man's death was ruled as suicide and a social media post showed that he had been shamed by his family for being gay. It was a terrible coincidence as there were so many police shootings nationwide that had led to the protests. And the first half of July alone, there were 112 protests and 88 cities.

It's important to mention the Atlanta March, because it does become a factor. In this case, though, there was no official March on the day, Diane McGyver was killed, but still specter of dangerous black lives matter. Protesters was raised by TexMacGyvers PR guy, a move that was seriously detrimental to MacGyver's defense.

Claudie MacGyver was born in San Antonio, Texas on December 22nd, 1943. He graduated from law school at the university of Texas before moving to Atlanta, Claude known as techs. All of his life worked for Fisher Phillips law firm for decades. He was a labor lawyer. But he didn't represent the little guy.

He represented the corporations by 2016. He was a long time partner. But recently he went from equity partner to income partner, meaning his income dropped from about $700,000 a year to about $120,000 a year. He was 73 years old. That's not unusual. Tex MacGyver was also a staunch Republican who served on the state election board for 12 years.

He was nominated by the governor in 2005 to be on the judicial nomination committee and even more telling he served on the American bar association committee on gun violence Tex was a man who knew guns. He didn't just know them. He loved them owning close to 40 guns. Some 22 of those being rifles. He was such a good shot.

He could toss a bottle in the air and hit it. Tex MacGyver, married his first wife, Nancy in 1966. They had three kids, two sons and a daughter Nancy filed for divorce in 1997, citing several affairs. She said Tex had specifically that he was having an affair with a woman that worked at their Putnam County ranch.

The 85 acre ranch was Texas crown jewel. He had horses and cattle and a big sprawling ranch house as well as a guest house. And pool techs kept the ranch in the divorce, but otherwise took quite the hit financially. It was an ugly three-year Corps battle. When they settled in July of 2000 techs had spent more than 100,000 on attorney's fees.

And he had agreed to pay Nancy almost $700,000 in alimony. Nancy also got half of his retirement account, which was valued at a little over 700,000 at the time of settlement and also half of their property, which was $400,000 techs also had to pay 100,000 for her attorney's fees. The settlement, even stipulated, how techs could visit their dog Malone quote, the wife shall allow the husband to use her garden hose if necessary to wash the dog.

After one of his visits, his daughter, and one of his sons stopped speaking to him after the ugly divorce to the point that he wasn't even invited to his daughter Meredith's wedding at the time of his divorce has assets totaled almost 1 million, but his monthly income was down to $17,000 a month. He used to bring in close to 60,000, but like I said, his age and semi retirement had changed a salary.

He met Diane the year of his divorce though. There is no speculation whatsoever that there was any overlap or that she was one of the affairs. Nancy accused him of, he met her through business associates and was immediately enamored of the beautiful 47 year old woman being 10 years. Her senior didn't deter him at all.

Diane Biddy Smith MacGyver was born on July 21st, 1953 in Auburn, Alabama. She had a kind of rags to riches aura about her, but she grew up middle class. The her relationship with her mother was always very volatile. She had never known her father and her mother was an alcoholic with several ex-husbands.

Diane had a brother who died in his early twenties. She moved to Atlanta with her family when she was in high school. And a business owner named Billy Corey hired her when she was just 17 years old. As a part time payroll clerk, she worked nights to earn an accounting degree from Georgia state university and her first job for Corey at U S enterprises.

She started out answering phones and soon became president U S enterprises is the umbrella company that Cory enterprises falls under. At the time of her death, Diane McGyver was the CEO of Cory enterprises and her net worth was estimated at 12 million. She had worked for Corey enterprises for 43 years.

She was respected as a formidable business woman, ambitious, uncompromising, and tough as nails. Diane didn't marry until she was 40 years old. She always just said that was a mistake. She never had children of her own. Friends later said it was a painful divorce and like Texas divorce. It was also ugly with the splitting of finances.

And Diane was estranged from her mother for 15 years before her death. She wouldn't even attend her funeral telling her neighbor that she would not shed one tear for her mother though. Tex and Diane had met before he started pursuing her more vigorously. When she moved into the luxury Villa Buckhead condos in Atlanta in the summer of 2000.

He slipped a note under her door, welcoming her to the building. She wasn't interested at first, but he wore her down. When she finally agreed to a date, it was dinner in Texas apartment. And Diane showed up in yoga gear and a ball cap. She was determined that this was going nowhere. The techs charmed her Rachel styles.

One of Diane's assistants said, quote, he was the perfect match for Diane. Diane was a very strong woman. She intimidated a lot of men. They just didn't want to compete with her. The techs didn't want to compete with her. He was just infatuated with her Diane didn't trust, many people that seem to trust those that worked for her, her best friend, Denny, Joe Carter, the one driving that night was her manicurist.

They had been friends for 40 years though. There was a 10 year period. They didn't speak because Danny Joe had a drinking problem. She got sober and was then welcomed back into Diane's life. Diane's other trusted confidant. That's where her two personal assistants at work. And the man who detailed her car and ran errands for her.

And that's about it. You would think a woman in her position would have many rich high society, friends, but Diane chose to trust people who worked for her. It's not that she didn't rub elbows with a well healed in Atlanta. She did, but her close friends were more down to earth. And I think there is something else at play here.

Diane could be a bit controlling. She was known as a very blunt person. She would tell you that you've put on weight, but then offer tips on how to lose it. It wasn't really malicious. She was just fastidious and she always thought she knew best. She could be really critical that everyone in her life accepted that as the other side of the coin, that was Diane because she was also very generous and loving and she was hard on herself too.

That's probably why she felt critical of others. She got up at 5:00 AM every day to work out and she kept weights in her office, but she can't always behave that way with your peers and get away with it. Diane did, but her friends were not exactly her peers. She was the CEO of a company, a self made millionaire.

Her friends were mostly employees and coworkers. She didn't have close friends in her own social standing, which isn't that unusual? How many female CEOs do you know? Her peer group would be mainly men in that sense. And before Tex, she had even decided not to remarry. I think that wealth can be insulating from the world's problems, but it can also be very isolating.

You never know if someone is your real friend or if they want something from you, at least with employees, you know, where you stand. But Diane wound up falling hard for Tex. They dated for almost five years before marrying in November of 2005 and a lavish ceremony at the ranch. Diane came down the aisle in a horse, drawn carriage, the horse wearing a flower crown was her maid of honor.

And they lived a jet setting, extravagant lifestyle trips to Paris, and the South of France, she in Tex would fly into Louisville for the Kentucky Derby, but have Danny Jo or her husband drive their limo up so they could have it to ride around town. And, but she was generous to Danny Joe with these trips, even if Danny Joe might drive the limo or handle some other things for her, she was getting to go on all these fabulous trips all over the world with her generous best friend and Diane often lent money to her friends.

Terry Brown was one of Diane's personal assistants at Cory enterprises. And he was in charge of keeping track of the loans. She gave friends. He told the AJC that around the third of every month, she would ask him if the money was all in, she loaned money, but with reasonable interest rates and she even loaned money to Tex.

It's important to note here that she in Tex made the decision before they married to keep their finances separate. Both had been through messy, expensive divorces. And both were still self made millionaires. At the time of her death, it was estimated that Diane was worth around 12 million, but most of that was in real estate holdings.

She had about 400,000 in the bank and Tex was worth about 1.7 million on his own. I told you before that his income had significantly decreased, but it's not like he was a poor man. The engagement ring he gave Diane was worth $60,000. The loan she made to Tex was to expand the guest house, making it a real party house on the property and the style of an old West saloon.

I've seen conflicting reports on whose idea this was friends told reporters that it was Diane's. She loved having huge parties on the ranch Tex was fine with that as long as she could pay for it, but she made it alone in his name with interest, he was paying around $1,500 a month on the loan, just the interest.

It was supposed to have been a three year loan, but in 2014, Diane extended the loan for another three years. Terry Brown said that Tech's always made us payments on time. But the interesting thing on this extension is that she put a codicil that of Tex defaulted. She could call him the loan and take controlling interest of the ranch.

Well, Tex had already willingly put her name on the deed to the ranch. When they got married, this is where their finances seem murky to me. If she really was the one who wanted the saloon party house, she certainly could afford to pay for it, but she expected Tex too. And that caught a soul was her insurance that he would pay for it.

But the same friends who claim the saline was her idea said that the loan through Tex was merely for tax purposes. She and Tex also made new wills in 2005, much was made at Texas trial about the possibility of another new will that Diane had recently made, but they never found proof of it. The other important person to point out when it comes to the MacGyver.

Finances is there God's son, Austin Schwab. His parents were divorced and he was the son of a Fulton County judge. They both doted on the boy, but especially Diane, who never had children of her own Austin called her mommy die. She threw him lavish birthday parties pay for private school and intended to pay for his college.

If there were issues with her will, it was discussed on and off for a few years. It was Austin. Diane wanted to leave him everything, but Tex wanted to leave all or at least part to the son that still spoke to him. But Diane never legally changed her will. Despite the rumors, the prosecution continuously brought up, there was no proof, no other will was ever found the prosecution even put out an ad for any Atlanta lawyer who might've worked on a will for Diane McGyver to please come forward.

Sunday was a hot day for September, even in Georgia. With temperatures rising into the nineties, Diane sex, and Danny Joe had been at the ranch all weekend. Any Joe later testified that techs got up that morning and brought her and Diane coffee upstairs before making breakfast for everyone. He liked doing little things like that.

He was always the quarterly gentlemen, even after 10 years of marriage. Tex. And Diane had given Danny Joe a horse and that Sunday, the MacGyvers went to meet a friend to play golf. While Danny Joe stayed at the ranch to ride her horse Tex later told investigators that his wife shot a 74 that day, while he shot a 92, they all had a lot of fun that day, despite the heat, after they finished playing golf, Tex and Diane picked up Danny Jo to head back to Atlanta.

Danny. Joe said they pour wine in a Yeti cup and sipped it as they headed to dinner and Conyers Georgia, on the way back into the city, they were meeting a friend and colleague of Diane's for dinner at the Longhorn steakhouse. There a bottle of red wine was opened Tex later, said he didn't drink much of it because he didn't like it.

But still, yeah, after dinner, Danny Joe took over the driving because Diane and Tex had been drinking and she was sober. As they neared Atlanta traffic on the downtown connector was a parking lot. Even at 10:00 PM on a Sunday night, you can count on Atlanta traffic being the worst. Diane told Danny Joe to take the edge wood Avenue exit, and then she turned around and fussed at techs to wake up.

He had fallen asleep in the backseat. Diane was in the front passenger seat and Tex was directly behind her. She didn't want him to fall asleep because she said he wouldn't be able to sleep that night. When Tex woke up and looked around, he said, quote, girls, this is a bad idea. This isn't safe. He was talking about the area of Midtown.

They were in. Diane said, we'll be on Piedmont shortly. But he said, quote, darlin, Hemi, my gun. And Diane reached into the center console and pulled out a snubnose 38 revolver wrapped in a plastic bag. And then she handed it to her husband. And here is where everything went wrong. Tex took the gun and laid it in his lap and then nodded back off to sleep, Danny, so that she was driving on Piedmont.

When she got stopped by a red light at either 12th or 13th street. And then she heard a boom. She thought at first that they had been hit by another car. But Tex quickly said I discharged the gun and asked if everyone was all right. Diane said, Tex, what did you do? Denny Joseph. She thought there would be a bullet hole in the floor of the car.

And no one realized Diane was shot at first, not even Diane until she started breathing heavy and slumped in her seat. And then she said, I've been shot at this Tex, leaned forward, cradling her head as Danny Joe stepped on the gas to speed for hospital. This isn't huge point of contention at trial. Why didn't they just call nine one one?

Danny Joe admitted. She was scared because of the location and wasn't sure how long it would take to get an ambulance there. She had Piedmont hospital in mind, but didn't know the way tech spoke up and directed her to Emory hospital, which was not the closest, even if it was the closest. Anyone from Atlanta can tell you that Grady Memorial hospital has a renowned level, one trauma unit.

It handles almost all gunshot wounds in Atlanta. At trial, the prosecution would apply that Tex intended to go to a further away hospital. But the truth is Emory hospital was a client of his as a lawyer at Fisher Phillips. He had represented the hospital and had been there many times. He knew exactly where it was.

And this makes sense to me, despite the fact that Grady was known to be the place for a gunshot wound, Tex went to the first hospital. He knew how to get to. What Tex and Danny Joe didn't know was that there was a firehouse some 300 yards or so from where the SUV was sitting, when Diane was shot, though, the exact distance is estimated because they were on a section of Piedmont where the traffic cameras were not working.

Danny, Joe also wasn't sure which stoplight she was at. So there were medics extremely close by. I think the decision to drive to a hospital, any hospital was a mistake they should have called nine 11. At the hospital, Texas scene on security cameras, jumping out of the SUV and waving Danny Joe through to the emergency doors.

He also helps get his wife into a wheelchair. Dr. Suzanne Hardy took Diane's case at the ER. Diane made a spontaneous comment in front of the doctor while she was examining her. She said, quote, it was an accident at trial. The prosecution focused on her only other statement. She said, I'm dying. And the doctor asked if she wanted to see her husband.

And Diane said no to this. I say, yes, Diane was dying. Who knows if she even understood the doctor's question at that? Her blood pressure was extremely low and she was about to be taken in for emergency surgery. The other spontaneous comment can be considered a dying declaration. It was not an answer to a question made under duress.

Diane just said it. The bullet hit where Diane's 11th rib met her 11th vertebra. Scattering pieces of bone and then traveled through her left adrenal gland and left kidney and severed blood vessels going into her spleen. Then through her pancreas and stomach sublet quickly started filling her abdominal cavity, the bullet mr.

Harper centimeters, that because it, Nick, those arteries, she bled out internally. Anyway, dr. Hardy wanted to transfer her to Grady, but Diane was never stable enough for transfer. And the operating room surgeons opened her abdomen only to find several liters of blood close to what would be the total blood volume in her body.

For over an hour, surgeons fought to save Diane's life, tying off damaged blood vessels and removing pieces of damaged organs. But her blood pressure kept dropping the attending surgeons report. Read. Her chance of survival was zero. At this stage, there is no disagreement whatsoever among anyone involved, including all of the surgeons and the anesthesiologist that we could have done anything differently.

And given her a chance to survive at the hospital techs called an old friend of his, this would wind up being a very bad decision. His friend was also an attorney, an attorney who had represented him before. Steven Maples is a Decatur attorney who defended Tex when he was charged in 1990, with three counts of aggravated assault for firing his pistol at a car with three young men inside the teens had been hanging out in the culdesac of Texas neighborhood, playing their music loud and annoying him.

He tried sticking his dogs on them before he got his gun out, but the charges were dropped when Tex agreed to pay for the damages to the teen's car. And this was the guy who sat on the American bar association committee on gun violence. It's an example of what the prosecution would later seize upon Tex was a politically connected white man.

He got away with that incident 15 years earlier, and now he was involved in another gun incident at the hospital. Texas, Steven Maples were overheard conferring and Tex was heard saying, what do I say? What do I do? Naturally, there was much made of this at trial, but honestly, if you had just shot your wife even accidentally, wouldn't you be scared, but optics are everything.

And his behavior, even while still at the hospital put people off. And at this point he had no idea that Diane had already told the doctor, it was an accident. He went up to Danny Joe and said, why don't you just say you weren't there. Things like this can get so turned around. Just say you came here to be with us as a friend and Danny Joe told him, no, she couldn't do that.

Quote Tex. I just drove you to the R I can't do that. Why would I be here at this time of night? On a Sunday without my own car. Danny Joe talked to the Atlanta police right away and insisted it was a tragic accident. She said there was no doubt in her mind. And this was even after his strange request for her to lie at the hospital.

She didn't tell police about Texas requests. The first time they questioned her, but she did the second time and a very different Danny Joe testified at trial. She did not change her story, but she was no longer on Texas side. She now believed the shooting was intentional. I think like everyone else, she was put off by Texas behavior after Diane's death, starting with him, asking her to lie at the hospital.

Afterwards, he went so far as to call Danny Jo's husband and tell him to get Danny Joe to retract what she told him. Yeah. Interestingly, Texas defense team found another reason for Danny Joe's flip. Diane had loaned her money also as she did for many friends and associates and Tex expected her to pay the loan.

Now, this isn't as heartless as it sounds, Tex was executor of Diane's estate. Danny Joe, wasn't the only friend expected to repay their loan and about Texas behavior. Well, first of all, Tex it and go voluntarily. Talk to police for two days. That does look bad. Why wouldn't you just sit down with them right away if it was an accident and why didn't the police insist on speaking with him right away?

I'm pretty sure if I shot my husband, I would be questioned that same day. Even with a witness saying it was an accident. It does show that Tex was getting preferential treatment. The police felt confident. It was an accident after taking Danny Joe statement. So maybe this isn't as bad as it looks, but again, optics are everything.

And to the world, this looked like a rich white lawyer with political connections. Wasn't being questioned by the police right away. And why would he choose to wait? Friends say Tex was beside himself. It wasn't to get a story. He was just in shock. When he did finally talk to the police, he said, said the gun was in his lap and it just went off.

Tex told police quote, I was handling the gun. I forgot it was in my lap and it just went off and I don't think he's lying. Tex was diagnosed with REM behavioral disorder, which means where most people don't act out their dreams techs often did thrash around bill Rankin with the AJC podcast. Breakdown explained this diagnosis very well.

He said, normally people have a wall between and their dreams and actual bodily movements in reaction to the dream people with REM behavioral, somehow quote, breach that wall specifically Tex would clinches fingers and thrashes arms a Massoud. Need any Anderson testified at Texas trial about his condition.

He often fell asleep while getting a massage, and she had to be careful about where she was standing in relation to his body. If he fell asleep or he might accidentally hit her. She also had to testify to deny allegations of a sexual relationship with Tex. I will come back to this in a moment. The next big state tax made was hiring a PR consultant by the name of bill crane.

He made an official statement to the press that Tex was alarmed about the recent unrest surrounding several black lives matter protests in the area and theory that they would be carjacked. This is the mistake that took this case. National black lives matter representatives across the country were outraged.

In fact, there is no evidence that there were protesters in that area on the night of September 6th. As many people have said, bill crane injected race into a case where it did not belong. I agree to a certain extent. First of all, Tex MacGyver denies, ever saying this. He said crane made that statement.

All he had said was that it was a bad area. Crane stands by his statement and testify that techs tried to get him to retract the statement. This would lead to one of the three charges, the prosecution indicted Tex four of trying to manipulate a witness. The other two counts for the same thing were for when he asked any Joe to lie and say she wasn't in the SUV that night.

And also for the message he left on her husband's voicemail, Tex foolishly left the voicemail for Denny Jo's husband from jail. This was before he made bond. He found out that Danny Joe told the police what he had asked her to do. And he called her husband to ask him to get Danny Joe to stop talking to the police.

Oh. And he also said, delete this message. Except all calls coming out of the Fulton County jail are recorded foolish, indeed. And that is what I think is Tex MacGyver's huge problem. He was arrogant and foolish, but before he had ever even been indicted, he made his next huge mistake. Within days of Diane's death.

He was taking inventory of her extensive collection of couture clothing, first shoes, hats, and jewelry. And then he auctioned everything off. He held three auctions actually, and this is really hard for people to swallow. It was tacky, it was unseemly and it definitely looked callous, but Diane's a state lawyer actually advised techs to do this until they could liquidate assets to cover not only her requests, but other financial issues related to her estate and just the wrapping up of her life.

But still this looked awful. The estate lawyer spoke with the AJC and defended the advice he gave saying those clothes would appreciate within a year when styles change. And also you need to sell winter clothes at the start of winter, Diane had 137 for coats. The auctions were held in early December.

Okay. I get all of that, but it's hard to believe that this guy and Tex both thought that this was a good idea, but then I think about it this way. Tex said it was an accident. I don't think he really believed that he would be prosecuted. So why not follow the lawyer's advice? He was not officially charged until December 21st after the auctions.

And he was charged with involuntary manslaughter and reckless conduct. One big point of contention with this auction as not only how it looked. There were some Ruby and diamond pieces that had been willed to a friend of Diane's with the same birthstone. If he was really auctioning to honor requests, why would he auction pieces for someone in the will pieces that she was supposed to get?

Well, she wasn't supposed to get those pieces. According to the AJC in total, there was a Ruby ring, bracelet and earrings that brought around $18,000 at auction. Now that's no small amount. But Diane had many other Ruby and diamond pieces. And in fact there was a ring bracelet and earrings valued at more than 100,000 that he did not auction.

He was saving those for her friend, Texas bond was set at $75,000, which he quickly made and was out until trial. By April prosecutor served multiple subpoenas for the MC Ivers financial records. Now it would seem that the DA's office did not agree with the Atlanta PD. They didn't believe this was an accident during the search of Texas condo, a Glock pistol was found in his sock drawer.

This was a violation of his bond. He had all other firearms removed from the condo and ranch, except this one, the judge revoked Texas bond. And then a few days later on April 27th, he was indicted on a charge of malice murder, Georges malice murder charges. What many States refer to as first degree murder?

The da Inditex on seven additional counts. He was also charged with felony murder, which is what other States call second degree murder, then aggravated assault with a deadly weapon, possession of a firearm in commission of a felony. And those three charges of trying to influence witnesses that I told you about.

And this trial would be dramatic in so many ways for one. They had a judge who allowed jurors to ask questions throughout the trial, not just in deliberations. This is highly unusual and something that defense attorneys didn't like if the state wasn't making their case clear enough, that's on them. This judge allowing clarification questions clearly gives the prosecution a leg up prosecutor, Clint Rucker, as one of those preacher prosccutors and natural born theatrical speaker.

He uses that thing where he says something and then repeats it for emphasis. He recites poetry or scripture, his booming voice and lyrical way of speaking is very effective in a courtroom in late October of 2017, three days before the trial was to begin, the prosecution asked for a continuance saying they felt the defense needed more time, which was some hilarious legal wrangling, because the defense strongly disputed this.

If they needed a continuance, they would have asked for it. Bill

Rankin with AJC said that the prosecution was actually still looking for evidence to support their indictment of malice murder. So they put it on hold for four months and then came back. The AJC also pointed out that they had some 90,000 email to go through between Tex and Diane position.

Is that Tex MacGyver needed not just wanted his wife's fortune. They also brought up the specter of supposed affairs. He was having, which was convenient as it was the reason his ex wife divorced him, but they could never find any proof of an affair Tex. Worshiped his wife, the state brought a woman named Annie Anderson to testify.

She was the misuse I mentioned earlier. She came over and gave massages to Diane and Tex regularly. Being wealthy people. They didn't make appointments at a salon. They had a personal misuse who came to their house and it's important to note that she treated both the MacGyvers and also considered them close friends as did many of their employees, any Anderson and Rachel styles.

Diane's other personal assistant, stayed with Tex the first couple of days after the shooting, because they were afraid he would mix up his medication and hurt himself and he slept on the floor and Texas room. The prosecution had a field day with this, but you know, what is gross? God's son, Austin was sleeping in the bed with Tex where they insinuating that he had sex with Annie, with his godson and the room for her part.

Any Andersen was angry and humiliated that this was even insinuated. She was a professional and this accusation was detrimental to her career. And what's more, she cared about the MacGyvers that is really clear in her testimony. But aside from imaginary affairs, all the state really had was money techs wanted Diane's money.

As I told you, his income had drastically decreased at his age. He was no longer an equity partner, but an income partner and his expenses at the ranch were exorbitant. And it is something he and Diane were talking about. And an email, the state found, he tells her, trying to reduce his monthly expenses.

She then playfully suggest that he take over the job of his ranch hand at the Putnam County ranch. He says, well, guess it's back to being a gigolo. And the state thought this was nefarious. The defense thought it was playful. Bad. Sure. Yes, there were money issues, but tech still made money and he and Diane were both millionaires.

They would work it out. To me, this sounds very much like playful banter. I would hate for a prosecutor to see some of the Tex I sent him my own husband when joking around Danny Joe Carter was the state's star witness at trial. They later even called her the, but the biggest problem with the state's case is all the promises they made in the opening statement.

They continue to allude to a second will, uh, will they could never prove existed. It was never found. It's why they wanted to go through all those emails. And when they did fund an email talking about wills, but nothing was formalized. The lawyer who was copied on this email told the AJC that drafting a will for people as kind of like selling life insurance folks, keep putting this stuff off because they don't want to think about it.

The lawyer didn't think it was fishy at all. And yes, the state proved that Tex was ever spending and his income had gone down. But in reality, Diane made more money than him. If he was really worried that much about money, it makes more sense for Diane to live. She was the breadwinner and every friend agreed that they were in love.

Ridiculously in love. The kind of couple who after five years of dating and 10 years of marriage still held hands all the time. Friends turned on Tex by the time of the trial because of his many bad things. Alice looking choices, he did auction off her things. And he also asked a colleague of hers. If he would be able to draw her social security benefits.

This was only a few days after her death. And that's the problem with Tex. He not only takes bad advice, but he makes bad decisions, but none of that makes him a murderer. I do think he was worried about how he would live out his days, how he would maintain this lifestyle. And he could also just be a greedy bastard.

That's true. But I don't think he killed her over it. She was the one keeping him in such a lavish lifestyle to begin with. And he adored her Eden friends who turned against him. Couldn't argue with that. It's why they found it. So shocking at trial Tex did not take the stand in his own defense. I'm not going to take you gavel to gavel through the trial of Tex MacGyver.

I would rather point you to the excellent podcast breakdown by the AJC that I've already mentioned. They're long form podcast on this case covers Texas trial extensively. So I will just give you some highlights. There were competing firearms experts. One sticking point is that no one knows if the gun was actually caught.

The police didn't ask that question right away and Tex later said he couldn't remember the difference is if it wasn't cocked, it takes 12 pounds of pressure to pull that trigger. If it was cocked, it takes less than two pounds. That makes a lot more sense for an accidental shooting. There was no way to know for sure, but I am willing to bet that after Diane handed Tex the gun, he cocked it to be ready and had it sitting in his lap.

And then he did not off back to sleep. And many people have difficulty with this. If he was afraid enough to ask for his gun, how could he just not off. To this. I say he was 73 years old. He had played golf and the hot Georgia sun for four hours and then had been drinking wine. The defense also made some really good points about why, if he wanted to kill his wife, would he do it this way?

Why try and shoot her in the car through the seat? There was a great chance that the bullet could have ricocheted back at him or get lodged in Diane seat. There's any possible scenario that would have made this a strange way to kill his wife? The first problem being that he did it in front of her best friend, but the prosecution did do a good job of making techs out to be the entitled white, rich, politically connected man.

He was, none of that is false. It just makes the police look bad for not going after him harder in the first place. However, I don't think the police were going that easy on him. The detective on his case had worked over 40 malice murder cases before he had an excellent record. He had an eye witness that said it was an accident.

He had a dying declaration from the victim saying it was an accident. I will say that they definitely should have brought them in for formal questioning that night, if for no other reason than protocol, if his connections helped at all, it was that they gave him those couple of days before their formal interview.

The problem was, but the prosecution and defense, when all or nothing and closing arguments, both as the jury, not to find him guilty of involuntary manslaughter, the defense wanted a straight not guilty. This was an accident. The state wanted premeditated malice murder. The original involuntary manslaughter charge was taken off the table.

The jury could choose malice or felony. Or they could find him not guilty, but that was it. During deliberations, the jury kept sending out questions that made the defense feel pretty good. They didn't seem to grasp the legal definition of intent. Things were looking pretty good for Tex. Especially once the jury sent word that they were deadlocked.

But the judge gave them instructions to keep deliberating. And then they came back with a confusing verdict. They found Tex guilty of felony murder, aggravated assault with a deadly weapon, possession of a firearm and commission of a felony and witness influencing the reason it's confusing as felony murder as like second degree murder, it means a person was killed in the commission of another felony.

In this case, that would be the aggravated assault charge. Meaning. There was no actual intent to kill Diane, but just to harm her. See what I mean by the jury, not understanding intent. So why did they decide this way with the conflicting verdicts? Why would Tex shoot Diane, unless he meant to kill her?

The problem here lies and what the jury was not allowed to ask. Malice murder and felony murder have the same punishments, but they were not allowed to ask how long Tex would go to prison for these offenses. They did ask, but of all the questions that this judge allowed, he refused this one and it is a matter of law except in capital cases, juries are not to consider punishment during their deliberations.

Maybe that felony murder was a lesser charge. When in reality, it's basically the same in terms of punishment. Tex MacGyver will spend the rest of his natural life in prison. He would have, if he had been convicted of malice murder. Also, I think the defense made a crucial mistake with all or nothing charged to the jury.

Typically all types of murder charges are on an indictment to give the jury and out if they don't believe it was premeditated, it's not surprising the prosecution wanted this charge removed, but it was the defense who really rolled the dice here. Texas now embroiled in a wrongful death suit with Diane's estate, but here's the thing.

So is Danny Jo Carter, she is named in the same suit. The suit says that she breached the duty of driving in a safe manner at all times, but specifically cites her decision not to call nine one one and to drive to an ER. Instead as of may of 2019, the lawsuit hasn't been settled. So I'm sure by now you guys know what I think.

I think Tex MacGyver was guilty of involuntary manslaughter due to reckless conduct. I do not believe he intended to murder his wife. I think he is an old man who had handled guns his whole life and never thought something like this could happen to him. I think it was a horrible tragedy and his behavior after the fact was shitty, he took bad advice and also made several bad choices on his own.

He really was his own worst enemy. But being a dumb ass does not make you a murderer. And you know what maybe race did belong in this trial, regardless of whether Tex made the black lives matter comment, or if it was really his PR guy, the specter of race, is there this bad spot of town they were stopped at?

Wasn't just about homeless people. It was about black people. Tex was an old white guy has automatic response to this kind of neighborhood is indicative of his own racial bias, whether he was conscious of it or not. And ironically, Diane McGyver had donated money to the blue lives matter campaign in Atlanta Tex message.

I may not have understood the black lives matter movement, but it would seem that his wife did either way. When he awoke on the stark street, he didn't feel safe. So he said, darlin, hand me my gun and Diane McGyver handed her husband the gun that killed him.

3 DOUBLE MURDER ON ROBINS AIR FORCE BASE

in the early morning hours of July 5th, 2004, a man placed a desperate nine one one call from the Robins air force base in Georgia. The call only lasted 34 seconds and the dispatcher could hear a man being attacked in the background pleading for his life. And then a woman's screaming. And then the line went dead.

Andy and Jamie schlep sick were found dead in their home viciously, stabbed to death with an army combat knife. Their friend Jason King had been there too, and was also severely injured. But managed to make it out the door, running to the first neighbor for help Jason King survived, but just barely and senior airman, Andrew Paul Witt was arrested for the double murder and attempted murder the next day.

So up to the events of this fateful night. Before this over the 4th of July holiday, Andrew with the and Jason King and his wife were all seemingly friends.

In October of 1941, the war department was looking for a site for an army air Corps Depot. They found a small town called Wellston Georgia, just 18 miles South of Macon. It was a tiny whistle stop town made up of just farmers and their families with the only landmark being the stop on the railroad line.

Colonel Charles Thomas who held from Atlanta was tasked with overseeing the building of the Depot. It was originally named Wellston air Depot at Robin's field. Colonel Thomas had named the field for his mentor, Brigadier general, Augustine Warner Robbins, who was considered the father of logistics.

Because he came up with an ingenious system for cataloging materials and supplies for the army. But Thomas wasn't technically allowed to do this. Regulations required a base to be named after the nearest town. So in 1942, the town of Wellston was officially renamed Warner Robins, and the newly built Depot took over the workload of two closed air force bases in mobile, Alabama, and Middleton township, Pennsylvania.

Robins air force base is not within the city limits of Warner Robins, but just across us highway one 29, that serves as a boundary between the base and the city today. Warner Robins has about 75,000 residents and is home to the museum of aviation, the largest tourist attraction outside of Atlanta in the state of Georgia Warner Robins is located in Houston County and the middle of the state with hot and humid summers, but pretty mild winters.

In 2004, when today's story takes place, there were around 50,000 residents in the town of Warner, Robins and Robins air force base employed around 25,000 civilians, contractors and military members. The residential population on base was around a thousand and on the 4th of July holiday in 2004, temperatures ranged in the mid nineties.

When it's hot and sticky and especially on a national holiday, people drink more, make bad decisions and tempers flare.

Yeah. And Jamie had been high school sweethearts. Jamie was more shy and reserved while Andy was charismatic and outgoing as Jamie's father put it, they completed each other. Andrew Richard slipped, sick known as Andy was born in Peoria, Illinois on April 3rd, 1979 to parent's day of and Jacqueline. He had two brothers named Jeremy and Chad.

He attended Richwoods high school where he was a popular and athletic student and he graduated in 1997. Jamie Lynn Beilin Birch lipstick was born on July 19th, 1979, also in Peoria to parents, Jim and Deborah. She had two sisters named Jody and Casey. Jamie also attended Richwoods high school, but only for three years.

And then she attended university high school for her senior year. She was on the swim team and graduated in 1998. Her teachers thought she was a pleasant girl with a good attitude, just an all around good kid. After high school, Jamie went to Eastern Illinois university where she graduated in 2002. Andy enlisted in the air force in August of 2000, by 2004, he was a senior airman in the 54th combat communications squadron of the air force.

His job was to maintain ground radar equipment. He was deployed in Iraq from April to October of 2003, his commander Colonel John lint described Andy as an outstanding troop and a natural leader. Andy moved to Robins air force base in 2001 shortly before he and Jamie got married. Jamie worked as a social worker for Houston County, Georgia.

Once she joined him on base, the couple married back in their hometown of Peoria on June 8th, 2002, friends and neighbors characterize them as lovebirds. They never lost that initial giddy spark, a falling in love on the base. They lived in a red brick, duplex, common to married couples, close to the other families on base there they met Jason and page King.

Jason King was a senior airmen in the 53rd squadron. He and Paige had a three year old daughter named Ramsey. The couple lived about a quarter mile from each other. Andy and Jason were both senior airmen and worked in neighboring units. One of their colleagues suggested that they play a round of golf together and the men became fast friends.

So did Jamie and Paige, they shopped and hung out at the pool on base together. Paige had initially struggled to make friends on base and was delighted to find Jamie by the summer of 2004, the couples were inseparable. Jason King later said he felt that he had known Andy his whole life. So he was really happy when Paige met Jamie and they also instantly clicked the 4th of July holiday fell on a Sunday that year on Saturday, the Kings hosted to get together.

Andy and Jamie brought a friend of Andy's along named Andrew Witt. They work together and when Jason met him, he was friendly and inviting saying any friend of Andy's is a friend of mine. The next day, Sunday was officially independence day. It is usually a big party atmosphere on military bases, but the schlep six and Kings just hung out together at Jason and page's place.

They drank beer girls, some ribs, and just hung out as little Ramsey colored on the sidewalk with chalk. It was a fun, relaxed day. Andy had made the decision to leave the air force and he and Paige were set to move to Chicago in two weeks onto a new adventure. Jason. And Paige were sad to see their friends leave, but they were already making plans to visit.

As the evening was winding down the couples considered going to the fireworks show, but decided to stay home page tired said good night to everyone around midnight. Andy, Jamie and Jason stayed up talking. Jamie had something bothering her and she hadn't said anything to Andy about it yet, but after a few beers and maybe feeling more comfortable.

She decided to open up and tell him and Jason, what was wrong? After the Saturday party at the King's home, Andrew Witt, the friend, Andy and Jamie had brought, had too much to drink and rode home with a to sleep on their couch. Andy went straight to bed and page was making sure Andrew was set up in the living room.

When he made a pass at her, he tried to kiss her. Jamie says she firmly pushed him away and said, no. And then went to bed. Andrew went to sleep on the couch and he got up and left the next morning before Jamie and Andy woke up, each lipstick was understandably livid. When he heard the story, Andrew Witt was his friend.

He had trusted him in his home. He decided to call him and

confront him at 1:37 AM. Andy called Andrew. The first time, the next call was at 2:21 AM and it lasted for 33 minutes. But it was the last call where the men actually spoke. At this point, there were two kinds calls between the two men and nine unanswered calls.

Jason later said he remembered a lot of calls back and forth, and then they just let the subject drop. I'm sure. Jamie was really, it's not easy for a woman in this situation. She had to know it would upset her husband, but she probably felt very burdened by the way it happened and needed to get it out.

And she felt comfortable with Jason there as well. Any woman who has spurned an unwanted sexual advance knows how awful it feels. It's much worse when it's someone you trust someone, you consider a friend it's a betrayal and it's embarrassing, even though, you know, you've done nothing wrong, having let the uncomfortable subject of Andrew Witt drop, but not ready to call it a night around 3:30 AM.

Andy, Jamie and Jason drove to the slip six. They had run out of beer and cigarettes and figured they would go restock at Andy and Jamie's house. Meanwhile, Andrew wed back at his own apartment had changed into his camouflage combat uniform and grabbed a combat. And from his closet, he put the knife in the trunk of his car and then drove to the base at around three 15.

Am he parked 50 yards away from Jason's house so he could watch everyone without being seen. Crouching outside. He watched them through the trees and bushes later from phone records. Investigators found that once Andrew, it was on base, he kept calling Jason and Andy. But this time Andy wouldn't answer and he talked to Jason.

Jason said he did seem apologetic in some of the calls, but in other calls, Andrew reportedly told Jason that he and Andy should quote, come over here and kick my ass to which Jason responded with. You need your ass kicked. Andrew Witt watched Andy, Jamie and Jason get an Andy's car and head to the slips of house around 3:30 AM.

He left his car parked where it was and follow them on foot. When they all got to the house, Andy went into the kitchen and Jamie went into the bedroom to get a sweater. Jamie had called Paige to let her know where they all were. So Jason had followed her into the bedroom and then they heard yelling in the kitchen.

Andy was screaming. Get out. When Jason ran into the kitchen, he said he saw Andrew wet and combat fatigues and figured he was there to fight. When Andrew went, saw Jason King, he said, Oh good. You're here too. Jason tried to pull Andrew off of Andy by putting him in a headlock, but then Jason pulled the combat and I thought of his pocket.

Andrew broke free and ran to the living room with Andy and Jason close behind Jason later said what happened next was so fast. He could barely understand what was happening. Andrew. And Andy were fighting while Jason was trying to pull Andrew away. And then Andrew turned around and seemingly punched Jason in the stomach.

Only it wasn't a punch. Jason felt a searing pain in his stomach and realized Andrew had stabbed him as Jason backed up into the kitchen. Jamie ran in screaming, my God you're bleeding. And then Andrew turned the knife on to Andy and he fell to the floor. Jamie kept screaming and ran back to the bedroom and locked herself in.

Jason was trying to get out the kitchen door, but was struggling with the deadbolt. Andrew Witt came up behind him and kept stabbing him in the back. Jason finally made it out the kitchen door and staggered to the nearest neighbor who had a light on the neighbor called nine one one as Jason collapsed in their driveway.

Andrew Witt later claimed he didn't want to leave any evidence. So he went back into the slips at home. After he at first, tried to chase Jason to the neighbor's house. When he got back in the house, he found anybody on the phone with nine 11. This was the call that only lasted 34 seconds. Andy can be hard pleading for his own life and begging Andrew not to hurt Jamie Andrew stabbed Andy twice smore and Andy died almost instantly.

Andrew Witt then went to the bedroom and broke down the door. He later said Jamie was on the ground in the fetal position. He broke her arm, yanking her up, and then he stopped her and kept stabbing her after he killed Andy and Jamie, Andrew went left and returned to his apartment off base. His roommate later said, Andy woke him up and they drove around for a while.

Police arrived at the slips at home and found the bodies of Andy and Jamie. They found Andy lying on his back in the living room with his open cell phone laying nearby. He had suffered three stab wounds. The first was to the left of his chest, penetrating his diaphragm and piercing his liver. The second stab one severed his spinal cord and he was instantly paralyzed from the waist down.

The third wound was to his chest piercing straight through his heart and killed him. Instantly. Jamie was found slumped against the wall behind the bedroom door. She was wearing only a shirt and underwear. Her Jean skirt was about 10 feet away from her body. A blood spatter expert would later say he believed the skirt was on Jamie before the attack and came off or was pulled off sometime during the attack.

Jamie had suffered five stab wounds for, to her back. She had been stabbed once in her chest collapsing, her left lung and piercing her spleen. The stabs to her back, went through her side, into her kidney and liver, and also collapsed her right lung. The final stab wound was under her right armpit and it entered her chest cavity.

Jamie also had what is called an incised wound to her back that cut into her sixth, seventh, and eighth ribs. An incision like that is slow and precise and makes you wonder if Andrew Witt deliberately cut Jamie that way to further terrorize her with her skirt found away from her body. It looked as though Andrew was attempting to rape Jamie, her autopsy showed Jamie wasn't.

Right, but you can only imagine her terror anyway, stabbed and about to be sexually assaulted knowing her husband was dead or dying in the next room. But then Andrew Witt ran off into the darkness when he heard the sirens coming. Jason King had been stabbed four times once in fighting with Andrew Witt, three more stabs to his back as he was trying to escape out the back door, that searing pain in his stomach that he had initially thought was a punch, was actually angled up and punctured his left lung.

Nearly going through his entire chest cavity, almost severing a major artery. He had serious wins to his spleen and kidney as well as a laceration on his arm. He was rushed to the hospital where he underwent emergency surgery. He had lost four and a half liters of blood. It was in the hospital for 15 days.

It was a miracle. He survived two weeks after his release, his lung collapsed again, and he got a staph infection. Jason later had five followup surgeries spending over 30 more days in the hospital. He later told reporter Kristin Davis of the air force times that everyday when his wife Paige came to his hospital room, he asked about Andy and Jamie, and she just kept telling him that they can't be here right now.

He finally began to understand. And on the third or fourth day in the hospital, he said to Paige, they're dead. Aren't they? She admitted they were in an air force. Chaplain came to see Jason soon after. His commanding officer and first Sergeant, as well as other airman and friends visited him frequently.

But Jason was bereft just two weeks before the attack at the slips at home, he had lost his best friend and wife and a car accident. And now he had not only almost died from this horrific attack. He was grieving for two more lost friends. Jason begged his doctors to attend the funerals and also the Memorial service held on base for Andy.

But he was still in intensive care. This wasn't possible. The Memorial well service on base was on July 9th. The joint funeral for the slip six was held in the same church. First federated church in Peoria, Illinois, where Andy and Jamie were married 2002 only one coffin draped with an American flag was in the charge.

Andy's body was in the coffin and cradled in his arms was the urn holding the ashes of his wife. The murders of Andy and Jamie were the first murders committed on the Robins air force base. And it's 75 year history.

Andrew Witt was arrested July 5th, 2004, by the air force office of special investigations also called the AAF O S I for short, he was held at the Houston County jail. So who was this guy that brought so much destruction on a beautiful young couple in their friend before the murders? Andrew Witt had no criminal history.

He was not married and had no children. Andrew Paul Witt was born in June of 1982 when he was three years old, his parents, Terry and Melanie divorced, and Melanie moved Andrew to Wichita shortly after Andrew saw his dad on school breaks. And Melanie said his dad never missed a child support payment.

Melanie remarried a doctor in 1988 and moved to Wisconsin having two more children and became a stay at home. Mom. Andrew's upbringing has been characterized as strongly religious with his parents being strict and over-protective, but both of his parents described their son as a joy to raise a happy and polite young man with no history of violence, but his life wasn't without some strife.

Andrew's dad. Terry had always struggled with drug and alcohol issues. And when Andrew was around 10 years old, Melanie and Terry agree that it was best if he didn't see his dad until Terry got clean. So Andrew didn't see his dad again until he was 12 years old by then Terry had remarried and Andrew didn't particularly care for his new step mom or her kids.

Melanie Andrew's mother voluntarily checked herself into a mental health facility in 1996 to deal with depression and stress. Andrew would have been about 14 years old at the time. As far as his education, he was homeschooled in the seventh and eighth grade. There's no reason given as to why. And it doesn't necessarily mean anything, but I am curious, those would have been the turbulent years when he didn't see his father and his mom was dealing with depression, but Melanie was also a devout Christian it's possible.

She didn't find public schools or a private school to her liking in those years. Andrew then attended a private Christian school in West Salem for his freshman year before he moved to Aquinas high school in lacrosse, Wisconsin. His teachers remember a friendly kid who played many sports, but was also in jazz band.

After he graduated. He spent nine months in England at Cabernet Bible school. His parents paid that tuition. And when he came home, his father gave him $30,000, which would be around $43,000 today to either go to college or begin his adult life. In November of 2001, Andrew joined the United States air force.

His dream was to become a pilot and then an astronaut at the time of the murders, he was a senior airman and an avionics technician for the 116th air control wing, but close friends. And his family felt that joining the air force changed Andrew. He seemed like a different person. When he came home for a visit in December of 2003, he now cursed all the time.

Something has evangelical parents would have whore and he bragged a lot about partying and having many girlfriends. It seems to me, he found a freedom on his own in the air force that he didn't find growing up. That's not unusual in any young person. And a lot of us were assholes in college and technically these were Andrew's college years.

Something that is notable though. Is that on February 22nd, 2004, Andrew was riding his motorcycle when he lost control on a patch of gravel and wrecked, just a couple of blocks from his apartment. He did lose consciousness for a little while, but then he got back on the motorcycle and drove to work. It was a coworker who noticed that Andrew had a cut over his left eye and that he seemed to shoveled and disoriented.

She said he was speaking slowly, almost slurring and walking slowly. So she insisted he go see a doctor. He went to the hospital and was briefly admitted for a closed head injury, but was released the same day. We're starting to learn a lot more about traumatic brain injuries and how they can cause aggressive, even murderous behavior.

You hear a lot about it in relation to football players, longterm because of injuries can even lead to dementia. In later years, this will be a sticking point in the legal proceedings against Andrew. Once Andrew will was arrested, he had basically the same rights as civilian, the right to remain silent warrants for search and seizure of his property and the right to an attorney.

But in the military, typically a military attorney would be appointed at no cost to the defendant. However, you can hire a civilian attorney with your own money. If you choose the main difference in civilian and military arrests, like these is that military personnel are not eligible for bail. Andrew Witt was eventually assigned to military attorneys and hired one civilian attorney to represent him.

The civilian attorney had experienced defending military cases that had no capital trial experience. On July 8th, three days after the murders, Andrew squadron commander charged him with two counts of premeditated murder and one count of premeditated attempted murder. And according to military law charges must be brought within 120 days.

Meaning the military members are denied bail. They couldn't just hold Andrew Witt indefinitely while they investigated. Once Andrew was officially charged the prosecution and his defense began their formal investigations. At some point in the investigation, which is unclear from court records, Andrew Witt did confess to the air force office of special investigations.

He said he wore his battle dress uniform, the camouflage combat fatigues, because he wanted to observe them unseen to see what was going on. He also said Andy was yelling at him during the calls. I'm sure he was. You tried to kiss his wife and his own house. Moving on. Andrew took the F O S I investigators to where he disposed of the knife, the combat fatigues and the cap and boots he was wearing that night DNA from the bloodstains found on the boots and fatigues was tested and found to match Jamie's DNA trace evidence of red fibers from the knife was tested and was found to match fibers from the shirts.

Andy and Jason were wearing the combat knife, had a six and a half inch cerated blade with a six inch handle. The F O S I interviewed Andy's roommate who told them that he also got a voicemail from Andy slip, sick early in the morning of July 5th, telling him that Andrew had made a pass at his wife.

Andy wanted the roommate to call him to talk about it. The roommate did not return his call. Andrew had told his roommate that he was going to wear his combat fatigues, because he didn't want to be seen. Andrew also told his roommate that Andy had threatened to get him in trouble by telling their superiors about the advances he made towards Jamie and an affair.

He was having making a pass at another airman's wife was bad enough, but the second part about Andrew having an affair with a married woman was much more serious. When Andrew had been home at Christmas, one of the conquests he bragged about was an older married woman with a 17 year old daughter. He also had designs on the daughter laughing about how cool it would be to sleep with a mother and daughter.

This is probably the affair discussed in court documents, but the other woman was not named. But the reason this is so serious as according to military law, if you're charged with adultery, you can receive a disciplinary action all the way up to a court martial or dishonorable discharge. Regardless of his anger over the confrontations about Jamie that fateful night, Andrew Witt would also have been worried about losing his career in the military.

If Andy Schlitz sick, turned him in for the affair. And though the roommate wasn't personally responsible and obviously cooperated later with authorities, you have to wonder if he really thought his friend was just going over to watch those couples, or if he was going to pick a fight, I would hope he did not know about the combat knife.

Andrew took with him. But that answer is not in the court records. At his first pretrial hearing Andrew saw crime scene evidence for the first time during the hearing and became extremely upset. He was crying and had to leave the courtroom to calm down a deputy sheriff consult Andrew, after you left the hearing and Andrew did not return to the proceeding that day.

In October of 2004, Andrew met with a forensic psychologist to prepare for trial. They met over two days for a total of 12 to 14 hours during their meetings. The doctor gave Andrew a series of psychological tests, including neuroscience, logical, intellectual and personality tests. They met again twice in June, 2005.

And once in September, 2005, as of September 17th, 2005, the doctor named as dr. B M in court records did not have a psychological diagnosis of Andrew. But after the trial began, dr. BM made the diet gnosis he testified that yeah. Drew had a personality disorder, not otherwise specified with paranoid and borderline traits.

After this doctor B M would meet with Andrew's defense team and would talk with them about his findings. But even after the doctor learned about Andrew's mother's mental health facility, stay. He never advised his attorneys, that they should get her mental health records to use an Andrew's defense after learning about Andrew's motorcycle accident, that event's talked to dr.

BM about the possibility of a traumatic brain injury that could have caused Andrew's actions that night. But dr. BM insisted there was no connection between the motorcycle accident and the murders. So therefore there would be no reason to conduct further neuro-psychology testing. Nothing else was done to see if Andrew had a traumatic brain injury.

A psychologist refer to as doctor am and court documents conducted the sanity board hearing and agreed with dr. BM that there was no connection, but he did order the original CT scans of Andrew's brain. First, a sanity board hearing is meant to determine if the defendant is mentally fit to stand trial.

Dr. Am examined Andrew CT scan from the accident and said, quote, A medical record review indicates that the CT scan of the brain was negative for any significant changes. Meaning despite the motorcycle accident, both the forensic psychologist who examined Andrew and the sanity board psychologist agreed that his head injury was not a factor.

Andrew Witt was tried by general court martial starting on September 13th, 2005. According to military.com military court marshals are the most severe sanctions under military law. And a conviction is the same as a federal conviction. There are three levels of court martial summary, special and general the level of court martial.

It depends on the severity of the offense. General court marshals are the most severe of the three levels. General court martial can only be convened by a high ranking official anyone from the president to a secretary of the military branch, a general or a commander can convene a general court martial.

For capital offenses, the jury panel consists of 12 officers and the general court martial can impose the sentence up to and including death drew, which trial was held at the bib County courthouse in Macon, Georgia, because the Robins air force base courtroom was too small to hold all the victims, family members, even though the Bibb County courthouse was bigger with more than 200 seats, it was still standing room only at Andrew's court-martial.

There were over 430 exhibits and 60 witnesses because Andrew had already confessed to the murders and attempted murder of Jason King. The court martial was determined whether the attacks were in order to prove premeditation the government primarily focused on Andrew's lack of remorse and callousness as well as many victim impact statements from the family and friends of Andy and Jamie.

Their case was basically that Andrew was, it was an evil man with the additional motive that he didn't want it each lipstick to tell his superiors about his affair or his advances towards Jamie Shalit sick. The government told the jury that if Andrew hadn't heard police sirens approaching the house, he would have raped Janie.

Considering her skirt was removed, not ripped during the attack. And the fact that he had already shown sexual aggression towards her. This is a logical conclusion. I also think back to the autopsy findings of the incised protracted wound on her back. I said before, it seemed like an attempt to further terrorize Jamie, thankfully, he was scared off by the sirens.

So Jamie didn't suffer the further degradation of rape the government called 14 friends and family members of the victims to give impact statements, a psychologist even evaluated the friends and family and testified. He said they suffered from mental health issues, ranging from bereavement and anxiety disorder to major depression, depressive disorder, and post stress disorder.

Losing a beautiful young couple, just 24 and 25 years old was simply devastating. Jamie's sister would later say it's not like it was a car accident. They were traumatized knowing the brutality of what Jamie and Andy went through. The government also had five people testify about Andrew's lack of remorse.

Evidently he acted rather callously in front of friends and law enforcers. After the murders. Also, Jason King surgeon testified about Jason's injuries. Surgeries and the aftermath of his suffering due to these grievous injuries, the defense needed to prove the attacks were not premeditated. They blamed it on adrenaline, which was brought on by anger, fueled by alcohol.

That was coursing through Andrew Watson. The defense insisted this caused his car functions to be impaired. The defense had a much harder job than the government, especially in light of Andrew's confession. They didn't have many people they could call to testify, not like the dozens who testified for the government.

They called a doctor to the stand, to testify about this logical and psychological effects of stress, adrenaline, and alcohol on perception and memory. They also called dr. Andrew's first forensic psychologist to the stand to testify about the effects of adrenaline. Dr. BM testified about the physiology of fight or flight and the cognitive effects of stress induced release of adrenaline and to the body.

He said, quit. These adrenal gland releases can impair cognitive functions, that guide behavior, thoughts, feelings, impulse control, judgment, decision making and insight. During the hearing dr. BM underwent direct examination by the defense. When the defense asked dr. BM about Andrew's diagnosis, dr. BM stated that Andrew had schizophrenia and borderline traits, which is not what he had previously told the defense team he had originally diagnosed Andrew with paranoid, not schizo traits.

I am not totally comfortable trying to explain the difference in those diagnoses, except that from what I've read in general, it is the paranoid type that tends to be more physically aggressive. Which would be an important distinction for the defense. They could pause it, that Andrew was not naturally aggressive.

It was the adrenaline from the arguments. It was the booze. Andrew Witt is not an evil man, but in this situation, I don't think that is the right context. Their expert doctor really screwed up by saying schizo weighed on the stand because that diagnosis would tend to show Andrew would not have mental health issues with violent traits that may have caused his actions that night.

An expert testifying to diagnose mental health issues is more powerful than blaming anger and alcohol people get drunk and mad all the time. Most don't brutally stab three people during cross examination. Dr. BM was forced to admit that he had incorrectly testified during the direct examination. He said the correct diagnosis was paranoid and borderline traits because of the doctor's error.

The government asked for an independent, psychological evaluation of Andrew. Andrew agreed to undergo the independent evaluation, but the government and defense settled on letting the government's expert witness dr. CR and court records conduct the evaluation rather than find an independent doctor. This is another crucial error made by Andrew wit's defense team, especially since the government's expert.

Dr CR testified that Andrew had quote no difficulty in the

areas of controlling anger, rage, or impulsivity. Furthermore, Andrew had been fully able to recount his actions that night, including his motivations and planning. This is not consistent with cognitive impairment based on the court records. It does not seem that this doctor was concerned with the terminology of schizophrenia or paranoid, because he did not believe that Andrew suffered from either personality disorder.

And he also insisted that Andrew did not suffer from a traumatic brain injury. His conclusion was devastating for the defense quote. Andrew Witt had a logical sequencing of behavior to accomplish his goals, abstract reasoning. The defense knew they could not recall dr. BM to the stand to talk about Andrew psychological evaluation, because he had already screwed up and then discredited.

So the jury might not believe his testimony. The defense team had time to ask for a continuance to find a forensic psychologist, to replace dr. BM as their expert witnesses, but they did not ask another mistake. And then basically, basically without expert testimony to refute dr. CR the defense, his whole case fell apart.

The defense had Andrew's roommate testify about the voicemail he had received from Andy, but they did not call anyone to the stand who could talk about Andrew as a person. There was no one willing to get on the stand to counter the evil guy argument. The government presented the 12 panel jury of officers deliberated for about 12 hours over the course of three days.

And they found Andrew Witt guilty unanimously because the vote was unanimous. Andrew was eligible for the death penalty. A unanimous vote is required for a death sentence to be even considered during the penalty phase and a court Marshall. Before his sentencing, Andrew said quote to the families to the slip six and be Lemberg's.

I am so sorry from the bottom of my being. I'm so sorry. I took your son and your daughter away from you and also to mr. King. I'm sorry. Sorry for hurting you. He also submitted a written statement that red. I would like to apologize again to the slip six, the Bloombergs the Kings, my family and the air force for my actions.

My life has changed dramatically since that night. And I plan to continue to make changes. I want you to know that I am firmly resolved to lead a productive life in the service of others and will not wander from this path. If given the chance, please allow me to live so that I can do this. He went on in the letter writing.

Thank you for giving me this opportunity to share my thoughts with you. I regret losing my focus on the air force mission. Looking back. I do truly love the air force and I've been proud to wear the uniform. I understand that my actions mean I will never wear it again once this trial is over and I am sorry for that as well.

I am sorry for the discredit. I have brought upon the air force and the negative attention I have brought to Robins air force base on April 13th, 2005. Andrew was dishonorably discharged, which was automatic because he had been sentenced to death. His pleas for mercy made no difference. He was the first airmen to be given a death sentence since 1992, when Jose Savoy was sentenced to death after he was convicted of robbing a bank and killing a police officer, the last U S military execution carried out was in 1961 when army private John Bennett was hanged.

He had been convicted of the rape and attempted murder of an 11 year old girl. The president has to confirm the death penalty before a member of the military can be executed. According to an article by Nancy Montgomery for stars and stripes written just 10 days ago, federal death row holds about 60 prisoners.

Right now. The last executions were during the Bush administration and the early two thousands. When the Oklahoma city bomber Timothy McVeigh was executed. And this was after a 40 year hiatus. The point of ms. Montgomery's article is that the current presidential administration has plans to reinstate federal executions.

Though so far, none have been carried out. The president seems more interested in giving clemency to members of the military who committed war crimes, regardless, just as in civilian court, there is an automatic appeals process for court martials as well. The us court of appeals for the armed forces is the highest court, but this court only reviews questions of law and their decisions can be appeal to the U S Supreme court.

Andrew appealed his conviction and sentencing on 88 issues. Oral arguments were held in October, 2012 and August, 2013. The court of criminal appeals found three issues. The defense didn't look into mitigating evidence had the jury known about these three issues. They may have different verdict had even one person found Andrew not guilty premeditation.

He wouldn't have been eligible for the death penalty. The first issue regarding the possible traumatic brain injury. Andrew suffer from the motorcycle accident in his appeal. Andrew said emitted information provided by yet another doctor that said quote with proper scanning. He could have found out whether Andrew had suffered a brain injury.

He also stated that Andrew's behavior was consistent with a traumatic brain injury though. He could not be sure without seeing a brain scan. The second issue regarded Andrew's mother's mental health history, the defense fell to quote, investigate the appellant's family history of mental disorder after their esteemed forensic psychologist.

Dr. BM who screwed up his testimony at trial, told them that they didn't need his mother's medical records. The defense should have requested them anyway, quote. They cannot simply hire an expert and then abandon offer the responsibility. It is the attorney who bears the responsibility to investigate and bring to the attention of mental health experts who are examining his client is facts that the experts do not request.

The third issue had to do with the defense. It's not investigating the testimony from that deputy sheriff regarding Andrew's breakdown at the pretrial hearing, the defense did not ask the deputy sheriff, if he would be willing to take the stand and testify to what happened at the pretrial hearing. When contacted by the criminal court of appeals, the deputy sheriff said that he would have testified the appeals court affirmed Drew's conviction, but they set aside the Senate and it's an order to rehearing to be performed by the judge advocate general.

However, four judges did not participate in this appeal decision because they arrived after oral arguments began, the government immediately appealed this ruling, asking the CCA to reconsider setting aside Andrew wit's death sentence. In October, 2013, the criminal court of appeals reconsidered, and found that the defense was not incompetent on the three issues.

And they upheld the death sentence. The reconsideration included judgments from three of the four judges who didn't participate in the original appeal decision. So now Andrew Witt appealed the reconsideration because it was wrong for those three judges to participate in the reconsideration. When they did not participate in with original appeal.

This would be the three of the four judges who didn't show up until after oral arguments began and on and on, we go needless to say, Jamie and Andy's families were devastated by the hearing for a new sentencing almost 10 years after the murders. There is a Facebook page dedicated to a Memorial fund for Jamie and Andy.

And on there is a very moving video by Jamie sister, Jody. You can also find it on YouTube. Her family wanted his death sentence upheld. She talks about how this appeals process further traumatized their family. It is a gut wrenching video to watch on July 19th, 2016. The U S court of appeals for the armed forces.

The highest military court ordered a new sentencing hearing because they found the criminal court of appeals had mishandled Andrew's original appeal by allowing the participation of those three judges and the reconsideration on July 6th, 2018, Andrew was recent it's to life in prison, just as Jody feared.

They were put back through this process. I hope now, even though it was not the outcome, the families wanted that they are at peace. There are no more automatic appeals for Andrew Witt.

Jason King suffered immensely after surviving the horrific attack. He was promoted to staff Sergeant while still in the hospital.

And he has always told reporters how much support he received from the air force during this difficult time. But that doesn't stop the nightmares and it didn't stop. The debilitating PTSD. He suffers from Jason tried to recover. He went to airman leadership school and also served in Korea. He officially retired from the air force in 2011, after he was diagnosed with chronic obstructive pulmonary disorder, a breathing condition most likely caused by the scarring on his lungs from the brutal attack.

He also started drinking excessively and became addicted to painkillers. And sadly his marriage to Paige buckled under the pressures of this tragedy. And Jason's continued suffering. The couple divorced in 2009 and perhaps the saddest part, Jason felt tremendous guilt for running out the door that night, though, he was running for help.

He hoped that by running for help, the sirens drove. Andrew went out of the house before he could rape Jamie, but he could not help a fill. Like he let his friends down and that by running, he was a coward. This is not true. Andy's call to nine 11 was only 34 seconds. And it was from a cell phone, not quickly traced.

If Andy didn't get his address out, which he didn't, Jason hadn't run for help. I don't believe the cops would've gotten there that quickly. To me. Jason King is a hero after his retirement. Jason King moved home to Johnson, city, Tennessee, and got sober. He worked for a while at the post office, but had trouble with the job physically due to his lasting injuries.

He told the air force times in 2013, quote, I couldn't physically lift things and I couldn't mentally do it. It was just too much too soon. I guess he had to fight for disability and won, but he felt conflicted about this quote. I don't like it. I don't like being one of those guys living off the system. I don't want to be inside jobless being a piece of trash, but as he said, he has to live.

This interview was in 2013 and I truly hope Jason King doesn't feel like trash for being on disability now. And though he will probably always feel guilty for running that night. He ended the interview in a very positive way. Quote, the message I want to get out there is that in your darkest hour, when horrible things happen to you, when you're facing life or death, there is always hope.

If it helps even one person than to me, it was worth it. Maybe this is the reason why I survived as for Andrew Witt and his recent syncing. I believe it was technically fair. His court martial appeal and reconsiderations were messy, not just by his defense team, but by the court of criminal appeals decision, to let those judges participate, who hadn't bothered to show up for oral arguments yet it does seem strange to me that two doctors insisted he had no traumatic brain injury, but 10 years later they found an expert who said he did.

No Andrew Witt did not have a history of violence before the early morning hours. After the 4th of July on Robins air force base in 2004, but after several arguments and threats to his career, he had the wherewithal to change into camouflage fatigues, arm himself with a combat knife, and then silently stock his prey.

This is what is called a cooling off period. He had time to change his mind. He made a choice. Andrew Witt forced his way into a home and brutally stabbed three people with a combat knife, killing a young couple and the prime of their lives and leaving their friend traumatized and permit disabled. I do believe it was premeditated.

He knew exactly what he was doing. And he ruined so many lives, including his own with a selfish, monstrous

4 THE MURDER OF CHERYL FERGESON

On a sweltering August day in 1980. Sixteen-year-old Cheryl D. Ferguson was up early on a Saturday. She was meeting the bus at her school at 7:15 AM. Those school didn't start for another couple of weeks. Cheryl was the manager for the girls volleyball team. And she was traveling with the team to plan a trip.

And I met at a high school in Conroe, Texas at around 9:30 AM. Cheryl went to, I used the restroom and never returned her teammates became worried after a couple of hours. And we're walking around the gym and auditorium shouting her name. The police were called a black janitorial supervisor named Clarence Brandley told another janitor that they had better help look for the girl.

They found her body hidden in a loft above the auditorium. She was nude. And had been strangled to death. Brandley immediately found one of the lease officers and brought him to the scene. But within days and clearance Brandley was arrested without any physical evidence. And before investigation had even really started.

What followed was more than a miscarriage of justice. The police prosecutors, three judges, and even the damn district court clerk alluded to frame Clarence Brandley with nothing but pure racism in their hearts. He spent almost 10 years on death row and there was never justice for Cheryl.

The seat of Montgomery County in East Texas in the Piney woods area between Houston and Huntsville today, Conroe has over 85,000 residents.

In 1980, there were only around 18,000. It was considered a sleepy peaceful East, Texas small town. But appearances can be deceiving. Conroe has an extremely ugly history of racism, public lynchings, and the presence of the KKK. In 1922, a black male was accused of raping a white girl. They were actually dating, but when caught, she was scared and said he raped her.

A posse of white men called the black man named Joe Winters and drug him to the town square. He was chained to the fence around the courthouse and in front of a jeering crowd, he was burned alive. The local newspaper reported in the headlines proudly the next day. Quote, Joe Winters burned here. Negro pays penalty for assault on 14 year old girl in 1941.

Another black man named Bob white was accused of raping a white woman named Ruby Cochran. Ruby's husband, dude Cochran decided to take things into his own hands. He snuck up behind mr. White and shot him dead. Right in the courtroom. It took an all white jury, less than a minute to declare dude Cochran, not guilty.

And he was given a hero's celebration in 1973, just seven years before the murder of Cheryl Ferguson, a black man named Greg still was shot to death in a jail cell at the Conroe courthouse. Two days before Christmas. He had been arrested for a bar room fight, but his family said he was dating a white girl and had ignored warnings to end the relationship.

The officer was put on trial and claim. Self-defense saying that Steele had pulled a knife on him. He was found not guilty, even though Greg still had been shot in the back three times. And there was no evidence of a knife or blood. Nick Davies, the author who wrote white lies, rape murder, and justice, Texas style began his research into the racist history of Conroe with his article called the town that loved lynching.

In his seminal book on the Brandley case, he outlines dozens of similar incidents in the last 100 years of history, since Conroe was established in 1881 before Sheryl Ferguson's murder 1980 and Davies points out that an almost all incidents. A black man is accused of attacking a white person in some way.

Normally I would not give you so many examples of the bad parts of a town before we get into a case, but historically these previous cases matter a great deal to Clarence Brandley and Cheryl Ferguson.

Cheryl D. Ferguson lived in the town of Bellville with her father buck Ferguson. She was born on August 10th, 1964. She was tall and willowy with dark blonde hair. Who's an artist and a budding journalist working on her school paper and painting a mural for the team sports at bell. Hi, she had a pad for rollerskating and even worked part time at the rink to earn extra money.

She lived with her father buck on a horse ranch, and she loved to wear Western style clothes, not just because of the urban cowboy craze of 1980, but because her daddy had been in the rodeo. She often wore cowboy boots and a belt with a huge buckle and her name stamped into the leather on the back. And she always wore a gold chain with a crucifix.

It was just her, her dad and her beloved cat at home. These days, her older brothers, Jerry and Jimmy had graduated and moved to Houston. Her mother Sylvia had passed away in January of 1979, just eight months earlier of cancer. Despite having just lost her mother, Cheryl was still a cheerful and upbeat girl.

She was a joiner belonging to many school clubs, and she had just become the manager for the girls volleyball team. On the morning of August 23rd, she was rushing around because she was late and she was anxious to make a good impression on the coach. But she got to the school on time, not missing the bus, taking the team to Conroe high school, about an hour Northeast of Bellville.

She wasn't late, but a team member was the bus arrived at Conroe high at nine, 10:00 AM. Since they were late. All the space in the locker room for dressing was taken. So the girls had to take a space in the warmup gym, Cheryl put down her stuff and then went to look for a bathroom. She just had a few minutes before the first match started instead of trying to go into the full locker room, she turned the other way down a long deserted hallway.

Barely a minute later, her coach came looking for her, but she had vanished. Clarence Brandley was working that Saturday morning, not just for the overtime, but in his position as supervisor of the janitorial staff, he knew there would be a lot of work to be done before school started. He hadn't even known about the volleyball tournament until he saw coach prop open a gym door with a garbage can.

He went and unlocked the doors for the tournament. Clarence Lee Brandley had been born in Montgomery, Texas on September 24th, 1951, his parents, Willie, and many Olaf were divorced. And he had a sister named Margaret and a brother named Roselle who went by OT in 1980. He was 28 and living in a housing project in Southeast Conroe.

He had recently moved from Houston after separating from his wife. He had five children with his ex Evelyn, but had struggled in Houston. As he told author Nick Davies, he had been living a fast life. His job at Conroe high school meant a great deal to him. He was also working to bring his oldest son Clarence jr.

To live in Conroe with him. Evelyn had no arguments about this. As long as he had settled down, he was determined to make this right. He had a girlfriend named Beverly and was working hard to change his life. Beverly dropped clearance off at Conroe high school at around seven 40 that morning. And he unlocked the maintenance store.

He spotted icky piece already waiting for him. Ickes real name was Henry, but that nickname had stuck since childhood icky stood about four foot 11, but weighed nearly 200 pounds. He was the only janitor who was friendly with clearance. Gary anchorman, a sullen white man, 21 years old showed up around 8:00 AM.

Along with John Sessom, who is a bit older, white, and a known alcoholic, rounding out the men working that morning was San Martinez, a young Hispanic man that Clarence generally liked though. He didn't know him. Well, Gary anchorman was openly hostile towards his new boss, calling him the N word. Even when Clarence was within earshot, Clarence turned the other cheek and made friendly overtures to men who still disrespected him in front of the other janitors.

Clarence told SESAM anchorman at Martinez to set up tables and chairs in the cafeteria. There was a meeting for all Conroe district teachers scheduled to be in there Monday morning. He went with to get icky set up to both the floor and the teacher's lounge. He was going to help, but icky assured his boss.

He could do it himself. So Clarence moved on, checking other parts of the building at around 9:30 AM. Clarence was worried about the heat. So we went to open windows and set up fans. As he went, walked by, he noticed his crew just standing around. None of them had been thrilled to work on a Saturday.

Clarence had graciously told them that it would just be a few hours of work, but that they could still claim the whole day on their time sheets. It didn't stop their attitudes toward him. Clarence went to refill the toilet paper in the bathrooms, but Gary anchorman stopped him and said, don't go in the girl's restroom.

Clarence. There's a girl in there. Clarence said he wouldn't go in there and then sent them in across the street to the vocational building. They had a few things to get done in there as well. He said he would meet them over there in a few minutes. He went to his office and had a cigarette and then went and let them in, into the vocational building at around 11:00 AM.

Clarence went to check the cafeteria to see if that work was done and sure enough, the men had half-assed the job. So Clarence and Nicky had to finish it up at 1130. Clarence told them, man, they could go home again, assuring them that they could claim the whole day's work. Anchorman sesamin Martinez left together.

Clarence asked if icky piece would wait and give him a ride home. As they walked outside, clearance spotted a police car. When he asked what the problem was, the officer told him a girl was missing. They walked back into the building and heard the girl shouting Cheryl over and over again. Clarence figured they better start helping look for the girl.

He Indeck. You took off to go look and he immediately noticed that one of the lobby doors from the parking lot was unlocked. That wasn't right. He had also noticed a garbage can propping up an outside door earlier. All outer doors were to remain locked. He then noticed the auditorium door was open too.

So he and Nikki went to check it out. Sure enough, a door to the left of the auditorium stage that led to the bathrooms was unlocked. And another door leading outside was also open clearance and achy made their way up to the dark loft above the auditorium, feeling around in the dark. Achy moved a wooden flat away from a wall.

And there she was Sheryl Ferguson was nude except for one sock. Her blue eyes stared up words. Her mouth was frozen, open screamed. And then Clarence told him to stay there while he went for the cops, achy, ran with him, terrified they alone the cop they had seen earlier and then went and sat down in the first row with auditorium.

Not sure what else to do. Police come the scene. And one cop took care of scene on Cheryl's thigh and put them in the cellophane of his cigarette pack for safekeeping. Her gold crucifix was found, but not the chain. Part of her bra was found and a paper towel was near her body after an hour or so. The cop asked if clearance and achy would come make statements at the station.

They agreed, but felt unsettled riding in the police car on the way. They both gave statements and were fingerprinted and then asked if they would go give blood samples. And they agreed. Clarence was then told to give a hair sample. And then the doctor took pubic hair samples, as well as the cop drove them back to the school.

Achy told Clarence he was worried he couldn't read or write. And he had asked the police if a sister could come read his statement before he signed it. The cops had refused, but icky had signed the statement. Anyway, as they got back to the school, the cops were searching Ickes car and pulled out weapons.

He wasn't supposed to have a couple of knives and a Billy club icky was even more scared. Clarence was watching all of this thoughtfully worried. One of the cops walked back over to clearance with achy and toe. Clarence said that the cop looked at the two of them up and down and said, quote, One of you, two is going to hang for this.

Then he looked clearance in the eye and said, quote, since you're the you're elected, the captain of detectives for the Conroe police gave his men Sunday off by Monday morning, a cleaning crew had come through and cleaned up the crime scene. It was a sloppy mistake. Despite his fear, Clarence got up and went to work Monday morning.

Before long, his boss came to get him. And so the Conroe police wanted him and the other four janitors on duty that morning down at the station. This time anchorman Sessom and Martinez made statements and Clarence and achy were asked to take a lie detector test and Houston, they complied. They knew they hadn't done anything wrong.

The polygraph examiner even told Clarence that he had passed and had nothing to worry about. Back at the school Cheryl's clothes were found in a dumpster behind the gym by Thursday, Texas ranger, Wesley styles was put in charge of the investigation and he immediately focused on Clarence and Nikki piece because they were the ones who found Cheryl's body.

He arrested Clarence Brandley the next day, without even beginning his investigation or interviewing any of the other janitors, the district attorney for the night it's judicial district in Texas, Jim Casey junior high called the supervisor of the polygraph examiner in Houston to look back over Clarence, this test, this time they claimed they found one deception.

This was what they use to arrest Clarence Brandley. At this point, none of the physical evidence had been processed nor has Cheryl Ferguson's autopsy been done yet. Her body was taken to Houston on Sunday after Clarence was arrested that Friday before by Saturday morning, Clarence, his family had raised enough money for a defense attorney, Ray Reeves, but he was not allowed to confer with his client.

Finally, they let him see Clarence who told him emphatically that he did not do it. That same day ranger, West styles took Ackerman Martinez and SESAM for a walk through the school to get their story. All three said that they had seen Cheryl Ferguson walked down the hallway and then they said they saw Clarence follow her up to the auditorium.

These men were never taken in for hair or blood samples, and this was an informal interview, but they all signed new statements. Sheros all types. It was conducted by dr. Joseph . There was semen found on Cheryl's body and swabs were taken three Caucasian hairs were found near her vagina. Her hymen was intact, but there is also semen found in her vagina.

The state's theory would later be that Cheryl was killed first and her hymen wasn't broken during the rape because her muscles had naturally relaxed after she died. I'm not sure I've ever heard of this as a reason before, but it's also possible that the ripest did not fully penetrate her. Her bladder was empty leading investigators to believe that she had just used the restroom, it fit with the other janitors stories that they had seen.

Cheryl walking towards the restrooms down the hall, there had been blood found on her socks and blouse, and it was tested as type a Clarence Brandley was type O she had bruises on her arms and the Hills of her hands. She had cuts on her knees and a four and a half inch abrasion on her neck. She had been strangled, but her fingernails were not broken.

It looked as though she had not fought back. Also, there was an indention of her crucifix on the back of her neck. It is more likely that those bruises are from someone holding her down, pressing her hands hard onto the floor. If the investigators had studied the photographs and consider the crime scene, it looked more like two men were involved.

One man holding her down on the floor, on her back, gripping her arms and maybe even kneeling on her hands on September 5th and a pretrial hearing. Clarence was granted bond at $30,000. It may as well have been 30 million. His family couldn't raise that much money. And then Ray Reeves made the mistake of letting Clarence testify before the grand jury da Jim Keshan kept firing and proper questions at him.

Had he ever raped a girl? Had he ever masturbated in the school auditorium or had sex with anyone in there before? He also brought up two women that clearance knew one was a prostitute named Jo Ellen parish who had once accused him of rape. She had stayed over at Clarence's apartment and when her pimp boyfriend found out about this, she had lied, but she had retracted the statement and charges were not filed against Clarence.

Kesha also asked Clarence if he knew of a woman who went by the name of pokey, Clarence said, yes, he knew her. Then he asked if it was true. If Clarence had raped her and Clarence denied it. Did she report you to the police? Keyshawn asked? No. Was the answer. Ray Reeves knew he made a huge mistake letting Clarence testify.

Keisha was bringing up unsubstantiated rumors. And if it had been at trial Reeves could have objected as it was. The grand jury was left with the impression that Clarence had a history of rape. He was indicted and his trial date was set for December of 1980. Reeves filed two motions with the district court clerk.

Peggy Stevens. One was to have the judge instruct Jim Keshan to stop interfering with witnesses and all those witnesses to be interviewed by the defense. He accused Kesha of unethical behavior and unprofessional conduct. The judge denied that motion. The second motion was a request for 18 pieces of evidence that's so far, the district attorney had refused to turn over to Ray Reeves in pretrial hearings.

Judge Lee Allworth refused to give the defense a copy of the autopsy report. He did not order photographs of Cheryl's body to be turned over nor any of the other scientific evidence. He also refused to hand over criminal records of any witnesses at the school, including the other janitors. All he allowed Reeves stuff have was a few crime scene photos and access to some of Cheryl's clothing, but he did not release them that time.

This was a basic discussion, very emotion and Ray Reeves was done and he should have already had access to all of this evidence. It was absurd. Ray Reeves knew he was out of his league. And by now Clarence's brother OT had the same feeling. OT found two seasoned trial lawyers in Conroe who worked together, George Morris and Don Brown.

They didn't want to take on the case, but agreed to assist Ray Reed. Yes. First meeting with Reeves, which was in a smokey bar. They knew they had to take over the case. Ray Reeves may have believed in his client and was fighting for him, but he was a racist. He said the N word several times in front of the two men, they took over the case and wrote up a blistering motion listing all evidence that had been denied by Keeshon and judge Hallworth and threatened to appeal to a higher court.

If they were denied on October 3rd, 40 days after the autopsy, the defense finally got to look at the report. But they still did not get a transcript of the grand jury proceeding. No copy of Clarence's statement, no photographs of the crime scene or the clothing that the judge had promised Ray Reeves. He shouldn't finally agree to hand over this evidence and he tasked ranger, Wesley styles with retrieving the box and bringing it to the attorneys, to their horror.

The attorneys found there was no rape kit in the box, meaning the vaginal swabs and other semen samples were missing. The only piece of clothing in the box was Cheryl's underwear, but it had a piece cut out where there had been a semen stain. So that would indicate that it had been sent for testing. So where was the lab report?

The one thing Ray Reed's had done right was to take what little money the Bradley family have raised and hired a private investigator. Lorna Hubble had come from Houston and spent six weeks interviewing people on her own. John Sessom told again about how he anchorman and Martinez had finished up in the cafeteria and then saw Cheryl Ferguson.

He said that then Clarence had told them to go wait across the street. That was basically all the prosecution had. Clarence had separated from the group when he went to his office for a cigarette, Clarence disputed their story, that he was gone for 45 minutes, insisting he could not have been gone for more than 10 minutes.

He knew the men were waiting outside the building in the heat. Wouldn't have waited for 45 minutes. Not these guys who barely followed his orders to begin with Hubble, talked to Gary anchorman who acted extremely suspicious. He just kept saying, what did John say? What did John say? He meant John SESAM.

Meanwhile, George Morris and Don Brown were fighting with the da Jim Kesha and judge Lee worth over every motion in pretrial hearings, time. And again, they were overruled. They pleaded with the judge to order samples of hair, blood, and saliva from the other janitors. They were denied as for the missing rape kit.

Keishon pled ignorance. He insisted that neither his office, the Conroe police department, nor the department of safety's lab had the missing evidence. Don Brown decided to call dr. Joseph Yakim sick himself. He was hoping to find out that the doctor either still had the samples or could testify that he had turned them over to the police, to his astonishment.

The seasoned medical examiner said, quote, Oh gosh, that's more than 30 days ago. I throw everything away after 30 days. In a rape murder, trial Brown exclaimed, the doctor said yes, unless the police asked for the evidence, he didn't have the room for storage.

The evidence would have been handed over after all testing was done, and it would have been stored with the police to safeguard the swabs until trial Brown and Morris had now decided to use their own collateral to make clearances bond. With all the missing evidence, they needed his assistance to put the pieces together.

Da Jim quiche, judge Lee Allworth and sheriff, Jean raves all work together to make sure Clarence didn't get bond in a heated, private meeting in judge's chambers, the sheriff and the da, both referred to Clarence Brandley with the N word insisting. He should not be released though. Bond had already been ordered.

Brown and Morris took a writ of habeas Corpus to the court of criminal appeals in Austin. Going over, judge, all worths head, all were found out and order the sheriff to release Clarence on bond. On the morning of November 14th that morning when Brown and Maura showed up to make bond, they were handed a motion from the da Jim Keshan signed by judge Allworth to raise the bond to 75,000 without a hearing Keyshon and all worth raise the bond.

It was illegal at this clearance. Attorneys had no choice, but to do what every lawyer, dreads, they filed a motion to have judge all worth recused, all worth stepped down voluntarily, but fixed it with the County administrative judge that he got to choose his replacement. The honorable Sam Robertson jr.

Would be taking over the case. He was known as a prosecutor's judge and he proved it in his first hearing by upholding keychain's new motion. Despite the illegality of the new hire bond, Clarence Brandley would not see the light of day for almost 10 years.

Attorneys for clearance Brandley had just about two weeks to prepare their case. Due to the Thanksgiving holiday, they poured over the evidence and felt sure that Cheryl Ferguson had been attacked by two men from the bruises on her upper arms and the palms of her hands. And with the indention of the crucifix on the back of her neck, it would appear that one men held Cheryl's arms, possibly kneeling on her hands causing those bruises.

And there were also two types of Caucasian hairs found. One

was black and one was reddish in color, neither were from a black man. And then there was the blood typing. It did not match Clarence. However, there were two hairs found that did come from a black man. They knew that Clarence Brandley had been forced to have pubic hair removed as well as hair from his head.

When they took his samples at the hospital, they strongly believe that those hairs were planted. After everything else that had already happened in this case, it was not all that far fetched to think someone had planted those hairs, but this was a dangerous argument to take in front of a jury. If they accused law enforcement of planning evidence without proof, they would likely be shut down quickly by the judge and alienate the jury.

Clarence Brandley was no OJ Simpson. Their next problem was judge Robertson. They had to get rid of him. Just eight days after successfully getting all worth to step down, they filed a motion of recusal on judge Robertson because he had upheld judge it's illegal ruling. This time they lost. And at the hearing judge Lynn Coker listened to our arguments and then ruled that Robertson could stay on the case.

Anyway, it was a nightmare. But the attorneys had no choice, but to carry on now in front of a judge who would be openly hostile after their attempt at recusal Clarence Bradley's trial began on December 8th, 1980 as the rest of the world was grieving over the assassination of John Lennon. Jury selection went exactly as you might suspect.

Da Jim Keshan made sure to use all of his peremptory challenges to cut any black person off the jury panel, five women and seven men, all white would decide Clarence Bradley's, fate Brown and Morris watched carefully as Jim Kesha put on the state's evidence, they were waiting to be ambushed with something.

They still found it hard to believe that Kesha would go to a capital trial with only circumstantial evidence. Especially when any physical evidence collected had supposedly been lost, but they were wrong. They also had to sit there and take it every time. Judge Robertson overruled their objections. And the three days that

Kesha put on evidence, they watched as law enforcement, the medical examiner and other experts got on the stand and sheepishly admitted to either losing evidence or not collecting it in the first place.

It was almost laughable except that a man's life was at stake. The captain of detectives had to admit in open court that many of the crime scene and autopsy photos were lost. When the camera had supposedly been put on the wrong setting, when Brown cross examined him, he asked if they had tried to have the photos developed.

The captain said, yes, they were taken to Fox photo, but they did not turn out Fox photo as a little shop in the mall where civilians drop off their film. Not the DPS lab in Austin, not the FBI lab in Houston, or even the Montgomery County lab Fox photo and the mall, the medical examiner took the stand and outlined his findings that Cheryl Ferguson had died from asphyxia caused by ligature, strangulation.

He speculated it would have taken about 30 seconds for her to lose consciousness and three minutes to die. But he insisted that her bladder being empty meant that she was attacked right after using the restroom, even though a human bladder fills with urine at the rate of two milliliters a minute, that means if it only took Cheryl three minutes to die, she would have had at least six millimeters of urine left in her bladder.

And the good doctor disagreed that she had released her bladder and death naturally as muscles relaxed while at the same time, insisting that her hymen was not broken because she was raped after death and her muscles had relaxed. He literally contradicted himself on stand. When asked about the missing Siemens swabs.

He first claimed that he had handed them to the captain of detectives and then backtracked and said, he wasn't sure. He may have forgotten. He also said he may not have taken swabs at the police. Didn't specifically ask for them. Dr. Joseph was either the most incompetent medical examiner I've ever heard of, or he was a liar and colluded with the prosecution, the defense put on their own expert from the forensic science Institute in Dallas.

She specialized in analyzing bodily fluids. Brown asked her if it was unusual to have no vaginal swabs from a rape victim, she replied it. Wasn't just unusual. That's the whole purpose of doing the rape examination, but the state's embarrassing testimony from law enforcement and other officials. Could not undermine the testimony of the other four janitors who had worked with Clarence Brandley that morning.

They all uniformly testified that Clarence Brandley was the only one with the key to the building and therefore access to the auditorium loft. They all said he went missing for 30 to 45 minutes, even icky piece. Clarence's only friendly employee. Now claim that Clarence had sent him up to that loft to check by himself three times.

The implication being that Clarence had wanted it, he to discover the body, it was all lies, but, and you have three white janitors and one Hispanic janitor, all telling the same story about a black janitor, who was this jury going to believe? One thing the prosecution had not counted on was a seasoned and fair juror named bill Shrek.

He had sat on three other jury trials and he was not a racist. He watched dumbfounded as the state put on such a weak case and was smart enough to read between the lines when the state and defense finished closing arguments. And the jury went to deliberate. Their first vote was 10 to two for guilt.

Only one of the women had voted not guilty. Now they went around the table, giving all their reasons. All of them said they believe the other janitors stories and that the defense had not given a good reason for the time that Brandley had been missing. They didn't care about the lack of physical evidence, the woman who had voted not guilty now, mumbled that she was undecided.

Bill Strack said straight away that he would be voting, not guilty. And quote, I want to tell you right now that I will not change this vote. I want you to understand it doesn't matter what happens in this jury room, because I believe this is right and I must not change my mind. 10 minutes later, they took another vote.

This time, the undecided woman voted guilty. And then bill Surak had to enter his fellow jurors, shouting at him and calling him ugly names. They sent a note to the judge, explaining the deadlock and the judge instructed them to continue to deliberate. Now the other jurors were pissed. They wanted to go home.

One woman wanted to get her Christmas shopping done. Bill Strack sat there and listened to 11 people care more about errands and getting home early than actually deliberating whether a man should live or die. They started yelling at him to change his damned vote and get us out of here. What are you? A professional juror, Brandley done it.

One yelled. What about that poor little girl? And then one said, quote, you're nothing but an hover at this bill rock, refuse to speak or take part in any discussion. And the judge was forced to declare a mistrial as he denied clearance Bradley bill. He said, quote, I am entering the following order, denying bail, pending retrial of the capital murder case in that I find proof is evident and that a dispassionate jury would not only find you guilty of capital murder, but would assess a punishment of death.

It was an extremely biased ruling. And what Don Brown told author, Nick Davies was the most brazen declaration of prejudice he had ever heard as jurors filed out, reporters were hurling questions, wanting to know who the holdout was. Bill's fellow jurors had no trouble pointing him out to reporters. And anyone else watching after the trial bill Strack was barraged with harassing phone calls.

Everything from heavy breathing to repeatedly calling him quote lover. He had to leave his phone off the hook. The minute he put it back on the receiver, the calls would start. He was convinced there was a monitoring device on his phone. This went on until he called the sheriff. They trace the calls, but then they told bill Strack that if he wanted to know who made the calls, he would have to get a court order.

The whole town. And every official was pissed that Bill's rock hung the jury, and they were not going to let him forget it. This harassment carried on through Clarence his second trial, his appeals, and even years on death row, bill would occasionally still get these phone calls. He changed his number once only for the calls to start back a day later.

Clarence Brandley second trial started on January 20th, 1981. As Ronald Reagan was sworn into office. Once again, an all white jury was seated this time. There was a new judge Morris and Brown had successfully run Robertson off the case with a blistering motion, charging him with bias and prejudice going point by point through his agregious rulings.

Texas had passed a new law January 1st that made it easier to remove prejudice. Judges from a trial Robertson was well aware. He voluntarily stepped down. Once he saw the defense's motion instead of facing recusal hearing, judge John Martin was chosen as his replacement for once the defense felt hopeful, Brown and Morris had both worked for judge Martins election.

They knew him to be a fair, clean cut defense attorney with a lot of trial experience. They considered him a friend. This was their first real win. They thought one Saturday early in the trial, George Morris received a phone call from a man named ed Payne. He said he had information to share. His daughter was married to Gary Ackerman and they lived in a trailer on his property.

He said the day that girl was killed, Gary came home pacing frantically and told them a girl had been killed at the school that day. This was completely different from the story he had been telling, which was that he had left before her body was even discovered along with Sesame and Martinez, but he told his relatives otherwise, And also said he was worried because he knew where the dead girls clothes were.

He had seen them in the dumpster, but didn't tell anyone Cheryl's clothes were not found until Monday following her murder, but they were found exactly where Gary Ackerman had told his family there would be on Saturday when he got home from work, the day she was murdered, this was huge Brown and Morris drafted a subpoena.

Lena. They now had a witness who could directly dispute Gary Ackerman's testimony. Maybe now there was hope, but on the day they plan to put ed Payne on the stand saved word, that pain was no longer willing to cooperate. They could still call him to the stand, but if he denied that story, it would only hurt their case.

And there were more bad tidings ahead. Their friend, judge, John Martin had flipped. They thought at first it was his attempt to show impartiality. But as he ruled against them, time and time again, it became clear Martin planned to make a name for himself at the Conroe courthouse. With this trial, he intended to show solidarity with the rest of the racist officials.

Brown and Morris were bereft, but they trudged on viciously cross examining ranger, West styles on why he hadn't collected any samples of blood hair or saliva from the other janitors. I did not because they hadn't had any contact with her. That's the reason he said the ranger had no way of knowing this, for sure.

He just chose to believe their lies over what their supervisor, a black man had told him. All the defense could hope for was that the jury could see the blind focus on Clarence Brandley when there were at least four other suspects in the building and they had gotten achy piece to admit that he had a set of keys to that was a win.

If a small one. The prosecution had always claimed that Clarence was the only one with keys to the building. Gary anchorman seemed more self confident this go around, I guess, threatening his own father or law and to not testify had made him feel cocky. Martinez testified down party lines again. Finally, John says some was brought into the courtroom for his testimony.

Jim Keshan stood up and said, quote, may it please the court that this mr. John SESAM, we would tend to him at this time to the defense counsel. And at this time the state rests, your honor, Morrison Brown admitted that this was a brilliant move. Sessom had tried to refuse to testify for the prosecution saying he no longer supported the other janitors stories.

So instead they threw him to the defense. The defense cannot cross examine their own witness. And they had no idea what Sessom would say. They rolled the dice and put them on the stand. They immediately tried to bring up his previous testimony and statements to which Keishon immediately objected as Sessom was now a defense.

They were not entitled to any of them, his previous statements for the prosecution. Morris tried hard to fight this. He said that that case was a mistrial, but that the judge had improperly revoked Brantley's probation and they were still fighting that appeal and had legal access to all exhibits from that trial, which included Sessums testimony.

But judge John Martin disagreed quote, this court is not concerned with revocation or the prior trial. The witness sits up here. If you want him fine. If not dismiss him. George Morris said, quote, is that the ruling of the court that we will not be given the two statements of mr. SESAM, any of the statements, not prior testimony?

The judge answered Mora said that mr. SESAM was not now and had never been a defense witness and passed him back. He was dismissed during closing arguments. Jim Kesha got up and started with his prior closing argument and then whipped out a surprise. He told the jury that Clarence Brandley had worked part time for a funeral home.

And it appeared that this girl was molested after she was dead or unconscious. George Morris jumped up with his objection to this inflammatory statement. He was overruled. In a later appeal, Clarence his former employer said his job was janitorial and he was never around or had any contact with anybody and the funeral home.

But the damage and this trial was done. Keyshawn had just done effectively painted Clarence Brandley as a necrophiliac. The jury went out to deliberate and came back in an hour. They convicted Clarence Brandley of capital murder. They were then sequestered for the night before coming back the next day to hear arguments or whether Clarence should be to death.

This time they came back in 45 minutes. Clarence Brandley was sentenced to death. Some Brown said about immediately to prepare clearances appeal and the case was starting to get attention outside of Conroe Houston city magazine ran a series that ran over two issues for the first time. Openly suggesting that Clarence Brandley had been railroaded.

Now the defense attorneys were waiting for the courthouse to release the official record of the last trial. Mary Johnson, the court reporter for Bradley's trial kept apologizing for how long it was taking Brown and Morrison went and filed a motion with district clerk, Peggy Stevens for an extra 60 days to prepare their appeal as they had not yet received the record.

Judge Martin granted the extra 60 days to the defense. This was in late October on January 21st, 1982. They received a formal letter from Peggy Stevens. That read quote. This is to advise you that the record is complete. You now have 15 days in which to file any objection to the record. So while the Conroe courthouse took months to produce the sprawling record, they gave the defense just two weeks to object to any factual errors.

The transcript was 2000 pages. There were photocopies of all exhibits and witness statements, photographs, et cetera, but something didn't seem right to Don Brown. The exhibit numbers were in a different order. And in court, there had been yellow sticky notes with a number. Now those exhibits did not show the yellow notes and he found that statements were missing.

Photos were missing as were Cheryl's clothing and other scientific evidence. Something was rotten. He could feel it, it wasn't just that things were missing. It was the strange photocopies. He went to Peggy Stevens who said, I'm sure I don't know what could have happened. Then he demanded to see the originals.

Peggy showed him what she had and they were the same photocopies. Finally, one day a man named Frank Robin pulled on Brown aside, Robin, a young attorney had recently been hired as Jim keychain's assistant. He flat out told Brown that all of the evidence from the Brandley case was missing and that the da, the judge, the court reporter, Mary Johnson and district clerk, Peggy Stevens all knew about it.

He was risking his job coming to the defense, but he felt he had to do what was right. Morris and Brown were cautious. They did not want to expose Frank Robyn as their source. So instead they scheduled a hearing for February 5th within their 15 day limit, but barely. They filed a motion about the discrepancies in the record and all the missing evidence.

They asked that the originals be brought to court. Judge Martin gave the state a week to produce the evidence. In the meantime, the defense heard privately from the court reporter, Mary Johnson. She was terrified, but determined to tell the truth. The evidence boxes with missing exhibits had been locked in her office as per protocol.

She came to work one morning and they were just gone. As soon as she found out, she went straight to judge Martin who called in Jim Kesha and district clerk, Peggy Stevens, Mary thought, they had been trying to work things out, but she knew it was improper for the judge to be involved with this privately and something else was bothering her.

She had witnessed Kesha going in, judge Martins, chambers every morning for private meetings during the trial. It is highly improper for the judge and da to meet out of presence of the defense and Morrison Brown were livid. They always felt that the judge and prosecutor your work colluding, they work too much like a well oiled machine at trial.

Mary flat out said that they were rehearsing rulings and objections. So now they had a witness, but Mary was terrified of losing her job. Furiously Morrison, Brown, drafted a motion for judge Martins, recusal. Instead of filing the motion, they simply went to the judge and said, if he didn't step down himself, they would file the motion and go public about the charges of the judge and district attorney meeting secretly and plotting trial strategies.

Judge, John Martin quickly stepped down. And judge Lynn Coker took over Don Brown, finally finished writing their official objection to the trial record and filed it. He was now working alone as George Morris had become ill diagnosed with lung cancer. George Morris would die before the end of clearances appeals.

There was then a negotiation to correct all errors in the record, but there was nothing they could do about the missing exhibit. They were gone. And judge Lynn Coker was not interested in hearing the attorneys argue over it. Don Brown wrote a 75 page appeal and filed it with a criminal court of appeals.

Several months later, the appeals court wrote back that they would only accept 50 pages. Brown now used to such bureaucratic bullshit. Calmly went to his own secretary. And asked if she could change the font and tighten the margins to make it fit 50 pages. She said, sure, no problem. And even left him an additional six pages to argue on making matters worse in a year Supreme court ruling that had nothing to do with Clarence Brandley.

The court had ruled that in death row appeals, if the defendant had first had a hung jury, the court would now only hear evidence of the second trial, which produced a conviction. This sounds like a movie, a comedy of errors, except it's not funny. It's about a man's life. This ruling by the Supreme court meant that the whole record of the first trial was wiped, including the prejudicial behavior of judge Sam Robertson, as well as the changing statements of the other janitors.

So the ruling by the Texas criminal court of appeals went, as you might imagine. They upheld every argument for the prosecution, finding no misconduct, despite the missing exhibits, which they said was unfortunate, but did not matter now. And now that he had lost the first appeal, Clarence Brantley's execution date could be set.

Judge John Martin managed to get back on the Brandley case at the behest of district court clerk, Peggy Stevens, just so that he could set the execution date. The reason why. Peggy Stevens wanted it to be January 16th, which was her birthday Pernett Davies book, white lies. The defense learned the truth yet again from Mary Johnson in 1986, Clarence Bradley's appellate attorneys received a tip.

The prosecution had gotten a call and interviewed a witness named Brenda Medina. She called the da to say that her former live in boyfriend, James Dexter, Robinson. Woke her up in the middle of the night and admitted to her that on August 23rd, 1980, he committed a rape and a murder. He said that he had hidden the body well, so that there would be time for him to gather his stuff and leave the state.

Before anyone found her, when she woke up, James was gone and there was a pair of blood splattered shoes, which she threw away. Brenda had been 16 years old and pregnant with his child. She was used to his lies and didn't believe him. She thought he was trying to run away from the responsibility of the child.

What's more, she had actually been raped by James and then became pregnant. She didn't want to explain that to her parents. So she moved in with him. Robinson was abusive to Brenda, so she did not want him back in her life. After he took off, she thought it was for the best until she heard about the Brandley case.

And the details were so similar to the story. James had told her James Dexter, Robinson used to work at Conroe high. When Clarence Brandley took over from the previous supervisor, all keys were supposed to have been handed over, but one set did not make it to Clarence. Robinson had kept his say keys, the da.

I said, Brenda Medina was untrustworthy and felt he had no obligation to tell Bradley's defense team about her tip. But Brenda Medina got a lawyer who contacted Bradley's defense, who took a sworn statement from her. And then the defense petitioned, the

Texas court of criminal appeals for a writ of habeas Corpus and the court then called for an evidentiary hearing at the hearing.

Brenda Medina testified and now Gary anchorman testified that he had seen James Robinson at the high school on the morning of the murder. John SESAM also agreed to testify and had changed his story. Now he said he had seen Gary anchorman follow Cheryl up the loft stairs. He said he had heard her screaming.

No. Gary threatened him and told him not to tell anyone. But Gary did tell someone it was Texas ranger, West styles, the ranger threatened to arrest John SESAM. If his story did not match the other janitors, this was explosive new evidence. And yet again, the appeal was denied. Clarence Brandley would not get a new trial.

By now the FBI had decided to get involved and Centurion ministries based out of Princeton. New Jersey took on the case. They worked with a private investigator named James McCloskey, a former clergyman who had now made it his life's work to fight wrongful convictions. McCloskey was able to get a videotape statement from Gary anchorman who confessed that James Robinson was the one who raped and murdered Cheryl Ferguson.

He quickly recanted, but by then other witnesses came forward. Two people gave statements that they had heard. Gary Ackerman say he knew who killed Cheryl Ferguson and that it wasn't Clarence Brandley with these new video statements and intervention by the FBI. Just six days before his scheduled execution date, Clarence Brandley was granted a new evidentiary hearing.

James Robinson, Gary anchorman and ranger, West styles, all testify for the prosecution. But they're shifting stories actually help the defense this time on cross examination. Robinson admitted that he did tell Brenda Medina he had killed Cheryl, but it was only to scare her. So she wouldn't come after him looking for child support anchorman under cross examination admitted that Robinson had been at the school on the morning of Cheryl's murder, even better.

Under a vicious cross-examination Texas ranger, West Stiles

admitted that he had chosen Brandley as the only suspect before he had ever interviewed any other witnesses. And John SESAM finally testified to the truth. He in San Martinez had been near the drinking fountain and saw Gary anchorman grab Sheryl Ferguson, a man that he didn't know, but who he said had no teeth.

Was standing there watching and ran up the loft stairs after anchorman the screaming, Cheryl Ferguson, James Dexter, Robinson was missing some of his front teeth. Sessom said this man had something in his hands. It was a belt. The prosecution had never been able to prove what ligature had been used to strangle Cheryl though, they insisted Clarence Brandley had a belt on that day.

Brandley had not worn a belt. And part of those missing photographs from the exhibits would have proven it. He had on pants with an elastic waistband. He had never changed his story about this. And the state had never been able to prove he wore a belt. Sessom had made a good witness this time. He had managed to stay sober the night before his testimony.

He told how Gary anchorman had threatened him as they drove home that day. And then how ranger styles had also threatened him weeping. He explained to the court that he had perjured himself at the previous trials out of fear. He said, quote, I run from people over this for a long time, but you can't run from yourself or your feelings or your own conscience.

Henry achy piece also only came forward with the truth. Remember how he could not read the original statement he had signed. He had told the police that Gary Aker had disappeared during the time that the girl was attacked and that Martinez knew the girl was missing before anyone came looking for her.

That was not what his statement had said. His statement, implicated Clarence Brandley and matched the other janitor statements. He signed it without knowing what it actually said, but all of the janitors knew the actual truth. Icky had been threatened by ranger styles who had snatched him up by his shirt and said he would blow his head off.

If he told the truth. Despite this achy piece had gone to the da, Jim Keeshon and told the truth and the da assured him that he would handle it. This was proof that Kesha has suborned perjury as by the time Clarence went on trial, all four of the janitors told the same story, anchorman and Martinez for their own reasons.

Sesamin peace because they finally gave in to all the threats. Mary Johnson, the court reporter for judge Martin also testified at the evidentiary hearing about the missing files, the secret meetings between the judge and the da, and about Peggy Stevens and judge Martin choosing the execution date for Peggy's birthday.

They thought Mary would find it funny too, because it also happened to be her birthday, Mary Johnson, sobbed on the stand, as she told the truth and said, she knew she would lose her job over this. Sure enough. She was called the next morning and told to take a two week leave. When she returned to work.

Judge John Martin fired her. She had come to the defense, terrified of losing her job. And she had been right. Not only that, she tried to freelance with other judges at the Conroe courthouse, but could not get work because no one wanted to be associated with her. She was now the enemy. She had betrayed them all.

During this hearing, Clarence Brandley finally had the public on his side. There had been a 60 minutes segment on the case and James McCloskey organized, peaceful demonstrations. They marched on the courthouse. They marched to the governor's mansion, holding signs and yelling justice justice. There were t-shirts bumper stickers and statewide mailings.

The demonstrations may Texas news, and then national news. The tide had finally turned after the evidentiary hearing. Judge Perry picket ordered a new trial saying that in his 30 year career quote, no case has presented a more shocking scenario of the effects of racial prejudice, perjured testimony, witness intimidation, and an investigation.

The outcome of which was predetermined on October 9th,

1987, the court of criminal appeals. Granted Clarence Brandley, a new trial. And yet Clarence Brandley was not freed until January 23rd, 1990, as the state decided whether or not to pursue a new trial on December 13th, 1989, judge Pickett called for Clarence Bradley's release.

The court of criminal appeals had turned over his conviction, and yet Brandley still sat behind bars. As the Conroe courthouse full of corrupt officials kept filing motions, begging for new hearings. The charges against Clarence Brandley were finally officially dropped in October of 1990. He had spent nine years, five months and 23 days behind bars, almost seven of those years on death row.

In the fall of 2014, the Conroe police department told a reporter that they had no intentions of reopening the case. Gary anchorman. Okay. James Robinson were never arrested or questioned much less brought to trial. Gary anchorman and his wife, Cindy divorced in 1996. She never spoke publicly against him.

He still lives today. James Dexter, Robinson married and divorced three more times and is still alive. As far as I can find John Sessom returned to his home of Mississippi and died in December of 2014. I could not find any records on San Martinez. We may never know what really happened to Cheryl Ferguson and that Conroe high school auditorium.

But most theories of the case are that Robinson raped Cheryl as Gary held her down. And also that San Martinez had watched the door. Well, everyone was so worried about Clarence Bradley's missing time. They forgot that Icky piece had also been on his own, working in the teacher's lounge. John says some new things, truth, but was too scared to come forward.

So he drowned himself in alcohol. Icky piece later admitted to having continuous nightmares about the case and his lies. Clarence Brandley came out of prison and began a new life. He became an ordained Baptist minister and married Melvina Sims in November of 1990. He filed lawsuits to receive compensation for his years on death row, but because he had never received a pardon or a new trial, he was not granted relief from the court on the basis of actual innocence.

Therefore, he could not legally receive compensation on top of that. As soon as he got out, he was hit with a lien for $50,000 in back child support, child support. He would have been paying in those 10 years, but couldn't because he was in jail and then prison for the entire time, he moved out of Conroe, never to return.

He struggled finding and keeping work, but he maintained his faith and was happily married. Along with not receiving compensation. He also never received an apology. Conroe will never admit to what they did. Declare in Spradley. Clarence Brandley died September 2nd, back in 2018 from pneumonia. He was 66 years old.

He has suffered for 10 years while three judges, two prosecutors, the Conroe police, a Texas ranger, and even the damn district court clerk all colluded against him to railroad this innocent man onto death row, all because of the color of his skin. Once Texas ranger West styles, refuse to look at any other suspect, the entire Montgomery court and Conroe conspired to make sure a black man went down for this crime, despite so much evidence to the contrary.

I believe that the missing evidence didn't just go missing. Mary Thompson pointed out that Jim Keishon had a key to her office. This was a criminal conspiracy to Lynch a black man inside the courtroom, rather than on the courtroom lawn, like they would have in the 1920s. This happened in 1980, though. I bleeped the N word.

I hope you truly feel the gravity of racism. Clarence Brandley faced when he was wrongly accused city County and state officials openly use that word throughout Clarence's case. And what about Cheryl Ferguson? An innocent young girl whose life was cut short. The corrupt officials in Conroe would rather see an innocent black man hanging for her brutal rape and murder than to avenge her death.

By prosecuting the men who are actually responsible. This case is a double tragedy. There is no justice for Cheryl Ferguson. There was no effort to further investigate her murder. Once Brandley was freed, she was forgotten. Pushed aside for politics in the Conroe courthouse. If they had reopened the investigation, it would be admitting they were wrong.

The racist officials did not and would not ever admit. They railroaded a poor black janitor rather than conduct a proper investigation and to Cheryl's rape and murder. And though he was released, Clarence Brandley was never pardoned and never received compensation for the 10 years. The state of Texas stole from him.

His life was never the same. He did not receive justice either. And he came within six days of being murdered by the state of Texas for a crime.

5 THE MURDER OF KATIE AUTRY

At 4:08 AM. A fire alarm went off at Poland hall dormitory on the Western Kentucky university campus students in all States of undress, most grumpy and hung over.

Glumly gathered outside and waited to be told it was a false alarm, so they could go back to bed. Some had only been asleep for a couple of hours. There had been a big frat party over at the pike house the night before, but the grumbling turned a gasping as two firemen brought out a smile, a young woman naked, except for the sheet she was carried in.

T-shirt tied around her neck. She had burns from her neck to her thighs. She would be taken by helicopter to the burn unit at Vanderbilt hospital in Nashville, Tennessee, where she would die. Three days later from third degree burns. Katie Autry had come to Western Kentucky university beating all odds.

She had been bounced between her mentally ill mother and relatives until she was placed in foster care. At the age of 10, despite her hard Scrabble upbringing, she worked hard in high school. She was a straight a cheerleader, an overachiever. A bubbly, always smiling, petite and pretty girl at Western. She did change a bit.

It was her freshman year and like a lot of new college students, she was drinking and partying too much. And she was also working out some of her demons, but she was finding her footing and her independence. She had a bright future ahead of her. Until it was stolen from her and the early morning hours that May 4th, 2003, when she was raped and then set on fire in her dorm room, two suspects would emerge one from a wealthy family with a resources for a first rate defense.

The other was poor mixed race and was assigned a public defender even 16 years later. A lot of locals, aren't happy with the investigation, the trial or the outcome. Many still believe that one of those boys got away with murder.

Bowling green as a midsize city nestled in Southern Kentucky among the Hills caves, beautiful foliage and humidity that dominates much of the South. It's probably most famous as the city that manufacturers Corvettes at the general motors Corvette assembly plant visitors can watch the step by step production of one of America's favorite sports cars.

The Corvette museum includes one of a kind prototypes that were designed, but never manufactured along with other Corvette memorabilia. In 2014, a huge sink hole opened up beneath the Skydome of the museum. Swallowing eight cups, STEM Corvettes. The sinkhole was 40 feet wide and about 30 feet deep, it made international news, but thankfully the structure of the building was not damaged.

And the museum sets at the same site today. The sinkhole has been credited with helping tourism in the area. And the anniversary is celebrated every year. Last year. One of the sinkhole Corvettes that have been restored was put on display. Bowling green is about 60 miles Northeast of Nashville and a hundred miles Southwest of Louisville.

And it sits at the edge of a karst region where caves Springs and sinkholes are common. Karst is landscape underlined by limestone, which is eroded over the centuries. The main entrance to mammoth cave national park is about 30 miles Northeast of the city. It's a cave system spending more than 400 miles.

Bowling green has its own large ancient cavern that sits in the middle of the city. The lost river cave is actually a seven mile cave system that originates outside the cave and flows in to it. There is an underground boat to her on the shortest deepest river in the world where you can see land formation more than 10,000 years old.

The cave was used for shelter by native Americans and civil war soldiers, the Louisville and Nashville railroad. Known as CSX transportation today came through bowling green in 1859, connecting the city with Northern and Southern markets though. Kentucky never left the union during the civil war, bowling green declared itself, neutral, hoping to escape the war, but because of its prime location and resources, both union and Confederate armies sought control of the city.

Today, the city of almost 70,000 is more diverse though. Still predominantly white. The 1990s brought a boom in immigration and along with the different cultures came more restaurants and retail centers and a shift in demographics, meaning xenophobia joined the racism, common to many small towns. There were already black neighborhoods, and now they had little Mexico as with any city that caused more racial tensions.

But ultimately the immigration boom also brought new businesses and breathe new life into the small city. But the relatively small Southern town was already a bit of a melting pot due to Western Kentucky university being located there. The students and younger generations had a more cosmopolitan attitude than the older residents.

WKU as a public university founded by the Commonwealth of Kentucky in 1906, with over 20,000 students degrees range from liberal arts, nursing and engineering WKU offers 12 graduate school programs as well, and has been repeatedly named as one of the top producers of Fulbright scholars in the United States.

WKU is more commonly known as Western. So that is how I will be referring to it. It was in this diverse, liberal, and yet still judgmental world that Katie Autry entered when she enrolled at

Western in 2002.

When 18 year old Katie Autry came to Western in the fall of 2002, she was studying to become a dental hygienist. Katie's real name was Melissa K Autrey, but her family had always called her Katie. She was born June 10th, 1984 to her mother, Donnie may Autry in Rozene Tuckey. She had a younger half sister named Lisa Lisa explained to us or William van meter that they didn't know who is Eddie's father was, and Lisa's father was in prison.

The sisters were just two years apart in age and extremely close, they really needed each other. And Lisa considered Katie, a mother figure. She also affectionately called her big sister, sissy. Their mother, Donnie suffered from schizophrenia and the sisters bounced between relatives until Katie was 10 years old.

They had been living with her aunt, but her husband went to social services and sign the girls up for foster care. They went to live with an older couple named Jim and Shirley and men and pelvic, Kentucky. Jim was ex-military and hand Shirley were in there. They had stringent notions of how young girls should be raised.

They were strict, but they did care for the girls. Katie and Lisa lived in a nice two story house. And for the first time in their lives, they got to travel a bit. When Katie entered Hancock high school, the teenage tension did begin. It's not unusual, any family, but particularly hard in a foster family.

Katie and Lisa both felt different. They felt like the foster kids, they were, Katie worked hard to overcome the stigma. She was an excellent student, an overachiever and a joiner. She was in numerous academic clubs and she was a cheerleader as a short, tiny girl. She was a flyer. What's your leaders call the girl at the top of the pyramid.

But despite all of this, Katie at heart was still lonely. She had one close friend in high school, but the girl moved away before their senior year. After that Katie got a job at Wendy's after school to start saving money for college. Her first semester at Western was a bit Rocky, Katie and her first roommate didn't get along.

The roommate criticized her for sleeping around, especially with black guys, perhaps because she had been through the foster care system. Katie didn't have the same prejudice about interracial dating. In fact, she preferred to date African American boys. But her roommate wasn't wrong about her reputation.

Katie was nicknamed the hoe of the second flow. Her room was on the second floor of the Poland hall dormitory on campus. Unfortunately, sexual promiscuity isn't unusual for someone who had been through as much as Katie had. She was volleyed between family members at a young age landing with an older foster family.

She never knew her father. But she did finally find a friend and ally as well as a new roommate named Danica Jackson, Danica and Katie were instant best friends, right from the start. Danica loved Katie and felt very protective of her. She looked out for her and just Katie didn't own a car. She gave her rides everywhere.

So during that first year, Katie did become more independent. She actually went to social services and had herself ascended from foster care. You can stay in foster care until you're 21 and still receive benefits. And the state paid her tuition, but it was important to Katie to stand on her own feet. So she dropped down to part time in her classes and got a job at a smoothie shop.

Also to the shock of many. Katie started working as a stripper at a club called tattletales on the edge of town in April of 2003. Danica did too, but only lasted for two shifts. It wasn't for her that Katie really, I liked it. She was good at it and she made a few hundred dollars a night. Her boss would later say that clients loved her.

It wasn't just her blonde, all American good looks. Some guys really just wanted to talk to Katie. And Katie didn't just like the work she was saving up to buy her own car. And she and Danica also wanted to rent an apartment off campus. Katie was determined to be more independent and she wasn't ashamed of the work.

She called her birth mom and aunt and told both of them. They were more concerned with her walking alone in a dark parking lot after work. But it was her body as far as they were concerned about her new job. Possibly one issue and Katie and Danica's friendship at the time of Katie's death was her dating a young African American football player named Maurice Danica.

Didn't approve of Marise because he had a girlfriend who lived out of town and she thought he was using Katie Danica was mixed race herself. So she didn't object to his race, but rather how he treated Katie. And while Maurice was seeing two girls, he told author William van meter that he really liked.

He thought she had a delightful laugh because quote, it was just so country. He said he was attracted to her because she laughed all the time and he did give her rides and cared for her in his own way. And to be fair to Marise the dislike with Danica was mutual. He thought Danica partied too much and was a bad influence on him, Haiti, but he was still unwilling to be exclusive with Katie.

She begged him for a ticket short of his to sleep in and he finally gave in and gave her an old, soft, turquoise colored shirt. She loved it and slept in it every night. She was wearing it when she was attacked in her dorm room. And the early hours of May 4th, 2003.

On the afternoon of May 3rd, Katie and Danica went shopping. And then that Katie took Danica's car to Arby's to get dinner. She called Maurice when she left the dorm out of Danica's hearing to offer him some food he accepted and she took him in his bag first, before returning to the dorm room. That night, the girls planned to attend a frat party at the pike house and they were pre-gaming in a friend's room down the hall, drinking what they called golden grain, which was pure grain alcohol mixed with Sprite.

By the time they arrived at the party, Katie was already very interested. This was another problem. She wasn't a happy drunk. In fact, normal cheerfulness would give way to tears and anger it's because alcohol removes your filter. Katie still had a lot of pinup feelings despite trying her best to work them out.

But Danica was annoyed. She did babysit Katie all the time when she was drunk. And Katie was particularly belligerent this night. She was all over the place at the party teetering on her high heels, dancing with many different guys. And during this, she was calling Merissa cell phone repeatedly begging him to come to the party.

He finally did, but he told her he wasn't staying long and refused to dance with her. As she became argumentative, he said he was taking a walk at this. Katie screamed, forget it. I hate you and slapped him. And then Maurice was done. I left the party, a security guard now noticed Katie. She was dancing aggressively with several young black men and it was causing issues with the other girls at the party.

She was getting into arguments and just becoming a nuisance. She was upset about Maurice and probably trying to make him jealous or she needed to feel wanted because rejection, it doesn't matter. She was very drunk and we all make poor decisions in that state. Finally the fraternity brothers asked the security guard to escort Katie out of the party.

Katie ran to Danica crying and Danica tried to take up for her friend shouting. She just broke up with her boyfriend, give her a minute. Danica told the guard she would take care of her friend, but right then a pledge named Ryan Payne walked up and offered to give Katie a ride home. The new pipe pledges were all acting as designated drivers that evening.

Normally Danica wouldn't have let Katie go with a guy in that condition, but Ryan was completely sober and it was his assigned job. And Danica had met a boy. She liked, he had invited her to his room and she wanted to go exasperated. She let her friend go with Ryan pain. She would later feel guilt ridden about this decision that she knew Ryan and was tired of babysitting Katie.

And it's not her fault. What happened next? Ryan didn't have his own car. So he borrowed a truck from a guy named Brian

Moon already in the truck, passed out with Steven souls. He scooted over to let Katie in the truck and they drove to Poland hall. Ryan later said he watched Katie drunkenly stumble up the concrete path and side.

And then Ryan reported that Steven souls said, quote, I'm going to go holler at her. Steven Lee was part of what was called the Scottsdale crew, a group of guys from Scottsdale, Kentucky, who didn't attend Western, but hung out with some of the students. He was 19 and a light skinned, mixed race, young man, his father, Danny was black and his mother, Jean was white.

He had an older brother named Daniel and when his parents divorced young, his father raised the boys. Stephen was especially close to his grandmother of Angelina and stated her tiny cottage more than he did at home. Because he was so light skinned has friends nicknamed him Guido because they said he looked Mexican.

Steve then took it in stride. He has been characterized as both a sweet, polite boy. And as a liar and a thief, I think it's possible. Both were true. He moved off of friends because he didn't have his own car or cell phone. And he was banned from the homes of several friends because when he would leave things with turnout missing, but he was also known to doubt when his grandmother and he had many friends.

On May 3rd, his friend Wesley picked him up with another guy named Chris already in the backseat. They all planned to get drunk and go to that frat party at the pike house so that they had heard about, they bought two 18 packs because of course, light and rode around drinking for several hours. Before going to the apartment of a girl named Sarah there, Steven used Wesley's phone to call a guy he knew named Luke Goodrich.

He had known him from high school, but he bought weed from him now. But Luke's roommate answered because Luke wasn't at home. Brian, good room was 21 years old, six foot, two inches tall with dark blonde hair and dark eyes. He was considered a fairly good looking guy. He lived in Scottsdale with his dad, Mike and stepmother.

Judy, his mother Donna was married to a man named Bruce to Goss. He was the grandson of Cal Turner, founder of the dollar general store chain. Luke's mom and stepdad lived on a horse ranch outside of Dallas, Texas. Luke spent most of his first years with his mother, but Donna and Bruce had many marital issues and Bruce was abusive to her.

She took out many domestic violence petitions on her husband and had in fact filed for divorce, but they soon reunited and right after they got back together in December of 1993, when Luke would have been 12, Bruce was imprisoned for vehicular homicide. He had caused a wreck that killed another man and tested positive for cocaine, despite their problems.

Donna stood by her husband while he was in prison. Even writing the parole board, explaining that she needed him at home. She had a young son who she was having trouble raising without Bruce, but when Bruce got out, he clashed with his step son, Luke was told he could go to military school or move back in with his real father and lucky he chose to live with his dad.

In Scottsville, Luke drifted, aimlessly. He got his girlfriend pregnant when they were still teenagers, but they married anyway. He and LaDonnaPatrik were already divorced and their son was two years old. In 2003, as patterns will go. Luke had been abusive to LaDonna and had many domestic violence arrests on his record.

Luke was a self proclaimed loser. He rarely worked preferring to drink, smoke weed and play video games. He also sold marijuana and sometimes cocaine for income. On May 3rd, he and his 17 year old girlfriend, Brittany had been hanging out. They went to the liquor store and when they got back, one of Brittany's ex-boyfriends called herself phone.

Luke picked it up, answered and was furious. Brittany denied talking to her ex saying she didn't know why he had called, but Luke threw the phone at her and slapped her in the face. Brittany fought back. But she later told police that Luke Pender down on the bed and slapped her twice more. Luke's roommate, Matt and his girlfriend witnessed all of this.

When Luke tried to stop Brittany from leaving, by sitting on her, when she got into her car, Matt's girlfriend called the police. Luke took off when he heard the sirens, Brittany would later say he was choking her as he sat on her. When Luke returned several hours later, Matt told him about Steven's call.

Steven was not welcome in their apartment. Because as I mentioned earlier, has habit of petty theft got him banned from many places. So Luke told Steven to meet him at the bowling alley. Sarah Jo Steven, over to meet Luke. He got in the car with them and went back to Sarah's apartment where the small group drank and smoked blunts and hung out, waiting for the pike party.

Friends from Western Damian Seacrest and Brian Moon came to pick up the Scottsville brew and take them to the party on the way to the pike house, frat party, Steven threw up in Damien's car. He had been drunk working heavily and smoking weed on an empty seat. Steven stayed in the car, passed out while the rest of the guys went into the party.

At 1258, am he called a friend and named Brian Richie and asked him to come and get him? Brian told him no, he didn't like Stephen's mooching either. And told him he had to be up early at 7:00 AM. The original plan that night for the guys was for Brian Moon, Damian and Luke to walk to Bemis Lawrence dorm, where Damien lived on campus, as Steven was still passed out in the truck, Ryan Payne was supposed to drop him off at the dorm after he dropped off Katie.

And then wait to take Luke back to his car at the bowling alley. So Steven should have been at the dorm when they arrived at 2:15 AM. They asked the residential advisor on duty if she had seen Steven. And she said, no, She remembered and recognized Luke. Good room later. She said he was quiet and just sat down on the lounge couch at 2:18 AM Damien called Ryan to remind him to pick up.

Luke Ryan showed up about 20 minutes later and took Luke to his car. Luke later said he was home at his father's house around 3:00 AM. After Danica left the pipe party. She got worried that she hadn't heard from Katie. She called her cell and the dorm room. Katie finally answered at 2:26 AM. Danica said it sounded like she was face down on her pillow.

Danica asked if she had made it home. Okay. And Katie said, yeah. And then Danica heard her door shut in the background. Katie said I'm scared. Someone just came into the room. Danica asked, well, who is it? Katie said, I don't know. I don't know. Her voice sounded muffled. Danica told her to hand the phone to whoever it was a male voice came on the line.

And when Danica asked him who he was, he said, quote, I'm the boy who brought her home. She got sick in the truck. So I just wanted to make sure she was okay. Danica instructed him to turn Katie on her side. So she wouldn't choke. If she vomited again. Then she thought she heard another male voice in the background, and then she heard the door close.

Katie took the phone back and said, I just want to go to sleep. I just want to go to sleep. And at 2:28 AM the call ended. Danica called their friend Amy down the hall to check on her. But the call went to voicemail. I would like to point out here that Luke was seen and identified by the RA at the Bema storm at two 15.

And wasn't picked up for at least 20 more minutes than Ryan said. He took him to his car bowling alley at 4:08 AM. The fire alarm went off at Poland hall, stern campus police officer was dispatched to investigate. He saw water seeping out from under the door to room two 14, used the master key to open it and then slammed it shut.

When the smoke hit him in the face, he ran and got a wet paper towel to use as a face mask to go back in as his shift commander radioed telling him to go get out of the building and wait for the bowling green sire department. Fire alarm calls. Aren't unusual in dorms, hot plates, cigarettes and pranksters are usually the culprit without major damage or injury.

Captain Bob Sanborn explained that 95% of these calls were already put out by sprinklers. When they arrived. He ended another firefighter put on their masks before entering the stairwell to the hallway. When Sandborne opened the door, he saw what they call cold smoke. Black clouds of smoke from a fire already.

Extinguished water was spewing from the overhead sprinkler. But it had also been draped with a blanket. Even though the room was almost completely black. He spotted something glistening on one of the beds, it was Katie's arm with a skin burnt off. It was the exposed flesh that he had seen. The bed was covered in blankets and clothes that were still smoldering.

He brushed all of that off. And then he saw Katie her face was wrapped tight with some kind of sheer cloth giving it the grotesque look of a Halloween mask. A white tee shirt was not around her neck and the remains of a turquoise. T-shirt still stuck to our shoulders. It was the tee shirt Maurice had, given her Sanborn was shocked to see her chest rise and fall.

He radioed immediately that he had a victim and needed help. He picks Katie up and her score sheet, and he said she was very slippery and couldn't weigh more than 110 pounds when he got her out into the hallway where he could see better, he was horrified. Just as he got out the door, two other firemen came into evaluate her.

All they could do was hold up the corners of the sheet, praying they were not further injuring. The poor girl, none of the men could scarcely believe it was a real person. They could hold their corner of the sheet. With one hand, Katie Autry was a really tiny girl. As soon as they got outside, they ripped off their helmets and screamed for a medic.

Sandborne instructed them to give her air from their mask. He rightly believed that case. He hadn't died from smoke inhalation. The cloth tied around her face acting as a filter. When the ambulance got there, the men were helping Katie breathe and she was fighting the mask, knocking it off with her hand in her pitiful, confused mind.

There's no telling what she was thinking. They got her in the ambulance and tried to insert an IV into her burn arm, but couldn't Katie kept mumbling weekly. Just take me home. Katie was welded to the see room of the bowling green medical center. She was covered in third degree, burns so thick. Her skin was hardened and her body was still smelling.

One of the attending technicians told author William van meter quote, with the extent of her burns, if you can call it a blessing, there was probably very little pain involved at that point. The burns would have killed away most of the nerves. So there wouldn't be much pain, but she had many other minor burns that could cause a great deal of pain.

She also had two puncture wounds in her neck. The technicians immediately noticed the tee shirt around her neck and her face also had extensive bruising. One text said it was so bad. It was almost an indention to the left side of her face. She had a black eye that was swollen shut and the burn pattern was strange.

She had no burns to her back or legs. It was all on the front from the top of her breast, down to her mid thighs in the groin area. This was unusual. People who fall asleep with a cigarette or some other way of setting a bed on fire always have burns to the back. She should have burns than one all the way around her extremities.

The text said she did not team leader. Dr. Lee Carter screamed get the police here. This was not an accident. The texts, bagged her hands, trying to preserve evidence and all the clothing or what was left of it for the police. Katie had a belly button ring that was melted into her flesh. A breathing tube was inserted into her throat and the staff did what they could to make her comfortable with sterile, cool water and towels, also trying to prevent infection.

And then they tried to insert a catheter. Normally there is a specific place to insert the catheter called the urinary myositis, which is the opening where your urine comes out. Katie's had been completely burned off. There was no distinguishable opening, so they just had to guess and hope they were inserting it correctly though.

The ER team had immediately called the police, the helicopter to take Katie to Vanderbilt's burn unit was already there. They knew this would wind up being a homicide investigation and they tried it. The city police, the WKU campus police, even the state police begging for someone to come photograph Katie before she was moved.

Finally a state trooper showed up and snapped a few pictures, but they could not hold the helicopter any longer. The entire ER team was in shock and upset, but one of the texts noted that dr. Carter, who was known to be a calm, stoic professional, picked up a chair and threw it across the room, they had done everything they could for Katie Autrey and they knew she was going to die.

Though Katie's birth mother heard of a disturbance at Katie's storm over a police scanner. It was her foster parents who got the call from campus police, even though she was emancipated, the Inmans would have been her murder. You see contact when she enrolled at Western Shirley and men called Katie's aunt Virginia.

And told them she was being taken to Vanderbilt. So 10 minutes later, Virginia, her husband and Barbie were flying down the highway to bowling green. As Virginia called everyone. She knew asking them to pray. They met the Inmans there and the family police drove together to Vanderbilt hospital in Nashville.

That would be the last of the civility between the two families. Danica and Katie's friend Amy, the one Danica called the got voicemail to check on her friend now called Danica to tell her about the fire. At first Danica's thought was great. Drunk. Katie burned down our dorm room, but then Amy told her that Katie had been pulled from the building and was taken by ambulance.

Danica raced back to the dorm and was met by police who told her that she was probably okay. Just had smoke inhalation, but they kept asking her strange questions where the scissors out, do you keep knives in the room? They finally explained that Katie had puncture wounds. They kept asking if Katie was suicidal slowly, they explained the gravity of Katie's third degree burns at Vanderbilt.

Katie was sedated and put on a ventilator. She had to undergo additional resuscitation due to low blood pressure. Her life was hanging by a thread. She had to undergo a procedure where they cut long slits into her skin so that her chest could rise and fall because her skin was too toughened to allow it.

They excise the burned skin and use skin grafts from a cadaver at 10:00 AM. She was listed as extremely critical. That was upgraded an hour later to severely critical Virginia and her family were made to sit in the waiting room as the Edmonds were allowed to go in and see Katie. Virginia was angry. The Inmans were not Katie's parents as she saw it.

I understand her loyalty to her sister, but the Inmans did raise Katie. They were not perfect, but they did love their foster daughter and raised her as best as they knew how I think this was all just so much raw emotion. People get angry, intense, or upsetting situations and want somebody to direct it at Katie's biological family lashed out at her foster parents.

When Virginia finally did get to see her niece, despite warnings from the nurses, she went into hysterics. Meanwhile, Danica and her mother, Donna Jackson were racing to Vanderbilt as well. Donna thought that if anyone could get Katie to wake up, it would be Danica. When they got to the hospital, neither of the officers or the Edmonds would let them see Katie.

It was, if they blamed poor Danica, Lisa Autry spent every minute she could in her sister's room. Cuddling her, especially cut around the machines. Lisa, her aunt, Virginia and cousin Barbie saying the song, my girl to Katie, but nothing would wait. Katie ever again at 7:10 PM on May 7th, Katie Autry died. Her cause of death was complications of thermal burns.

She had third degree burns over 40% of her body with

extensive injury to her genitals. The contributory calls listed was blunt and sharp force injury to her head and neck. The manner of death was homicide. Antibacterial hand lotion had been put inside her vagina and squirted into her and also smeared on the door knob of the dorm room.

A can of hairspray was found that was used as an accelerant. She had been sprayed specifically on her breasts in general, and then settle on fire. Students at Western we're in the middle of a candlelight vigil for Katie. When they received word of her death, the vigil was now a Memorial. At 7:00 AM on May 4th brand Richie woke up and found Steven souls on his couch.

This was the friend who had refused to give him a ride the night before he asked Steven how he got there. And Steven said he walked from the university to his house. Brian thought this was bullshit because Steven was too lazy. This time he gave Steven a ride to Sarah's just to get rid of him. There was a child's purple bicycle lying in his front yard.

At Sarah's Steven found that Westlake was still there and Wesley drove him to his grandmother's house in Scottsville. His grandmother was awake, so he went to her bedroom instead of the couch. He took off his clothes and there was a feces stain on his shirt. He folded the clothes and had the money or a baby bed, evangelists, and kept for visiting grandchildren.

Then he took a shower and went to bed. He woke up later that afternoon, a waltz next door to a lot with a foundation, but no house and dropped a handful of jewelry into some cinder blocks. He was on the phone with a friend when a special agent from the ATF called his grandmother's phone and asked for him, he lied and said he was his cousin.

And that Steven was in Louisville. On the evening of May 4th, Luke was at home watching basketball. When someone knocked on his door or it was Brittany's father. And he said, stay away from my daughter before he punched Luke in the face. Naturally gentlemen, Luke called Brittany the next day and told her if she dropped the charges against him, he wouldn't press charges against her father.

Then not long after that, Luke and Brittany got back together.

Katie's murder could have fallen under Kentucky state police jurisdiction, or the city of bowling green, both of which offered assistance. Other agencies that helped were the ATF. The bowling green fire department and the FBI WKU police chief Robert Dean was a retired Detroit police officer who homicide, but not since 1989.

He put Western police, detective Mike Dowell in charge of the case. Well, had a degree in general studies and had once worked as a dispatcher for the Kentucky state police before he became a patrolman at Western. In 1996, he was made an investigator. The other detective assigned was Jerry Phillips who had never investigated a murder rape or arson.

Dowel had only investigated rapes, but none that had gone to trial, the only violent crime he ever invited was a student punching a taxi driver. And William van meeters book bluegrass, a true story of murder and Kentucky, the author said this was a highly unusual precedent. I'm sure it has happened before, but I couldn't find another example in my research, but I did find that in state owned schools, campus police have the same authority and jurisdiction afforded to state police.

In Kentucky, the campus police are granted the same authority as a County sheriff, including power arrest authority to carry firearms on and off duty on property owned by the campus or surrounding streets in certain situations, Kentucky County plus police can assert jurisdiction, but it is usually in conjunction and agreement with another agency, whether it is the state police city or County.

Kentucky campus police are required to be trained and certified as peace officers through the Kentucky justice and public safety cabinet law enforcement training center, unless they have previous training records acknowledged by the state. I am still baffled after that, this explanation, it seems incredible to me that the state police didn't enforce jurisdiction or bowling green or Warren County Sheriff's department or the FBI.

Anyway, one of these agencies could enforce jurisdiction over the campus. I don't believe that these institutions to not care about the Katy Autry case. In fact, they did assist the WKU police. So I just don't get it. And the campus police investigation would be heavily criticized. Not that normal police investigation wouldn't have been criticized in some way, but still letting the campus police department handle the crime.

Seeing and investigation was a big mistake. As far as optics were concerned. As they processed the crime scene, they found the bottle of hairspray that had washed out into the hallway with the water. The smoke alarm was ripped from the ceiling and Katie's Afghan blanket was tied around the sprinkler.

The door to her room had been locked from the outside with her own key. When Danica was allowed back in the room, she told him that Katie's jewelry was missing the RA on duty at Poland hall that night told police that Katie came in around one 30 or 2:00 AM and took the elevator. She said she was alone.

The Western campus police and other agencies had already gotten wind of the Scottsville crew being at the same party as Katie. They already had the names of Stephen souls and Luke Goodrich among others. But the RA on duty that night would insist. She didn't see Steven or Luke come in. As they questioned the fraternity brothers about the party they learned of Ryan Payne, the designated driver, they learned from the security guard that evening, that pain had given Katie Autrey a ride home after she was asked to leave the party.

Police picked up Ryan Payne and questioned him. He truthfully told about taking Luke to the bimah storm, but a story about giving Katie a ride was shaky in his first story. He said he asked her she would be okay, and then watched her go into the dorm. He didn't mention Stephen souls until he was directly confronted.

And then he admitted that yes, he was in the car with him, a agreed to go to the hospital for sexual perpetrator testing. But he wouldn't talk to the police again without an attorney. I don't get this kid. Why would he protect you, Steven? They weren't friends. Maybe he was afraid of being implicated. Maybe he felt guilty that he allowed Steven to follow the drunk and Katie up to her room.

He later met Brian Moon for dinner and they commiserated at heaven. I did take the hospital perp tests and they talked about Steven souls. Ryan told Brian about Steven going back into Poland hall after Katie and Brian said that he and seen him all night after he passed out in the truck. On Wednesday, May 7th, uh, bowling green fire department, Sergeant and the ATF agent showed up at Stephen's grandmother's house to question and him, he claimed he had never been to Poland tall.

And didn't remember any girl getting into the truck. Steven claimed Brian Richie picked him up from Bema storm Richie originally backed him up, but then called the police and arranged meeting with a detective and an ATF agent. This time, he told the truth about Steven's late night call to him and then finding him on his couch at 7:00 AM.

The next day warning. He explained that out of loyalty, he covered for Steven, but then went and questioned him himself. And that Steven kept changing his story, quote I'm his own friend. And his story kept on changing and changing to me. Steven kept ducking authorities, but now his family knew something was up.

His father, Danny kept in touch with the police, assuring them that Steven would come in for questioning. His father finally called a detective and told him Steven had admitted to having sex with Katie Autrey and that his son was scared. Steven had agreed to talk to the police if they would let him get some rest.

The detective in question agreed and showed up at Danny's house at 7:00 AM the next morning, why they knew where he was. I wouldn't let him sleep. He admitted to having sex with Katie. That should have been enough for an arrest warrant, and yet they waited. When Steven souls was finally picked up for questioning, he was taken to a state police outpost in bowling green.

He told them about his stride with Katie and Ryan Payne. And that Katie had jokingly called him sick boy. He and Payne dropped her off and he had gone up to make sure she got inside. All right. He claimed that she invited and him into her room and then she took the elevator, but he took the stairs because he was afraid of elevators.

This would explain why the RA didn't see him that night. The stairs were not in the direct line of sight. The way the elevator was. Steven said they had sex and then she got sick again around two 30 or 3:00 AM. So he left and was at Brian Richie's house by three, three 30. Am he repeated this same story?

At least three times. And even admitted to speaking to Danielle on the phone, finally, police started grilling him and showed him the hairspray can with his fingerprints on it. Steven claimed he didn't know, but maybe he picked it up. When he was looking around her room. He admitted, he often took things from friends apartments.

The detectives fired away at him. Quote, somebody hurt that girl. How did things go bad? Are you covering for someone else? Steven, at this Steven said I didn't hurt that girl. Somebody kept calling her phone and I don't know who it was, but it could have been her boyfriend. When I was leaving, there was some dudes standing in the hallway.

I don't know if he went in and done it, but I hadn't heard that girl. Steven claimed he didn't know the guy that he hadn't seen him before. And didn't know that many people on campus. They asked him if something went wrong during the rape and Steven insisted, it was consensual that he wasn't that type of person, the cops kept asking leading questions.

Was it a buddy of his that had bye and hurt? Katie? Were you scared, Steven? I bet you didn't know what to do. You were scared to death right at this. Steven started nodding and staring at the floor, or he mumbled scared to death. Now to be clear, they are allowed to ask leading questions. But in this case, they planted the idea and Steve his mind to try and pin it on another assailant, an additional man in the room that night.

And if that was true, why was it not in Steven's original story? Steven then said, quote, we was in there messing around or whatever, you know, we was having sex. A buddy of mine comes in there. I guess he knew the girl or some shit like that. I guess he talked to her at the party. The police already had Luke good room's name as one of the Scottsville crew guys at the party.

But this was the first time he was implicated. Steven said, quote, I started talking to her and asking if we could run a train on her and shit like that. He told the detectives that Katie had said no. And Luke had become forceful with her. He said he had started hitting her and put a pillow over her face.

Then he claims that he walked out into the hall because he didn't know what to do when he came back in, he said, Luke was raping Katie again, the detective leads him. Has Lucas been known to do stuff like that before? Get violent like that. Steven heartedly agreed and said, that's why he was in bowling, green quote, him and his girl got in a fight.

He hit her and stuff and thought the police were after him. They asked him if Luke made him help hold the pillow or anything. And Steven said, no. Were you scared of Lucas? They asked, well, he's bigger than me. Steven answered, you know, I'm not a fighter or nothing, but I was just shocked. They asked him if he let Luke in.

And he said, no, he had knocked. And Katie got up and let him in. They asked him if Luke was there when Danica called Steven said, no, he arrived shortly after. That's an interesting answer because he couldn't have known that Danica thought she had heard two voices. I bet he would have said Luke was there if he had known, they asked you sure he was the last one up there.

Steven said yes, because I left. As soon as it happened, as soon as he was hitting her Steven, then insisted he left and didn't see the rest of the right or Luke setting Katie on fire. But then he claimed, he saw Luke put the blanket on the sprinkler, the detective pounced, and said you therefore knew what he was about to do.

Steven claimed Katie slapped Luke, and then he pushed her down on the bed and put a pillow on her face. He just kept having sex with her. And I guess he got done and shit like that. I was just standing there. So his story just changed again. Now he was there when Luke finished raping Katie not leaving as Luke was still riping Katie, as he had said, he said, Luke got up and ominously told him you didn't see nothing.

Then Steven said, Luke spreader with a hairspray. And that's when he, we walked out, the detective asked him to show him and Steven mimics spraying Katie's body and the bed. They again, asked if he saw Luke set the fire and Steven denied it. He said, no. Cause when I got outside, I ran down the steps. I ran, I knew he was gonna do something crazy.

So I just left. I just ran and ran. They also found out how Steven got to Brian Richie's house to be on his couch by 7:00 AM. The next morning he had stolen a girl's purple bicycle and rented there, leaving it in the front yard. Steven was then sent to the hospital for the sexual perpetrator tests. When he came back, he was more steady yet the police did not arrest him.

At the very least. He had watched a rate and asked me Mark Ritchie to give him an alibi. He had lied to police multiple times and historic had changed many times, but instead of arresting Steven souls, the police, let him go and got a warrant for Lou good or him to go to the hospital for perpetrator testing.

They then brought Luke in for questioning. He truthfully gave a time, one of the night's events meeting at the bowling alley, going to the pike party, going back to the Bema storm. After the party, they asked him if he saw Katie Autry at the party and he admitted he had seen her dancing and that she was really drunk.

He said she never danced with him. And he knew that Ryan Payne had given her a ride home. They asked him if he had talked to Steven and he said, no, sir. They asked him if Ryan would do anything like that. He said, no, sir. I play football with him. I'd vouched for him. He explained that after Ryan dropped him off at the bowling alley, he got his car and drove to his dad's who was up and shoot him out for being a bad father.

The cops asked why, and he said, quote, cause I'm a loser. I don't work. I quit a good job. Like an idiot. A detective claimed, he thought Luke was a straight shooter and straight out, asked him at any time, did you go to Poland hall that night? Luke said where with a puzzled look on his face, then he said, quote, I don't know where that is.

The only dorm I went to was Brian and Damien's meaning that Bemis Lawrence storm, the detective tried to scare him by saying there was security camera footage, and Luke insisted. No, I did not do that to that girl. I swear to God. So they asked him who did one detective told him not to cover for anyone because no one would cover for her.

Him. Luke said, quote, sir, I know that Brian and Damien was with me the whole night. And the girls saw me come in and sit down in the lobby of that. Or by the girl, he meant the RA who had already verified the story. He described the clothes, he had worn that night. And again said that his dad was up and waiting for him when he got home.

Then the detectives try the old, well, how does your fingerprints get in her room at this Luke yield? What, sir? I don't even know that girl call my dad right now. The detective kept on saying other people had ratted on him. Luke never budged one. Detective claimed they had hair samples from the bed and would get DNA.

Luke replied, quote, them test will show you ain't done nothing again. They went back to the fingerprints. They supposedly had. Luke said, I don't know. Then they said, what about the security footage tapes? And Luke said, well, let me see the tape. He had just called her bluff. There were no tapes and there were no fingerprints.

Again, the police are allowed to lie when questioning assess

SPECT, just like they could ask leading questions to Steven, but unlike Steven, Luke never changed his story. As Luke kept denying everything that detective asked, why people would lie about him. Luke shouted, people are jealous of me. I have a nice car.

I have a pretty girl friend. I don't know. My mom and stepdad are pretty rich after this. The Western police chief Robert Dean came in and conferred with the detectives and then Lou Goodwin was formally arrested and charged with capital murder and taken to the Warren County jail. On May 12th detectives found Katie's jewelry next door to eventually the soul's house, right.

Where Steven told them it would be only, he originally claimed that Luke put it there, right? Luke went to the house next door to Stephen's grandmother and had the jewelry. It was preposterous. And on further questioning, Steven admitted, he had the jewelry himself and that he had stolen it. So we have more lies from Stephen souls and the more the police questioned him, the more elaborate the lies became.

He now claimed that he did not have sex with Katie first. And when Luke came in and started attacking her, he was yelling for Luke to stop. He claimed that Luke threatened him and his family. If he didn't shut up. He also now said that Luke had put on a condom before he raped Katie. I think at this point he understood that his DNA would be the only one found.

So again, to cover his ass, he kept embellishing. He even said that Luke put the condom in his pocket when he was finished and then forced him to put the hand sanitizer and Katie's vagina. Then the most incredible lie. He said that Luke forced him to take his turn and ripe Katie, and then he did it out of fear.

And now he explained his fingerprints on the hairspray bottle by changing his story yet again, and saying, Luke made him Katie's breasts and genitals. And now that was the song he was singing and he would not get off that chorus. Luke made me do it. Luke made me do it on July 22nd, 2003, the Commonwealth of Kentucky filed notice that they were pursuing the death penalty.

I guess Luke and Steven Steven's family had raised the money for a defense attorney. His case was now handed over to the public defender's office. The attorney, the family hired had no prior experience with death penalty cases, which was a requirement and a capital trial would extremely raised the costs associated with a good defense on August 28th.

2003, the DNA results finally came back. The vaginal swab taken from Katie was tested against Luke, Stephen, and the boy Katie was seeing named Maurice Stephen souls was a positive match while the other two men were ruled out. Regardless, Lucas Gudrun remained in jail. Both men were denied bond due to the serious nature of the crime.

And town gossip and the media, Luke and Steven were pitted against each other as the rich boy against the poor boy as author William van meter pointed out. And this was not exactly true. Luke was not close to the Turner dollar store family. He was not raised by them. His stepfather was their relative, and he had only helped raise Luke for a few short years before his own incarceration.

And then he sent Luke back to his real father. But to be fair, Luke's family could afford a good defense attorney. His mother was still married to Bruce Dugas who did come from money. They hired famed bowling, green defense attorney, David Broderick. He was known as a showboat in the courtroom, but also as one of the best criminal defense attorneys in the state in March of 2004, Stephen souls was offered a deal by the Commonwealth.

If you would testify against Luke Goodrich, he would get life without parole, or he could roll the dice and risk his life at a capital murder trial. He later insisted that his defense attorney pressured him into taking the deal. And a later appeal has attorneys argue that Steven was not given enough time to consider this still and felt too pressured.

He lost that appeal. I could not find where Luke Goodrich had been offered the same deal first, and I don't believe he was it's difficult to understand why the police were so focused on Luke when they had no physical evidence against him. It was only the word of Stephen souls who had already admitted to taking part in the crime.

But the Commonwealth was determined to convict good room. Maybe it was some of the rich boy versus poor boy prejudice. If you look at Reddit, there are claims that physical evidence was suppressed. The Volkswagen Renet can speculate all they want just as the town gossips can. But if the Commonwealth had had any physical evidence tying Luke good room to Katie's right there, murder, they damn well would have used it.

Almost two years had passed. I looked good, or him sat in the County jail, awaiting trial. As he did, three inmates came forward and claimed that Luke had confessed his participation in Katie's murder to each of them. At different times, jailhouse snitches are notoriously unreliable, and one of these men didn't come forward until after the trial had started, they proved to be terrible witnesses at trial Lucas gutter, and finally went on trial in March of 2005.

The trial was moved 60 miles away to Owensboro due to the publicity in bowling green. Stephen stills was the star witness, of course, but his testimony was weak, especially in the face of all of his changing stories and lies. Luke had several good character witnesses, but one of these was not Ryan Payne, the designated driver that night.

He was supposedly Luke's friend and had played football with him, between his questioning, with the police. And then later on the stand, Ryan Payne, the claim, he didn't remember anything. I do not understand his shiftiness. In this case, there is no physical evidence suggesting that he was tied to the crime and he had alibi witnesses, but he came off as uncooperative and suspicious, but Luke had better witnesses.

One was a character witness against Steven souls who had witnessed him setting fire to a truck. He had stolen. They also played homemade rap tape. Steven had made with a friend with very violent and misogynistic lyrics. It was rightly pointed out that those types of lyrics are common in the right genre.

But the effect of hearing those tapes on the jury can not be discounted. There were also expert witnesses, one, a retired FBI agent who believed that the police had planet the notion of a second accomplice in Steven's head. Steven had told his story numerous times without mentioning Louis Goodwin's name until the day have suggested that there was another man there.

Then at night, they also had a professor of forensic science testify to low cards. Theory. Low card was a pioneer in the field of forensic science who had stated that a perpetrator will always bring something to a crime scene and leave with something from the crime scene. It is a common police principle and extremely relevant in a case with literally no physical evidence against the defendant.

The Commonwealth prosecutor had tried to suggest that physical evidence such as hairs would have been washed away from the sprinkler. It's still holding to the theory that Luke had used a condom as to why there was no DNA found on Katie's body. The forensic professor replied that the water would not have washed away selectively only one suspect's hair.

And let's not forget that not only with Steven soul's DNA, fennel Katie's body, his shirt with the feces was found. Without going into very graphic specifics. The multiple felony charges included sodomy. One of the last witnesses at trial was Western police, chief Robert Dean. His testimony was cringe-worthy as broader.

It got him to admit that he did not check out Luke's alibi witnesses. Remember there were more than just his parents to say what time he had come home. Katie spoke on the phone with Danica at 2:28 AM at literally the same time. Lucas good room was sitting on a couch in the Bemis Lawrence dorm. Not in Poland hall, Luke himself was an excellent witness.

He spoke clearly and was not rattled by the prosecutor's questions on cross examination. The jury reached a verdict within three hours, not guilty on all counts on May 12th, 2005. Steven souls was officially sentenced. Though there had been a plea agreement. It was within the judge's discretion to Senate souls, how he saw fit.

He had several family members stand up as character witnesses pleading for leniency. Most eloquent was his father, but Danny souls still insisted that Luke was the actual leader in this crime, not his son and his eloquence could not matter the fire of Lisa Autry's victim impact statement. She addressed Steven souls directly saying quote.

You and your family may think Katie was nothing or nobody. But to me, she was my, everything. She was my mother figure my best friend, my big sissy. And she's a girl that could have accomplished anything in life, but I will never know where her life would have taken her. Thanks to you. Sick boy, she practically spit out the name.

Her sister had teased her attacker with. In his sentencing. The judge said, quote, one person we haven't heard from is of course, Katie Autrey, her lips are sealed. And mr. Soles, you saw of that. And he then sentenced him to life imprisonment without the possibility of parole, it was over Steven souls would spend the rest of his natural life in prison.

And Luke Goodrich was finally free to get on with his own life, but that was not easy for him. In the bowling green and Scottsville communities, as well as Western, there will always be an era of suspicion. Lou good room was a punk. He beat the women in his life. He rarely worked his mom and stepdad kicked them out, regardless of what his upbringing, he has the aura of a rich kid who got away with murder.

I think a lot of this attitude has to do with Western insisting on taking control of the investigation. The crime scene evidence will always be in question because of it. No Luke Goodrich is DNA and fingerprints were not found. There has never been any evidence against him except the word of an admitted rapist and murderer who was trying to deflect responsibility from himself.

Luke Goodrich was a violent asshole. That's a fact that he has maintained at least publicly that he holds no animosity towards the

Commonwealth, the Autry family, or anyone else involved. He told William van meter quote, I think it was karma for how I treated women. I would like to leave you with something positive, but I'm afraid.

I really can't Western Kentucky university settled a lawsuit with the Autry family for $200,000 for failure to properly secure the dorm. Katie lived in eight days after her murder, the university formed a campus safety task force and announced that new magnetic locks would be installed at all. Dorms security cameras would be installed and alcohol would be banned from fraternity houses.

Unfortunately, the university president, Gary Ramsdale went on record with the Louisville courier journal after this and made it extremely problematic and defensive statement. He said, quote, I'm going to make a point this year, unlike in past years, because I'm more conscious of it, of individual responsibility and prudence and your personal activities.

No, when you're in a high risk situation and remove yourself from it. And by all means be sober enough to do so. Thank you, mr. Ragsdale for blaming the victim and further contributing to rape culture that is still so rampant on our college campuses. Katie Autry may have been drunk, but she got a sober ride home with someone she and her friend knew she made it into her dorm room, but someone else slipped in behind her due to the lack of security in her dorm.

And after he brutalized her and set her on fire, he locked the door with her own key on his way out. The brutal rape and murder of 18 year old, Katy Autry is no one's fault, but sick boy, Steven souls, shame on you.

6 MARK BARTON THE SPREE KILLER

Mark Orrin Barton is a family Annihilator and a spree killer.

He does fit some of the statistical molds. We characterize these killers by, but by definition, a spree killer is someone who kills two or more victims in a short time and multiple locations without a cooling off period. Barton did do this in Atlanta on July 29th, 1999, killing nine people and wounding 13, his total body count what 12, when police found the bodies of his wife and two sons, children, what sets Mark Barton apart from these types of killers is that he had killed before.

Six years earlier that breaks the mold we've come to use for understanding the motivations of a family Annihilator or spree killer. Mark Warren Barton quite simply may have been a serial killer.

Stockbridge Georgia as part of the Atlanta metropolitan area, meaning it is a suburb of the famous bustling Southern city. It would take a commuter about a half hour to go to work in Atlanta, though with the infamous traffic snarls.

I'm sure that commute is closer to an hour these days. The city of Stockbridge is located in the Northern part of Henry County, Georgia, which was founded May 15th, 1821. The County has an area of approximately 331 square miles located in the Piedmont section of Northern Georgia. Henry County lies South of the cab where Atlanta is located Stockbridge.

Isn't one of the more prevalent suburbs cities like Marietta or Alpharetta, which have larger populations. It's a sleepier city. More famous for it. Small town hospitality, beautiful parks and above average public school system. Today Stockbridge has around 30,000 residents in 1999. When today's story takes place, it was much smaller with under 10,000 residents calling the suburb home.

The original old stock bridge was a crossroads community when it was settled in 1829. About the time the Concord Methodist church was organized near the present day old stagecoach road, there is a bit of controversy about the name Stockbridge with some insisting. The town was named after Levi Stockbridge, a traveling professor who passed through the area multiple times before the post office was built in 1847.

But others insist Stockbridge is named for Thomas stock. Who is state surveyor and president of the Georgia state Senate in the 1820s, either way, the Southern railroad came in 1881 and was built from Macon to Atlanta. And Stockbridge was swept up in that economic boom, but it remained a small city retaining its suburban charm into the 20th century.

This is where 44 year old Mark or in Barton moved with his new younger wife Lee in around 1995. 17 years, his junior Leann Vandiver began an affair with Mark Barton in 1992. She was a receptionist at the chemical company, Lantech international in Douglasville, Georgia, where Mark had recently found work as a salesman, the couple moved to Stockbridge with Mark's two young children after the murders of his wife.

And mother-in-law in 1993. Though officially unsolved Mark Barton was, and is the only suspect in the vicious double murder.

Mark Oren Barton was born in Clovis Curry, New Mexico on April 2nd, 1955. He was the only child of Truman and Gladys Spartan Truman Barton was in the United States air force and was stationed in Germany when Mark was born, some sources list Barton as being born in Stockbridge, Georgia, and also Sumter

South Carolina.

But this confusion is probably caused by journalistic errors after his death. Probably because the Barton family was restate and Sumter, South Carolina, where Mark was officially given a social security card in November of 1967, Gladys was a housewife and the kinder, gentler parent and the Barton family it's been reported that Truman was harsh often cruel and always decided and delivered the punishment of young Mark.

Mark struggled in school and center. He was intelligent, but an introvert. He also stood six feet, four inches tall and weigh 205 pounds by high school. Despite his physicality, he didn't play sports. He was an academic, but he was a misfit with no friends, much less girlfriends. And he started rebelling against his disciplinary and father with petty crimes.

He was caught robbing a drug store at age 14, Mark excelled in chemistry. He was so good. He started making his own psychedelic drugs. He had heard about extracting powder from morning glory seeds and mixing the powder with a chemical solution. And so he tried it creating a drug similar to LSD. Mark suffered a terrifying overdose of this drug landing him in the hospital where a psychologist diagnosed him as delusional.

Mark said he saw demons coming through the floor and he lost his ability to read. He shaved his head and immersed himself in religious fanaticism, relearning how to read by studying the Bible. In later years, he considered himself a Jehovah's witness. All of this behavior did little to help with the bullying he faced at school.

He had shaved his head and isolated himself even further from his peers in 1973. Mark graduated from Sumpter high school. He attended Clemson university for a semester, but dropped out after having another psychic episode for the remainder of the school year, Mark received anti-psychotic drug therapy after finishing the drug therapy, Mark enrolled at the university of South Carolina, where he majored in chemistry.

While in college, Mark began making and selling

methamphetamine. He was also a user and still a petty thief. And so he was arrested again when he was 20 years old. When he tried to burglarize a drug store, he received probation in 1979. Mark managed to finish college, earning a bachelor's of science degree in chemistry from the university of South Carolina.

It was while he was attending the university of South Carolina, that Mark finally met a young woman who showed him some interest. Debra and was born on November 29th, 1957 in Savannah, Georgia to Paris, bill and Eloise. She had one sibling, a brother named John. Not much else is known about Debra's early life before her ill fated marriage to Mark Barton.

The two were married in Atlanta, Georgia. Shortly after Mark got a job in Texarkana, Texas as a chemist at TLC manufacturing within five years, he was a manager with an ICLE yearly salary on February 15th, 1988. The couple had their first child, a son named Matthew David. Matthew a boy scout was said to love playing video games though.

The Barton scape the image of a happy marriage. It was only on the surface. Mark's erratic behavior. Again was controlling his life. He thought everyone was out to get him and began recording conversations with coworkers at work. He was also known for his outbursts of temper, often throw in things in the office.

He also abused Debra. He was very controlling having to know where she was at all times often accusing her of infidelity. Eventually TLC manufacturing had enough of Mark's behavior. He was fired on September 13th, 1990. His coworkers noticed he left the building very unhappy on September 20th. Mark broke into TLC, manufacturing and stole confidential data off of two computers.

When he was finished, Mark wiped, the hard drives clean. Then he found install hard copies of all the data and took it home with him. Mark Barton was the obvious suspect in the burglary. When detectives visited market home, he admitted what he had done. He was arrested and charged with felony burglary, but he was only in jail a few hours before TLC manufacturing agreed to drop the charges against Mark in exchange for the return of their files.

And Mark Barton was required to move out of the state of Texas as part of this deal. So Mark Deborah and Matthew relocated to Macon, Georgia, their second child, a daughter named Michelle Elizabeth was born there on May 27th, 1991. Michelle is often described as a beautiful and sweet little girl. Mark found work at a chemical company called Lantech international in Douglasville, Georgia.

Douglasville is a little over two hours from Macon. So the family moved again and bought a home in Lithia Springs. About 15 minutes from Douglasville, not long after starting his new job. Mark began having an affair with a married receptionist named Leanne Lang. They flirted openly at work and were often seen together at after hours gatherings.

Leanne van diver was born on February 18th, 1972, and make a bit of County Georgia to Paris, Patricia and Jo. She had three siblings and grew up in Lizella Georgia. She had only been married for about a year before the affair with Mark Barton began when Mark started seeing Leanne, he bought a new wardrobe and began tanning.

Naturally. This made his wife suspicious, though. Mark told Debra she was just being paranoid. Other friends say that Deborah did indeed know of the affair, but chose to ignore it. Whatever Deborah did or didn't know about Leanne. She wasn't aware that Mark took out a $600,000 life insurance policy on her.

Deborah kept plodding along in a painful marriage. And in June of 1993, Mark left town with his mistress. They went to meet up with Leanne's friends in North Carolina. Well there. Mark told him that he had never loved anyone more than Leanne and that he would be able to marry her by October. A couple of months later, Leanne left her husband and moved into her own apartment on labor day weekend, just three months after his trip to North Carolina.

And just one month before October Debra left for her own

small vacation, she and her mother Eloise traveled to the Riverside campground on Y slake in Alabama to a Lakeside trailer where they plan to fish and relax. Debra had left five-year-old Matthew and two year old Michelle at home with Mark Bill's by the, also skip the trip because he was recovering from a heart attack.

The women had planned to be home by Sunday, but by late Sunday evening, others at the campsite became worried when they noticed that the camper and mrs. Bobby's Thunderbird were still parked in the same spot. Everything was eerily quiet as the other campers decided to check on the women. They walked in on a gruesome crime scene, backed out carefully and called the police.

Both women had been hacked to death with a small acts and were unrecognizable. Eloise had been a hit eight to 10 times while Deborah's skull was split in half with at least 20 blows to her head and face. There was blood and other body parts splashed all over the walls and curtains of the small trailer.

The police immediately found bloody footprints leaving the crime scene and also found that the murderer had vomited in and around the toilet. This indicates the killer probably knew the women vomit can sometimes be a good source for DNA, but we don't know that for sure. In this case, the crime scene appeared to be a staged burglary.

The murderer want a police to think a burglary had occurred, but police found $600 in cash and Eloise's overturned purse and no signs of forced entry. The police called bill and Mark Barton to come to Alabama and noted that Mark did not seem upset at all. And he quickly became extremely uncooperative.

A witness at the campground said he had seen a man fitting Mark's description. But a Georgia detective would later reveal that the witness had never seen Mark Barton and a lineup. Investigators sees the floormates of marks for Taurus and told him not to clean his car, but it was days later before they tested the rest of the vehicle.

And by then it had been cleaned, but technicians were able to find blood splatters on the steering wheel console driver's door and gear shift. They also found blood in Mark's garage and kitchen, wall and sink. Mark said the blood was from when Deborah cut her hand and he outright refused to undergo a polygraph.

Luminol was used to find the blood evidence, but there was not enough blood for DNA testing. Detectives had also found out that market called the company that creates luminol and would have probably known that while the cops would be able to find traces of blood. There wouldn't be enough for DNA. At one point, Mark, even sarcastically said, if there's a ton of blood in my car, why aren't you arresting me?

Why am I not in handcuffs? Alabama police decided the only way to get a murder conviction was to have more fast, but he would not budge. He said he was home with the kids, although he definitely had time to drive to the Lake. And back in the end, an investigator insisted that all they had was circumstantial evidence, but no physical evidence to tie into the murder.

Mark had not only cleaned his home and car diligently, but he refused to give a DNA sample that could have been tested against the vomit at the crime scene. I'm not sure why the Alabama police didn't get a warrant for his DNA. Yes, the evidence was circumstantial, but it was overwhelming. Mark was the only suspect and he had a motive, a mistress plus a $600,000 life insurance policy on his wife.

And as a healthy 38 year old man, he certainly had the means to brutally murder two uncertainty. He also had opportunity as there was plenty of time for him to drive from Georgia to Alabama and back in one night, no credible alibi. Other than that, he was alone with his two small children. He easily could have murdered his wife and her mother as his children slept later, a Georgia detective scoffed and said that if Alabama police had done their jobs, maybe 12 people would be alive today.

In October, the family held a funeral for Deborah and Eloise. It's reported that Mark sat expressionless in the last Pew. And as soon as the ceremony ended, he bolted out the door, skipping the burials, Leanne was waiting for him and her Mustang convertible with a music blaring. He hopped in the car and they sped away.

Leanne moved into the Barton home pretty quickly in October after the funerals and her own divorce was final. Mark was in, in a fight with a life insurance company over the policy he had on Deborah because they believe he killed her. Despite the failure of Alabama police and arresting him, they wanted the money put into a trust for her children, but Mark refused and the company eventually settled with him in early 1997.

He received $250,000. And the remaining $350,000 was put into a trust for Matthew and Michelle Barton less than a year after the murders, Leanne and Mark married on May 26th, 1995, and quit their jobs at Lantech. They moved with the children tomorrow, Georgia, where Leanne became the quintessential soccer mom to her new stepchildren.

Mark also continued to tussle with Alabama authorities over his first wife's murder, still adamantly refusing to give a DNA sample or submit to further questioning. Alabama detectives did keep a close eye on him with one telling CNN that they put psychological pressure on Mark Barton. They knew he did it, and he knew they knew it was a dangerous game of chess.

And the Alabama authorities had no idea just how high Mark Barton's body count would go. Through all of this Mark second marriage wasn't very much better than his first. He and Leanne fought often with her leaving for a few days, but always returning. Mark was also burning quickly through Debra's life insurance money with get rich, quick schemes and day trading.

In February of 1994, Michelle who was almost three years old, told the daycare worker that her father had molested her. Mark was ordered to undergo a clinical psychiatric assessment. The test showed he was quote, certainly capable of homicidal thought and homicidal action. However, given Michelle's age, it was difficult for the state's attorneys to build a solid case around her, against Mark, or prevent him from keeping custody of his kids.

After Mart Barton spree killings, the Douglas County da reviewed the 1994 custody hearing records and said, quote, It was disturbing enough to have a trained psychologist and competent prosecutors reporting these things back to us back then. It's absolutely chilling to think about it now over the next four years, Leanne and Mark's relationship, completely crumbled.

He was abusive and controlling towards her. Mark also stopped working and Leanne was supporting him and the two kids. Mark had lost over $100,000 by June of 1997. Almost all of it on volatile internet stocks in 1998 Mark's behavior got even worse. He had run through most of the insurance money. He also killed a family cat, but then took his children out to search for this missing cat.

In February of 1998, Mark began working for all tech investment group. Mark started with a self funded $50,000 trading account by March. Mark had drained the account and owed Alltech over $11,000. Because his account was negative. He was forced to stop trading in April. He came back to Alltech and told them he invented a new soap and made a lot of money.

And he did repay his debts and resupplied his $50,000 trading account. But by may, Mark was back to where he was before this time he owed the company $30,000. Mark told his boss, Brett Doonan, that he would go back to making soap and he would be back soon with a 30,000. He owed them Brent and Mark did remain in contact in October of 1998.

Leanne finally left Mark, according to Leanne sister, Dana Leanne left, because she was tired of supporting Mark while he wasn't working. However, there had been marital problems since the beginning, but land Barton now, mr. Stepchildren. She had raised them as her own for five years. And so she let Mark and the kids move into her Stockbridge apartment and late June or early July of 1999.

Mark got a new job trading stocks at momentum securities. Okay. He soon owed momentum securities money as well. Except this time it was much more than what he owed Alltech by June 26th. Mark owed momentum securities $187,000. The walls were closing in on him on Tuesday, July 27th, 1999. Mark bludgeoned, Leanne Barton to death with a hammer.

As she was sleeping, he hit her body in a closet behind boxes and clothes. The next day, he stayed home with his children, 11 year old Matthew and eight year old Michelle. Mark also bludgeoned his children with a hammer and then put them face down in the bathtub to make sure they were dead before drying them off, redressing them and tucking them into their beds.

Matthew was found with his favorite video game next to him and the shell was found with her Teddy bear. Then on Thursday morning, July 29th, Mark went to his attorney's office and made some changes to his will. He then headed to momentum securities in the Buckhead area of Atlanta's financial district at around 2:20 PM.

After chatting nonchalantly with his ex coworkers for a few minutes, Mark learned that the day had been bad for stock trading. Mark then said, quote, it's a bad trading day and it's about to get worse. And then he pulled out a 45 caliber, Colt and a nine millimeter Glock and opened fire. First he killed 38 year old Kevin dial with two shots, one in the back and the other in the heart.

After killing Kevin, Mark walked down the rows of workstations. 30 year old Scott Webb was the second to be shot. The bullet entered one of his lungs. Andrew zapper, Zella and James Jordan were shot at next. Andrew was not hit, but James suffered two non fatal wounds, one in the side and the other in the arm.

Next Brad show. Mel was shot twice once in the back and once in the shoulder, 58 year old Edward Quinn was fatally shot in the neck. And then Mark had a, towards the receptionist, Marcy Brooking and shot her point blank, but she miraculously survived next. Mark fatally shot 42 year old Russell Brown, three times.

Employees were hiding under desks. As Mark Barton continued to stalk around the building shooting both guns. Mark went up to Scott Webb and shot him again. He also shot Brad show Mela.

Third time. By the time Mark left the momentum securities building, he had killed four people. Edward Quinn, Kevin dial Russell Brown and Scott Webb.

The first call to nine one one was a 2:56 PM. Mark then walked across the street to the Alltech investment group building. As he walked into the building at 3:00 PM. Mark said, I hope I'm not upsetting your trading day. His previous manager, Brent Doonan thought Mark was coming in to repay the money. As he had promised Mark aspirin.

If the two of them could talk, Brett said yes, but he needed a minute. Well waiting for Brent Mark ran into another office that have manager Scott Mann speaker and his assistant Kathy van cam. The three were chatting when Scott noticed that Mark had red splatters on his arms, hands and shirt. As the three of them walked back to the main office.

Mark closed the blinds. He then left the office and headed back to the conference room where Brent was, he opened the door and said, Brent, come here quick. Really? You're going to love this. Brett followed Mark into the main office. Once in the office, Mark closed the door and told Brent Scott and Kathy quote today is going to be visual.

Then he lifted up his shirt and took out the two guns he had in his waistband. He immediately shot brunt twice and then shot at both Scott and Kathy Scott was hit in the arm and gut while Kathy was shot in her face, Mark then left the main office and headed out into the open trading floor and began shooting.

45 year old GM she'd have OSH was shot in the back by Mark's nine millimeter dying where he fell use of liver. Son was shot in the head and Fred herder was shot in the back, but both survived. Dean Della Wala 52, tried to make it to an exit, but Mark shot him in the back before he could make it. He was shot again, as he fell to the floor.

48 year old Allen tenon ball was shot in the upper back torso and right shoulder Joseph desert 60 was shot twice by the 45

caliber once in the shoulder. And once in the chest, all of the men died almost instantly. Meredith Forester was shot in the lower back, but survived. As they were seeking shelter, Charles Williams, Harry Higginbotham sing Yoon and Meredith, when it were all shot, Charles suffered a chest wound, hairy a head wound saying a head wound and Meredith of back wound.

And yet somehow they all survived. Meanwhile, Britton Doonan was attempting to escape from the conference room. When he came out, he spotted Mark Barron, still shooting, although he was badly wounded. Brent was able to tackle Mark as he aimed to shoot another employee. After the tackle Mark got up quickly, Brent took off running a smart shot off two rounds at him.

The first bullet hit Brent's left arm and the second hip Britt's left shoulder blade, but Brent spotted an exit and headed down the hallway. He found the elevator and press the down button. As he waited for the elevator. He saw Martin Martin appear at the other end of the hallway. Brent was able to close the elevator doors just as Mark pointed the gun and fired off a round.

Brent also miraculously survived and lived to write a book about the massacre. As police responded to the nine 11 calls from the momentum securities, building an employee inside the Altos building called nine 11, the operator misunderstood the caller and believed the address she had just received was the same one as the momentum securities building.

She told the caller police were already there because police did not respond to the Alltech office. Mark Barton was able to leave the building, get into his minivan and leave undetected. Five people were killed in the Alltech office that afternoon. Alan Tenenbaum Dean Della wallah, Joseph desert. Jim she'd have OSH and Varroa morale, Tahara, who is not an Alltech employee, but had been in the building taking a computer course after Mark left, Brent stumbled into another office in the same building.

The employees of that department called nine 11 at the same time, a motorcycle officer, her gunshots coming from the Alltech office building. The officer went inside and found the crime scene.

He called for backup, but the operator said he was at the wrong building. It took 30 minutes before commanding officer figured out that there were crime scenes at two different areas.

An Alltech employee thought to go through the HR records and found Mark Barton's file and handed it over to police. Police called in SWAT and searched nearby buildings. They set up roadblocks and searched all cars. They had three helicopters searching for Mark Barton and his minivan, but they had bad information.

Mark's minivan was green and they had been told it was white. And authorities had no idea where he was headed. For hours officers with shotgun searched the parking decks at Piedmont center and several office buildings, employees remain locked in their offices for their safety police dogs sniff the bushes and FBI agents dressed for war searched.

The area along Piedmont road or hours passed before authorities heard from someone who had seen Mark Barton. Security officers of the town center mall and Kennesaw about 20 miles from Buckhead saw Mark's unoccupied van and the mall lot around 7:40 PM. At about the same time a woman who had been shopping at Rich's approached her parked car, Mark walked towards her and said, don't scream or I'll shoot you.

And then she backed away and he said, don't run or I'll shoot you. But she ran. And thankfully this time Mark Barton did not shoot. After he left them all parking lot. Police caught sight of Mart driving. They began following him and saw Mark enter in Acworth, BP gas station parking lot as he circled the station, police cruisers blocked both entrances to the station.

When Mark pulled around, he saw the Acworth police. As the police surrounded the vehicle, they ordered him to throw his gun out of the window, exit the van and lie face down on the ground. But Mark Barton had no intention of being taken alive. He pointed the 45 at his left temple and the nine millimeter to his right.

Only one of the guns fired, but it was enough. Mark Barton,

family Annihilator and spree killer was finally dead

in the van. Police found four handguns, 200 rounds of ammunition and a large amount of cash. The on-scene Sergeant called for an ambulance and then headed to Barton's apartment. When police arrived at the apartment, they found a typed letter in the living room that read to whom it may concern. Leanne is in the master bedroom closet under a blanket.

I killed her on Tuesday night. I killed Matthew and Michelle Wednesday night. There may be similarities between these deaths and the death of my first wife, Deborah . However, I did not kill her and her mother, there is no reason for me to lie. Now. It just seemed like a quiet way to kill and a relatively painless way to die.

There was little pain. All of them were dead in less than five minutes. I hit them with a hammer. I'm so sorry. I wish I didn't, whereas cannot tell the agony. Why did I, I have been dying since October to wake up at night, so afraid, so terrified that I couldn't be that frayed while awake and has taken its toll.

I have come to hate this life in the system of things I have come to have no hope, killed the children, to exchange them for five minutes of pain for a lifetime of pain. I have my self to do it, to keep them from suffering so much later. No mother, no father, no relatives. The fears of the father are transferred to the son.

It was from my father to me and for me to my son, he already had it. And now to be left alone, I had to take him with me. I killed Leanne because she was one of the main reasons for my demise. I really wished I hadn't killed her now. She really couldn't help it. And I loved her so much Anyway, I know that Jehovah will take care of all of them in the next life.

I am sure the details don't matter. There is no excuse. No good reason. I am sure. No one will understand if they could. I wouldn't want them to, I just write these things to say why. Please know that I love Leanne, Matthew and Michelle with all my heart If Jehovah's willing, I would like to see them all again, and the resurrection to have a second chance.

And then Mark's last words were chilling. He wrote, I don't plan to live very much longer, just long enough to kill as many of the people that greedily sought my destruction. You should kill me if you can. Signed Mark. Oh, Barton on Matthew's body police found a handwritten note that read. I give you my son, my buddy, my life.

Please take care of him on Michelle's body police found a handwritten note that read. I give you my daughter, my sweetheart, my life. Please take care of her. Finally, police found a handwritten note only, and spotty that red. I give you my wife, Leanne Barton. My honey, my precious love. Please take care of her.

I will love her forever. Leanne's funeral was held on August 1st, 1999. She was buried in the old Valley Grove, primitive Baptist church cemetery in Irwin County, Georgia Matthew and Michelle's funerals were held on August 2nd. They were buried at sunrise Memorial gardens and Lithia Springs. I would also like to give you short biographies of all of Mark's victims.

Keep in mind that day traders were not always full time. Employees at the companies more targeted for some, it was part time work for others. It was a hobby. One poor woman was just in the building taking a computer class. Alan was a father of three who worked at his family owned grocery. He was the president of the synagogue and he loved to golf and jog.

Dean Della Walla was a devoted father of two. He came to America from Pakistan in 1973 and Pakistan, he had been a lawyer and a banker Kevin dial was the son of Pittsburgh Steelers and Dallas Cowboys wide receiver buddy dial. He was described as a happy, very bright and wonderful man. He was a graduate of the university of Texas and he was known for his sense of humor.

Edward Quinn was a father of three who have recently retired from ups. He loved working on his lawn, fly fishing goth. He was a devoted family. Man. Who'd become a grandfather for the first time. Just three weeks prior to his death, they want mural to Hora was a mother of two. She was a quote, very sweet spirited person who was dedicated to her family.

She was a native of Trinidad and Tobago and the wife of a pediatrician. Scott Webb liked to bike and jog. He was described as popular and athletic. He graduated with a degree in biology from Loyola university. He was very close to his father and he was a gifted tennis player. Joseph desert was an avid golfer.

He attended a prayer breakfast every Friday morning. He was known for running and races. He had many friends, it was known to say positive and encouraging things to everyone. He encountered. Russell Brown was quote, so kind. He couldn't bear to kill a hook. Doug. He was great at math track and swimming. He was a seat PA and had left law school with one semester left take care of his brother and father who were dying of cancer.

He had a blow loved cat named sweetie Mick Mac. Jam sheet of OSH was a leader in his community and a sports fan. He had a bachelor's degree in chemical engineering and two graduate degrees from Georgia tech. He was a father of one

as for Mark Barton's surviving victims, many sued, Alltech and momentum for not looking into Mark Barton's background when he was hired. But all of the cases were dismissed. Brent Doonan moved home to Wichita, Kansas. In 2001, he published a book called murder at the office and is working in his family's trucking business.

He's married with a son, Scott Mann speaker also moved back to Wichita, Kansas nail Jones stayed in Atlanta. She went back to real estate law and was semiretired in 2009. Kathy VanCamp was blinded by the shot to her face. As of 2009, she had gone through 15 surgeries to repair her face. She eventually moved to Hawaii with her husband.

Sadly. She said the last thing she ever saw was Mark Barton's face Forrester's chance of survival was one in a thousand. After going through 115 pints of blood Meredith survived, two emergency surgeries. She is missing a disc in her lower back. She has scoliosis in her upper back nerve damage in her right leg and extensive scar tissue throughout her abdomen.

She was wheelchair bound for a while, but it's miraculously walking again, according to the Taipei times, Fred herder committed suicide in December, 2001. He had lost $400,000 and three years through day trading, but we cannot discount the trauma he survived and had to live with after Mart Barton's massacre at Altec, I consider him to be the 10th victim of the killing spree that fateful July day,

as I said, in the opening, it's possible and fair to call Mark Barton, a serial killer. Because even within academic literature, there is debate on how to distinguish a spree killer from a mass murderer or a serial killer. Was there a cooling off period where the murder is done in commission of other crimes where the murders for revenge or for attention where the victims random or targeted adding to the confusion is the fact that the terms are not used consistently by law enforcement academics or the media.

Spree killers don't resume their normal lives between murders. And yet we know that Mark Barton did, he attempted to live a new life and put six years between his murders, his rampage at momentum securities, and Alltech fall within the spree killer definition. But he also murdered his entire family, including his first wife.

And mother-in-law putting him squarely in the family Annihilator category. And he killed for money. It was not for the thrill of killing as his vomit at the first crime scene illustrated and from his letters for the police in Stockbridge, he did seem to feel guilty about killing his children. And second wife though, this guilt did not stop him.

He planned the murders carefully. I do find it odd that even in his suicide note, he still denied the murders of his first wife. And mother-in-law. Why would he lie then maybe Alabama did get it right. And maybe Mark Barton just would not give Alabama the satisfaction of a confession for those murders.

I'm not sure that Mark Martin can be put into any one

classification, but considering that he checks boxes and just about every category, maybe he can simply be called a serial killer. But does it really matter? He killed 15 people, mass murderer, serial killer spree, killer family, Annihilator. These are all labels for the same thing.

7 BONEY & CLAUDE

A decade before Canadian married couple Paul Bernardo and Carla whole mocha shocked the world with their depraved crimes. Alvin and Judith Neely went on a remarkably similar spree crossing three Southern States. Both couples worked as a team to kidnap sexually assault. Torture and murder. And when they were caught, they turned against each other.

The trials of Bernardo and are legendary with Carla's plea bargain, being dubbed the deal with the devil by the Canadian press. But the sadistic Neeley's didn't garner the same attention United States for one, they were not an attractive couple, like the Canadian Ken and Barbie killers. And they also didn't choose victims that the media would be captivated by one was a 13 year old girl who lived in a children's home, a victim of abject poverty, sexual abuse, before she even met the Neeley's light.

Carla, the defense tried desperately to paint Judith Neely as an abused and unwilling accomplice. Also like Carla, no one believed her, but Judith hadn't made a deal before she confessed. Alvin was the one who got the deal. So at 18 years old, Judith became the youngest woman sentenced to death in the U S in 1983.

Alvin and Judith Neeley were from different areas. I committed crimes and Tennessee, Alabama, and Georgia. Normally I would give you the history of the town County or even state to give you a feel for where the victims or killers lived. That's not really possible in a case like this, but I will give you short descriptions of those places as the story progresses.

Alvin Howard Nealyjr. Was born in Trion, Georgia in July of 1953. Trion is a small town of less than 1800 people located in Chattanooga County. The Northwest corner of the state dotted by Hills and pond forest triumphs claim to fame is being the Denham capital of the world because of the Mount Vernon manufacturing plant that employs some 4,000 people from all over to, to get County.

But the triune cotton mill was established there in the 1840s and the small town was fairly prosperous. Growing up in the fifties and sixties, Alvin Neeley didn't come from a rich family, but it was a happy family. He was the youngest of three children, the pet, according to author, Thomas H. Cook, who described him as a jokester with a charming smile, a disarming smile.

He would keep his whole life. His childhood was spent hunting, fishing, swimming, going to boy Scouts and church, not the usual upbringing for what Alvin Neeleyjr. Would become. Judith Ann Adams was born in Murfreesboro, Tennessee, less than an hour from Nashville and Rutherford County. I've seen Murfreesboro described as a CD trailer park town in June of 1964 when Judith was born.

But that's not exactly accurate. Not that the town didn't have it. Sheriff trailer parks and honkytonks, but it wasn't quite as dismal as often portrayed in any bio you read about Judith Neely. By 1965 middle Tennessee state university had been established in Murfreesboro and the economy had already felt a boost after world war II.

Today it's often called a suburb of Nashville with people choosing to live and raise children in Murfreesboro, but commute to Nashville or the cost of living has skyrocketed in the last couple of decades. Judith grew up in the Walter Hill area of Murfreesboro, more rural than, and now. Her father was a construction worker and part time carpenter.

And her mother was a housewife, one of five kids. She had an older brother and sister and two younger brothers when she was nine years old, her father died in a motorcycle accident. He had been drinking and had a guardrail. It said that his death had quite an effect on Judith who was always considered a quiet child.

After his death, her mother changed Barbara Adams, put a trailer on the eight acres of land. Her husband had left her and took a factory job. She struggled as would be expected, but she also soon took up with a teenage boy. Judith found out when her mother and the boy were in a car accident and she was outraged.

They had been drinking and Barbara Adams was charged with contributing to the delinquency of a minor soon. Barbara began seeing many men. She had a CB radio installed in the trailer and went by the handle. Indian princess, strange men started showing up at the trailer at all times. There is no evidence that Judith was abused by any of these men.

In fact, according to her and Alvin, she was a Virgin when they met, but there was a simple sheet hanging to separate her room from her mother's and she became very bitter about her mother's act of sex life. In 1979, when Judith was 15 years old, she met 26 year old Alvin Neely. When he came to her trailer with another man answering a CB call from Indian princess.

Judith was no beauty. She had very pronounced buck teeth, and she was as big boned as she was tall. She stood five foot, 10 inches, but Alvin thought she was statuesque like a model and he loved her long black hair. The two talked until four in the morning. And within days they were spending every spare moment together.

They traded sad stories. Judith told him all about her dad and problems with her mother. Alvin's worst problem was his rejection from the Navy. It was his lifelong dream. But his application was rejected because they found a heart murmur. When he was 17, he began stealing cars. He served a two year stint.

Once a judge finally tried him as an adult, Alvin and Judith were obsessed with each other, but Alvin finally had to admit the truth. He was already married to a woman named Joanne. He said she was a liar and a cheat. Yeah. Told you to the marriage was over Judith. Wasn't phased by this revelation. She was in love by the beginning of her sophomore year in high school, she left a nasty note for her mother and he loped with Alvin.

Judith didn't actually marry right away, but hit the road for awhile. They stayed with his family and then moved to Rome, Georgia, where Alvin started working in a convenience store a few weeks later, some deposits went missing and so did the couple. They moved on to North Alabama, and then back to Georgia, this nomadic lifestyle defined their lives.

Only. They quickly learned that no matter how hot they were for each other, having no money, put a damper on everything, they would get jobs at convenience stores or markets only to move on. When the cash from the till would go missing the actually married on July 14th, 1980 after Judith turned 16 and they kept traveling from Texas back to Florida.

Stopping to stay with relatives, forging money orders to get by. They were enjoying their crime spree and started calling each other bony and Claude a spoof on the infamous Bonnie and Clyde. Alvin had blown up on a diet of fast food and sweets, common for travel. He still had his voyage smile, but much of the charm was lost, but Judith lost weight becoming noticeably thin a characteristic witnesses would remember as well as her buck teeth.

But the good times finally came to an end. However briefly, when Judith was arrested for robbing a woman at gunpoint at the Riverbend mall in Rome, Georgia, Judith was eight months pregnant with twins at the time. Alvin was picked up with her and senates to five years in a Lafayette prison. Judith was sent to the Rome youth detention center because she was under age and it was there that she gave birth to their twins, Jeremy and April, the couple had always exchanged love notes.

But their letters in prison and youth detention were voluminous. It took a detective a couple of days to read through all of them. Once the couple were caught for their more serious crimes, they were lovely letters that turned jealous as the years, went by. Judith got out of it. Youth detention in November, 1981 and moved in with Alvin's parents who had taken the twins just a week later, she was arrested for robbing an Exxon station, but was back out of jail by March, 1982.

Just in time for Alvin's early release from prison in April of 1982, they had a lovely reunion, but it didn't last long. Reportedly Alvin told her he didn't want her sexually anymore, but they stayed together committing petty crimes. They broke into post office boxes and cash checks and kept forging money orders on September 10th, 1982.

A Rome youth detention center employ can Dooley's home was shot through four times. The following day, fellow employee, Linda dares home was firebombed with a Molotov cocktail. The day before Ken Dooley's home had been shot, he had received a call from a woman claiming to be a friend of his wife's coming through town and wanted to know their address.

He didn't think anything of it when he gave it to her. The next day his wife got a call, but Ken was out. When he got home, she told him a girl had called and thought she was from the detention center. She wanted to know if Ken was home and his wife said no, but he would be soon. Not long after Ken came in the phone ring again, it was the same woman mrs.

Dooley put Ken on the phone. But instead of a woman, a man's voice said, quote, you've screwed the last girl you're going to screw and you're going to pay. Dooley was briefly shocked, but because of his job at the detention, yeah, Senator he wasn't as alarmed as some might be. He figured it was a prank call set up by one of the girls, less than an hour later, someone fired four shots at his house and then sped off into the night.

The next evening, Linda Adair and her husband were getting ready for bed and also got a phone call. Her husband answered, and a woman asked to speak to his wife when she got to the phone, no one was there. Her husband said the woman sounded young. But Linda just shrugged it off and hung up the phone at almost the exact same time.

Her phone rang again, and someone started banging hard on her back door. She looked up to see her car port and flames from the window. It was her neighbor on the phone, screaming that her house was on fire. The young man at the door had just been passing by dropping off his date for the evening and had witnessed someone throw the Molotov cocktail.

He was able to describe the car and said it was a couple inside though. He didn't get a good look at them. The crude bomb was made from gasoline and a grape soda bottle, and hadn't done much damage. It never made it past the car port as investigators. We're still on the scene, the phone ring again, Linda answered and it was a woman's voice.

She didn't recognize. She said, I'm calling about the shooting at Kendall, at least house last night and the attempted firebombing of your house tonight. And you will both die before the night is over then at almost 2:00 AM with investigators still at the Adair home, a woman called the Floyd County police department.

She said she was calling in reference to the shooting at Ken Dooley's house. And the firebombing of Linda dares home when the officer answered. Yes. She said quote, uh, for the sex abuse, I went through at the YDC, the officer said, okay, what kind of abuse did you take? She said sex abuse. And for the abuse I took, they're both going to die and who knows?

It might be tonight. And then she hung up. The YDC stands for youth detention center. Then on the evening of September 29th, 1982, a call came into the Rome police department. The caller said, quote a yes, y'all looking for Lisa and Milliken on run from the harps tome, the officer who answered, said Lisa Ann, who the woman said, Milliken, I can tell you where she is.

He calmly answered where she at the woman said go up to little river Canyon in Alabama. Just as you cross the bridge, turn to the left, go up into the national park. You'll see, on the left, some picnic tables in a big rock parking area and look off the side of the Canyon, where there is a power line going across it.

Look straight down the Canyon and you'll find her where I left her. And then she hung up. Despite the other recent anonymous calls involving the youth detention center, the room police didn't immediately make the connection. They also thought it could be a prank. Rome lies in the foothills of the Appalachian mountains in Floyd County, Georgia.

And it's about 20 miles from Cedartown. We're a home for girls called harps. Tome was located. It wasn't for delinquents, but rather for indigent girls, Lisa and Milliken lived there though. I've seen it referred to an older papers as a home for troubled girls. It was more like a foster home at the time.

Today it is called the Murphy harps children's center and it offers treatment and counseling for at risk youth abused and neglected children and teens, the officer who had taken the strange call then called the harps home and found out Lisa had been missing for four days. They thought she was a runaway and hoped she would return it.

Wasn't uncommon at harvest. Many girls missed their families, but would often return. Lisa was originally from Lafayette, Georgia, a small town in Walker County in the middle of the state. And she had voiced her and happiness at the harps tome and talked of wanting to return home to her family and Lafayette, the officer called Walker County to see if Lisa had been picked up there.

She had not. Cedartown where harps home is located as a small city in Polk County, Georgia, Cedar towns, pop culture claim to fame as a country music song by Waylon Jennings released in 1971. That is eerily precious. And Lisa Milliken's case. It's a murder ballad called Cedartown Georgia. He's saying tonight, I'll put her on a train for Georgia going to be a lot of kinfolks squalane and aggrievancecause that Cedartown gal ain't breathing.

The mystery color also called in a tip to a roam radio station. Claiming the Rome police knew a girl had been murdered and that her body was in the little river Canyon and the police were covering it up. She said the girl had been shot by a juvenile detention officer. The radio station took the information straight to police.

The Rome police had already called a cow County Sheriff's office in Alabama, where the Canyon was and to cab reported that they had found no body. The deputies had gone to look, but the Canyon is deep and treacherous and they didn't go very close to the edge. When pairing over the Canyon had McCobb stories that have been told for years, author Thomas H.

Cook said that the locals claimed that Satan has held demonic rights on the Canyon floor. A more valid rumor was that there was evidence of crimes. Especially murder and the dangerous Canyon. It was a good spot to dump something you didn't want found soon after the radio station call the same woman called the DeKalb County Sheriff's office, making the same claims that gave a more precise location, telling them to go left on County road one 76 and go about a mile until they found a place where there were power lines down.

She again, ended the call with that's where I left her. This call came in at 6:15 PM. And the date we're concerned that they better go rush and look again, as it was, it's getting dark that night by the beam of a flashlight to cap County. Sheriff's deputies found the body of 13 year old Lisa Ann Milliken.

It was after 7:00 PM and already dark. When the deputy these arrived, they had to crawl out and lay on their stomachs to appear into the Canyon. And first bought it a pair of blue jeans hanging on, on a limb. They kept looking until they saw Lisa's white checkered blouse, there's blood on it. She had been shot in the back back and lay crumpled over a fallen tree.

Investigators brought her body up out of the Canyon by a rope the next day, and found three use syringes among the debris into which she had fallen. The blue jeans spotted were womens and covered in blood. They hung on a limb, dangling over the precipice where Lisa was found because the Canyon had so much garbage authorities.

Couldn't be certain that everything they found was relevant to Lisa's case, but they bagged it all anyway and delivered it to them. Alabama department of forensic science in Huntsville and hopes of a lead though, Lisa was found into cab County. The Sheriff's deputies quickly realized by the anonymous calls that she had probably disappeared from Rome.

The harps home administrator said she had left with a small group of girls to go to a nearby mall in Rome called Riverbend. Remember the Riverbend mall was where Judith was first arrested for robbing a woman. When it gunpoint Lisa's case was assigned to detective Ken kines due soon found that her life had been assessed as it was short.

She had been removed from her parents' home. Along with her three siblings, following allegations of sexual abuse. She had been placed in and removed from four different foster homes and had spent 30 days at the open door, home, another youth facility in Rome before she landed at the harps home in Cedartown.

Lisa had been sexually abused by her father and her mother had known about it. She told authorities, he had put his hands inside of her, but her mother told her to forget about it and not to worry because quote. He would be too drunk to screw her. Then her mother took up with a man named slick Harris who took an interest in both mother and daughter.

He molested Lisa as well, like many children who are sexually abused. Lisa became promiscuous. She was also angry and acted out. She did poorly in school. She had all the signs of an abuse victim girls at Harper said she had a few boyfriends and evidently she got into many fights with girls over boys. So she wasn't well-liked at harps and she came from my family who acted like she was an acquaintance when they were told of her death, no crying, no concern, no questions.

As depressing as these interviews were for the detective, he still found she didn't have any real enemies though. She was neglected and abused. Her family hadn't murdered her. The best leads were the anonymous phone calls. Ironically had the location of Lisa Milligan's body not been brought to the attention of DeKalb County authorities.

She may have remained undiscovered for years. It was an 80 foot drop from the precipice to the floor of the little river Canyon where Lisa's body was found. The area was densely wooded and used as a garbage dump by locals, a caseworker from the Walker County department of family and children's services was brought in to listen to the tapes.

He had handled Lisa's case file from when she was removed from her home and Lafayette detective kind sat in while he was listening and the caseworker picked up on something right away. Y'all looking for Lisa and Milliken on run from the harps home. The caller had said the phrase on run rather than runaway or on the run as an insider expression, commonly used by people who have been through the juvenile justice system, the caseworker guests, the caller had a juvenile record.

As detective kinds pursued this lead. The Neeley's were still in action. Five days later on October 3rd, a 22 year old woman named Diane Bobo was walking down shorter Avenue in Rome because her car had run out of gas. A man in a red car stopped and offered her a ride. She first refused, but he had a small child in his back seat.

So she thought he seemed safe. He made awkward conversation, but he did give her a change for a phone call so that she could have her husband pick her up He dropped her off at a phone booth in a deserted parking lot. After she called her husband, she sat down on the curb. She hadn't noticed another car pull into the parking lot, but now she saw a Brown Dodge with a CB antenna coming out of the trunk.

She looked away and a few moments later, a woman approached her and asked, are you Patricia? Diane said, no, I'm not. And told the woman her name. Diane said the woman was tall and very thin and looked like she hadn't bathed or changed clothes in days. She also didn't look like she had slept. The woman said she was just riding around and thought she recognized her and then asked Diane if she wanted to ride around with her.

She said she was lonely. Diane told her, no, sorry. Her husband was on his way to get her Diane later reported the woman didn't want to take no for an answer telling her. I can take you wherever you want to go. But Diane remained firm and the woman finally drove off Diane's husband arrived and took her to work where she told her coworkers about the strange incident.

She had a bad feeling. She later told her landlord the story, but our landlord was also a police officer and insisted she reported. So she did on the same afternoon of October 4th, a 13 year old girl named Debbie Smith was walking home from school and her cheerleader uniform. A woman in a Brown car pulled up beside her and rolled down her window.

She asked, are you Michelle? Debbie tried to ignore the woman. I kept walking, but she persisted is your name, Michelle. She asked again, Debbie said no firmly and kept walking. She saw the woman very well. She thought she was young, maybe 19 or 20. And she was very unkempt, but she noticed her long dark hair and distinctive buck teeth.

She kept questioning Debbie, who tried to be polite, but kept walking. Then Debbie got near the open door, home, the other youth facility in Rome. One that Judith Neeley would know. Debbie decided to walk up to the home and go in to get away from the woman. After that Judith Neely hit the gas and pilled off.

And Debbie Smith walked on the home. She told her mother what had happened. And mrs. Smith immediately called the police. Diane Bobo came in just a few hours after the Smiths to give her statement well, and just down the hall, another man was being questioned. His run in with Judith Neely had not ended as well.

On the same day, October 4th and the evening hours, a 26 year old man, unfortunately named John Hancock and his 22 year old girlfriend. Janice Chapman we're walking down shorter Avenue. They were actually considered common law married at the time as they had been living together for about a year and a half, when they had met, he had instantly liked the geneal young woman author.

Thomas H. Cook said he soon learned that she had a sad history. Janice had been married and divorced and lost custody of her two children. She had very little education and was intellectually disabled because of this. She was often taken advantage of. She took rides from strange men who used are for sex.

And that wouldn't even drive her home. John felt protective of Janice and thought she would be better off living with him than her mother who did little to protect her disabled daughter. As they walked along the street that night, a woman in a Brown Dodge pulled up beside them. She got out of the car and said she was out of town and sort of lonely.

She said she was just riding around and hoped they might want to ride with her. Janice was confused, but not scared and wanted to go. John was hesitant. He thought the woman looked rough and like, she hadn't slept in a while. He told her no and said they were just walking home. The woman immediately said, I'll drive you home.

He said, no need we're three blocks away. But then he looked at Janice, who is smiling broadly. He finally shrugged and said, okay, he didn't think the woman was dangerous. And maybe Janice would enjoy riding around. Janice got in the back seat and he got in the front several hours later after dark a truck driver In Gordon County, Georgia Solomon in the middle of the road, waving his arms, frantically and staggering.

The trucker stopped. And the man said I've been shot. The driver got him in the truck. I took him to the nearest hospital or the getting nurse asked his name. And when he answered that John Hancock, the entire emergency room bursts out, laughing. But the next day, the GBI was called in because of the story.

John Hancock had told he had been shot in the back of his

right shoulder, but the bullet had been easily removed with no major damage. He was sent home, despite what he told doctors that they did call it in the GBI agents question, John Hancock at his home, and didn't really believe as bizarre story. So they passed him over to detective kines who was interested.

John told him he and Janice had been out walking the evening before and accepted a ride from a woman in a Brown Dodge. The woman said she was lonely and wanted to talk. And during the ride, she called a man on her CB radio. His handle was Knight rider, and the woman called herself lady sundown as John and Janice listened Knight writer and lady sundown made plans over the radio to meet.

They met up on a dirt road North of Rome. Knight rider drove a red car and had two small children with him. They told John to switch cars and ride with him, leaving Janice in the car with lady sundown. John felt uneasy, but not really threatened. Alvin had two small kids in the back of his car and Judith went and gathered them up and put them in her backseat.

Jenise had already happily moved to the front seat. Both cars started driving aimlessly again, eventually meandering into Alabama and back. John told Alvin or night rider that he had to pee. So he radioed Judith and let her know and they agreed to stop again. John walked away to urinate, but noticed Alvin didn't, even though he had said he needed to as well, instead, he walked to Judith's car.

John could see the two staring at him, and then he overheard Alvin and say, quote, if we're going to do it, let's get it over with. And then Judith walked straight towards John pointing a gun at him. She told him to walk on down the road with his back towards her. After about 300 feet, she told him to head into the woods and then said, stop.

Then he heard Alvin yell, hurry up and get it over with John said, meekly, can I ask a question? Judah said, hell no, keep your back to me. And then she said, don't worry about your girlfriend. We'll take care of her. And then she shot him in the back or rather in his shoulder. But he fell to the ground and instinctively played dead.

He lay on the ground for awhile, scared they would come back before he ran out to the road, after telling detective kines his story, he said he could definitely identify the couple and would be glad to work with a sketch artist. He also was more able to identify the cars Alvin and Judith were driving.

He even remembered they had out of state license plates, but wasn't sure where he thought Kentucky or Tennessee when he was finished. Another officer came in to escort John out. As they walked down the hall, Debbie Smith was in another room, listening to the police tape from the anonymous woman who had called in about Lisa Milikin

They wanted to see if she could recognize the voice. John overheard the tape as they walked by and suddenly yelled. That's the damn woman that shot me soon. Another detective in Floyd County got wind of the anonymous calls. He was investigating the attacks on the Rome youth detention center employees.

And immediately connected the cases that Walker County caseworker had already suspected. The caller had been a juvenile offender. Detective kinds requested the records for all girls who have been placed in the YDC from out-of-state. For the last few years, he got back 25 names. The detective spent days finding the women on the list, checking their alibis if they were still in the area.

And he finally had the list narrowed down to one name, Judith and Neely. He created a photo lineup with her latest mugshot and other similar looking women and call John Hancock, Debbie Smith and Diane Bobo back in John and Diane thought Judith's picture looked like the woman, but didn't positively ID her Debbie Smith.

However was certain. Now he had a name and he began his search. It didn't take long Judith and Alvin had gone back to Murfreesboro, Tennessee Judith's hometown. On October 9th, she had been arrested at a motel for passing bad checks. Her husband, Alvin Neely was arrested a few days later. And detective kinds finally got word.

His suspects were in custody on October 14th, but he now knew for sure that Janice Chapman was dead. She hadn't been with Neeley's when they were arrested. The detective felt sure there was no way they just let her go. Kinds along with other detectives from Rome and to cab County rushed to Murfreesboro where they were being held and the other for County jail to their surprise, Alvin Neeley almost immediately waived his right to remain silent, though.

He did ask for a lawyer and then gave a long detailed statement, implicating Judith as the mastermind and all of their crimes. Given his choice, detective kinds, chose to interview Alvin and let the other detective take Judith. You would later regret that Alvin told him that Judith planned and carried out the attacks on the YDA workers and that she had murdered both Lisa Milliken and Janice Chapman.

She's a dangerous person. Alvin said claiming he was scared of her. He then drew him out the exact location of Janis Chapman's body kinds, thought Alvin was a fat slob and quote, a complete wimp. He stepped outside of the room as they waited for Alvin's lawyer to finish his interrogation. He walked past the room where Judith was being questioned and saw how dirty and unkempt she was and the black circles under her eyes.

Then he heard her voice and it stopped him in his tracks. It was the coldest voice he had ever heard all while Alvin was supposedly singing like a bird blaming Judith for everything, of course, and living out his own part in the attacks, the repeated rapes of Lisa and Janet. After a bit of hemming and hawing with Judith repeatedly refusing a lawyer.

She finally sighed and answered every question. She was asked calmly and in great detail, she said she attacked the YDC workers because Linda Adair had forced her to have sex with Ken Dooley, both adamantly denied this happened, and I don't believe it did either. I think she had a grudge against some juvenile detention workers doing their best at a tough job, but she was not abused there.

There is no evidence of that at all. Besides her claim, she also claimed she was part of a prostitution ring run out of the facility. And those allegations were proven false as well. And then she calmly and coldly recounted the kidnapping and murder of Lisa and Janet. So far, she was leaving out details of the sexual assaults.

Judith said she had noticed Lisa Milikin because she looked like Joanie Cunningham the character from the old TV show. Happy days, they were both in a video arcade in the Riverbend mall in Rome. And Judith had walked up and started talking to the girl. Judith said Lisa had gone willingly with her because she didn't want to return to the harps home.

This does make sense, given that Lisa had been vocal about not liking it there that night, they had driven around for hours with Alvin and Judith's twin toddlers in the backseat before finally checking into a motel for the next few days. She and Alvin kept Lisa handcuffed to a bed frame. She said it was so Lisa wouldn't run off and get her in trouble.

She told the detectives that after a few days, she decided that Lisa had to die. She was now afraid. She might go to authorities and tell on her. The detectives already knew from Lisa's autopsy reports, what had been done to the girl, but it was chilling to hear Judith Neely calmly say she had decided to get syringes, filled him with liquid Draino and liquid plumber.

She said that she had seen somewhere that it was a painless way to die. She got Lisa up and drive her to the edge of the little river Canyon. As her children slept in the car. Judith walked Elisa over to a tree and told her to lie down. Judith said, I told her I was going to give her a shot to put her to sleep so I could leave.

And she wouldn't know where I was going. She then injected liquid Draino into the left side of Lisa's neck, but the shot didn't seem to work. So she gave Lisa another injection to the other side of her neck, this time of liquid plumber. But Lisa was still conscious. Judith then tried injecting both of Lisa's arms.

And then each of her buttocks, she sat there while the little girl cried in pain for a half hour. Judith said, Lisa told her that the shots burned and begged her to take her back to the harps tome promising. She wouldn't tell anyone what had happened to her, realizing that the injections weren't going to work, or at least not fast enough.

Judith forced the girl to get up and walk to the side of the Canyon and turn her back to her. As Lisa kept pleading for her life, Judith shot her in the back, but Lisa fell backwards instead of into the Canyon. So Judith said she had to go push her over the edge, getting blood on her jeans. She then changed her jeans in the car and threw the bloody jeans over in the Canyon too.

She also threw the syringes into the Canyon. Investigators had found those syringes and already knew they contained Draino and liquid plumber. Judith story was right on track. She says she then drove to Fort Payne with her kids and rented another motel room waiting for Alvin to join them all this time.

At least for now, she refused to implicate Alvin in any way. She emphatically told the detectives that he was the only man she ever trusted. She was sporting a black eye, but she insisted that she had gotten into a fight. I should also mention that she was, again, several months pregnant. Her baggy shirt hit her growing belly, but with her otherwise emaciated figure, it wasn't immediately evident as Judith and Alvin sat in interrogation rooms, giving alternate confessions investigators took the map.

Alvin had helpfully drawn and went and found Janis Chapman's decomposing body. Right. Where Alvin had said it would be, she had been shot once in the back and twice in the chest. After the confessions were taken in Tennessee, there were some jurisdictional issues to be worked out with the Neeley's Lisa Milliken had been murdered in Alabama and Janice Chapman and Georgia as Alvin led the cops to Janice's body.

He was extradited to Georgia while Judith was sent to Alabama, where she had tortured and murdered. Lisa Milliken in Georgia, Alvin was cooling his Hills and the Chattooga County jail. When the GBI stepped in with roam police and to cab County detectives. They were there to take hair and saliva samples, Alvin didn't look so good.

He hadn't slept much. And he wasn't as sure of himself as he had been the first time, this time the cops went in hard. They accused him of raping Lisa Millican, which he first tried to deny and then said, well, she was on the pill, but he still denied raping her. When the detectives told him that semen was found in Lisa Milliken's vagina and they would soon be able to match it to him, he got nervous.

He then told an outrageous story that Judith had quote, jerked him off, collecting his semen in a Dixie cup. He said his wife was bisexual and she was the one having sex with Lisa. He told the cops, she poured the Dixie cup onto Lisa's vagina before she had oral sex with her. It's not that the cops didn't believe it was possible that Judith Neely was a pedophile, but Alvin's story was beyond ridiculous.

They told Alvin to stop the bullshit and he slowly broke down. He still insisted. It was all Judith's idea and that she made him have sex with a girl and that they took turns. His story became even more insane as he claim the 13 year old girl had willingly had a threesome with a couple. He ended the story by saying that Judith got up one morning after a couple of days and announced that she and Lisa needed new clothes.

She said they were going to Kmart. He decided to take the twins and head to his parents' house. And when Judith met him there, Lisa wasn't with her. He claimed he didn't know what had happened to her, but he never saw her again. Then he told the story about John Hancock and Janice Chapman, his story of how they picked up the couple and then Judith marching, John down the road and shooting him, matched exactly what John Hancock had told the police.

He said afterwards, he, Judith and Janice, I checked into a motel with the twins. He claimed that Janice undressed immediately and said, Hey, you want to get it on. He said they had sex right there on one bed. As the twins lay in the next bed, then he said Lisa had sex with her. He said, the next morning Judith was loading the car.

While Jenna stood in the doorway, not handcuffed and saying nothing again. He said he left with the twins while Judith took Janice. He said, when he met his wife back in Rome, Janice was not with her. And Judith simply said she got rid of her. Alvin then claimed that Judith had kidnapped Lisa and Janice for him, supposedly, because while he was in prison, Judith had sex with black men.

Alvin quite the racist was enraged. So Judith offered to pick him up some girls to make it up to him. He said he at first questioned his wife and then she claimed she had done this before. He said she showed him newspaper clippings of unsolved murders and Albany Columbus and Chattanooga. He said that Judith did all of this to set him up so that she could control him.

Quote, that's the whole thing with Judy. She likes to have control over people. Even after years in prison, he still insisted he did not murder Lisa or Janice. He said Judith had some sort of rage inside of her. She was always mad, but I could never figure out why.

When it came to charging this sadistic couple Alabama investigators and prosecutors felt stymied, no matter how hard they tried, Alvin would not call it to the murders and Judith repeatedly exonerated her husband. They knew he hadn't shot John Hancock through John's story. It definitely sounded like he was in on the plan though.

And they had no physical evidence to tie him to the Canyon where Lisa was found, the best they could do was leave him in Georgia and let the Georgia justice system deal with him. He could definitely be charged with kidnapping, rape, and various other crimes, but for now they had to focus on Judith. Her trial was scheduled for March 7th, 1983.

She had given birth to her third child, a boy, while in jail, awaiting trial, public defender, rubber, French was chosen to defend Judith and right from the start, he could not stand her and didn't want the case, but he didn't have much choice. He was a good lawyer. And despite how he felt about his client, he set out to rigorously defend her.

He began by seeking youthful offender status for her as she was under 21 years, years of age. But as motion was denied, French then asked that psychological tests being administered to determine her fitness for trial. Judith was found quite fit for trial with superior intelligence and no tendency towards delusion or suicide.

French also arranged for her to have dental work on those buck teeth, which were also terribly chipped and he bought nice conservative clothing for her to wear at trial. District attorney Richard. had no idea how French plan to defend Judith until jury selection. When the questions French asked seemed to be leading to a battered woman's defense though, that phrase wasn't really in the vernacular at the time in the majestic to cab County courtroom, the same courtroom where to kill a Mockingbird had been filmed, Judith and Neely sat meekly at the defense table, mostly staring at her hands.

From his opening statement, Bob French laid every bit of the sadistic crimes that Alvin Neeley's feet quote, every move, every act, every thought, carrying out the perpetration of this hand, this event was planned, calculated and instituted by Alvin Neely. He told the jury Judith story beginning with her troubled childhood and adolescents.

She had fallen for Alvin at age 15. I'd had left home to be with him. And within a year he claimed Alvin was beating her savagely. Judith catered to Alvin's. Every whim bathing him, feeding him and eventually becoming brainwashed. French claimed Judith was Alvin Neely slave. The first witnesses for the prosecution were Diane Bobo, Debbie Smith.

And yet another woman named Suzanne Clontz who came forward because she was approached at Riverbend mall the same day that Lisa was kidnapped, all three women positively identified Judith, and they also said she did not appear to have any visible signs of abuse. John Hancock was up next to tell the story of his in Janice's abduction.

The da tried to emphasize that Judith was in control the whole time, but on cross examination, Bob French had John point out that Alvin was directing her from his car, but on redirect, John admitted to the prosecutor that she did not look upset or nervous, she was the one personally giving him orders.

And she was indeed the one who shot him. The first defense witness French called in was Jo Ann Browning, Alvin Neeley's first wife. She had been married to Alvin for three years in the mid seventies and was a mother to three of his children. She testified that Alvin had beaten her throughout their marriage, even when she was pregnant and that he had drugged and tried to rape her teenage sister, she claimed she had tried to leave him several times, but then Alvin would threatened their children.

He was the one who finally left when he met Judith. The prosecutor, Richard managed to damage her credibility by pointing out that she had remarried before her divorce from Alvin saying that made her a big chemist and a liar. She had also estimated that Alvin beat her around 800 times, but I grew pointed out that she had never had a broken bone.

Joanne left the witness stand very angry. And in tears, I have trouble with this and more detail later about Judith's possible abuse at the hands of Alvin. Not all abusers break bones. Some even actively try not to leave a Mark that will show by hitting in places that can be covered up. It is unfair to disbelieve a woman who claims abuse simply because she's never had a broken bone.

The next day, Judith Neeley took the stand in her own defense. Her appearance, a demeanor immediately conflicted with a portrait of a victim. And that was the one thing Bob French tried to explain right away. The jury had watched as Judith left easily and chatted at the defense table. So French asked her, how do you handle fear or nervous?

She said, I smile a lot. And she did indeed smile through all our

French's questions. She reiterated that she left home at age 15 with Alvin willingly, because he had been a very romantic suitor, but then she claimed that Alvin changed and his sexual advances were crude, selfish. And becoming more and more violent.

She said she was his servant and claimed that she bathed him, combed his hair, cooked for him and even tied his shoes. When she didn't perform these tasks to his satisfaction, she claimed he taught her robbery and forgery and that he was insanely jealous without cause. Judith claimed she had never been unfaithful contrary to what Alvin had told police.

She also said the made up stories of abuse. She suffered at the Rome youth detention center were Alvin's idea, but there was no real explanation of why he would want to target the YDC when he had never been incarcerated there. Judith also went into excruciating detail about beatings and rates. She suffered gradually.

She was appearing more sympathetic. On her fourth day of testimony, French asked her about Lisa Milliken's abduction and murder Judith claim that Alvin had wanted a Virgin. So she found one for him. This does line up some with Alvin story. Although he claims it was her idea to make up for cheating on him.

She claimed that she took part in the beatings Lisa received because Alvin forced her to. She said she washed his Alvin repeatedly, raped the girl. And so did their young children. She also claimed that Alvin was there when she shot Lisa and pushed her into the Canyon. Judith said he had chosen the spot and was at her side the whole time.

This is a direct contradiction to her own confessions to police. She also claimed that after he was surely, so was dead. He masturbated. Then he instructed her to make the anonymous phone calls to the Rome and Fort Payne police departments. Judith also admitted to the abduction and murder of Janice Chapman.

Again, claiming Alvin forced her to do it. And that she feared for her life. She said that Janice was also handcuffed to a bed frame and that Alvin repeatedly raped her. The da Richard went in hard to counter fridges, domestic violence defense. He pointed out that though Judith had claimed to have been beaten countless times.

She had only suffered two broken fingers and a chipped tooth. Again, only suffered. It's possible to have doubts of whether or not Judith Neely was telling the truth about being abused, but to emphasize that she only suffered small wounds is degrading and salting and would be unacceptable in a 2019 courtroom.

I go dig, get her to admit that she acted alone when she shot Janice Chapman. She said the first shot was because Alvin had ordered her to shoot Janice, but then she shot her twice more because Janice wouldn't stop screaming and Judith was afraid. Someone would hear. I grew then produced a series of photographs featuring Alvin and Judith posing merrily with various guns and family members in each Judith was smiling, happily.

She countered that Alvin arranged all the photos and order her to smile. When I asked her about the murder of Lisa Milikin every time he said, why Judith answered, because Alvin told me too, she claimed the only decision she made for herself for when to eat and go to the bathroom. That absolutely everything else about her life had been dictated by her husband on redirect.

French said about to convince the jury of Judith's claims by showing pictures of her with bruises, then prosecutor, I GU called a psychiatrist from the Alabama department of mental health, who testified that Judith knew the difference between right and wrong and made the conscious decision to kill Lisa.

The doctor also minimized the bruises shown in one photo that Judith claimed. Came from Alvin swinging a baseball bat. The doctor said she could have gotten that from a pinch when French cross examined the doctor, he tried to get him to say that Judith had been brainwashed in an established clinical definition of the term.

The doctor refused to agree. He was the last witness for the prosecution and he had been very damaging to Judith's case. French's closing argument was dramatically Southern. He made reference to the Bible and the Chinese principle of yin and yang pleading with a jury to live with their Christian witness and allow their feminine side, their love side to shine through.

He compared Alvin to Svengali prosecutor, I GU was more simple and also more effective. He reminded the jury that a psychiatrist insisted Judith was not brainwashed. And he doubled down on how she could not have suffered the abuse she claimed because she didn't have visible scars. I won't bitch about this again, but I am pointing it out one more time.

Quote, Judy planned carried out and enjoyed her crimes. Alvin didn't have the nerve, but she did. That was Judy Neely not spend. Golly, The jury was given instructions at four 30 in the afternoon and returned their verdict shortly before 11:00 AM the next morning. Judith Neeley was found guilty of the murder and abduction of Lisa Millican that afternoon, the prosecution and defense delivered arguments in front of the jury and the sentencing hearing later that night, the jury delivered at sentencing recommendation to the judge by a tend to vote

Yes, recommended that Judy be sentenced to life in prison at the time in Alabama, however, a jury's recommendation and a capital case was only a recommendation. The final decision line with the judge himself. On April 18th, 1983, judge Randall Cole sentenced Judith Neeley to die in Alabama's electric chair.

She was 18 years old, the youngest woman in the country to be sentenced to death. A bill was signed into law in Alabama in the spring of 2017. Barring this tradition of a judge overruling, a jury's recommendation. It is now back in the hands of the jury. But after her first conviction, Judith was anxious to avoid another death sentence and pled guilty to kidnapping and the Chapman Hancock case, and also agreed to testify against Alvin Alvin afraid of Judith's testimony, pled guilty to kidnapping with bodily harm and intent to murder in the Chapman Hancock case in Georgia, he was sentenced to two life terms

In August of 1984, a woman told Murfreesboro, Tennessee police that she had been abducted two years ago and had recently come across a picture of her abductor in the newspaper. The picture was of Judith Neely. The woman went by the street name of Casey and she was the final victim. Judith had picked up right before her arrest.

Casey said, Judith bragged about her crimes claiming she had killed a girl in Chattanooga among others, and that she had newspaper clippings documenting all of this. Casey said Judith talked all night and never once appeared afraid. Judith told her she liked to see the look on people's faces when she pulled a gun on them.

It was the next morning, October 9th, that Judith had been arrested for bad checks before the Georgia and Alabama authorities got to her. Casey said that Alvin held her at gunpoint in the bathroom as they took Judah the way. And then Alvin, let Casey go. This KC has never been identified. And it's anyone's guess if she knew the details of the Neeley's case, the media coverage was mainly local to Alabama, so maybe not, but a lot of what she said backs up Alvin's claims about Judith and it still leaves the open ended question of where they're really more victims as with any capital case.

Judith's went slowly through the appeals process over the years. But in 1998, Carla Faye Tucker was executed in Texas, like many on death row. She was a born again, Christian at the time of her death and Christian fundamentalists strongly opposed her execution because of her religion. And because she was a woman.

Meanwhile, the Supreme court denied you to spinal appeal and late 1998, it looked like she would be, be the first woman to be executed in Alabama and 40 years. Judith had also claimed a Christian conversion. She was very lucky that Alabama's governor at the time, father James was also a Christian fundamentalist in January of 1999.

He commuted her sentence to life in prison without the possibility of parole. But the Alabama attorney general pointed out that while the governor did have the power to commute sentences, he had no authority to regulate parole and Judith would be up for parole in the standard 15 year. Wait after her change in sentencing.

In 2003, the Alabama legislature passed a bill specifically aimed at Neeley, effectively changing her sentence to life without parole. She filed a lawsuit in 2014 when her 15 year wait ended and actually won in federal court, a judge ruled the law was unconstitutional. So she has been up for parole a few times, but she's always been denied.

Alvin and Judith Neely are dichotomies within themselves. They are both liars. Who also tell the truth. They'll tell you what they did, Judith, rather matter of faculty while Alvin minimizes, but they won't tell you why they did it. They both claimed you too had been sexually abused, but there's not a shred of evidence in her childhood or teen years at juvie to actually prove this.

And yet she is often seen bruised. And in fact, Alvin's alleged abuse of her was her actual defense. He did date her when she was still a child, impregnating her with twins at 16. She initially and adamantly denied any abuse until her lawyer needed it for a defense. And Alvin always denied it. Alvin claimed he was scared of his wife.

The same breath claimed to have had a consensual threesome with a 13 year old girl. They both claimed that the other had to have complete control to the point where the other one was either terrified or a brainwashed slave. Both of them denied that they were sexual status. But they both were. So, which is it?

I think it could be all of it, but I think some of that could also the bullshit. I do believe it's possible. Judith Neely was abused and if she was sexually abused, It happened in her home when she was a very young child, her early quiet years or angry teen years, that turned into violent late teen years.

She does have the markers. I do believe it's possible that Alvin physically abused her. But I also think it's possible that she got into a lot of fights. She told police that I imagined that they were both violent within their marriage. I believe Alvin, when he said it was Judith's idea and why she did it.

He had no problem calling himself out as a racist. And this is where she is very like Carla home for me, Carla, wasn't a Virgin. So she sought versions for her husband to make up for it. But she liked it just as much as he did Alvin found Judith when she was a Virgin, it seemed to me a lot to both of them.

I believe he was angry at her for cheating on him in prison with black men, making it even worse for a racist like him, but like Canadian Karla Homolka. Judith was also a sadist. She wanted to kidnap and rape those girls. She also wanted to bring girls to her husband to make up for her transgressions. I also believe the Neeley's were on some sort of drugs and alcohol.

It is speculation though, because it, oddly isn't mentioned at all in this case, but riding around aimlessly at night, losing all that weight, looking sleepless, I think at least Judith was on something. Alvin was notably overweight. I'd peg him as more of a drinker. But does it matter whether they lied about parts?

Judith was abused, many victims of abuse to not grow up, to be sexual status and murderers, two girls are dead, their families still grieve and it's possible. There are other victims out there as well. No, I think this is a case of two status fatefully meeting, bony and Claude. As they affectionately called themselves, started their crime spree, small check, hiding and petty theft before moving to robbery.

And then they needed the next buzz, something bigger. And that's when their mutual depravity blossomed. But unlike the Canadian, Ken and Barbie killers, Alvin and Judith wanted to get caught. You don't make that many anonymous calls, especially when leading to a body that might never have been found. If you don't want to get caught.

I suppose they needed the attention and validation for their crimes. As much as they needed the depraved rush of terrorizing and torturing girls. To me, they display that particular brand of psychopathy that shows no empathy for others. Alvin Neely died in prison in 2005. Judith comes up for parole every five years.

This past time in 2018, she tried to wave her hearing before the parole board claiming she didn't want to put the families through it all again. She had found God, I hate to be cynical, but most cons eventually do it makes life easier on the inside, whether they are true believers or not. But I'm sorry.

Judith Neely can talk about Jesus until the cows come home, but you'll never convince me that she's not a monster.

8 THE NOVACK MURDERS

Most of us can't understand what it means to be truly wealthy. There's a reason it's called the 1% a peek behind the curtain to those unicorns who are born into the privilege and glamour of the Uber. Rich is often irresistible Ben Novak, his wife, Bernice, and their son, Ben jr. Known and childhood has Bingy encapsulated everything about the rich and famous in the 1960s.

Ben sr built the infamous fountain blue hotel on the strip of Miami beach in 1954. Ben and Bernice Novak were held as King and queen of Miami beach. And Benji came up the lonely Prince in the tower, living on the 17th floor, waited on him, hand and foot his, every whim, granted Ben know that jr. Only friends were really employees.

This colored his adult life. In many ways, he had trouble making and maintaining intimate relationships, but he was a brilliant if called businessmen, the saga of the Miami beach Novak family ends and the bankruptcy of the fountain blue. And two brutal murders scandals, which captivated the nation spurning lawsuits, which are still winding their way through probate court.

Miami beach is a coastal resort city and an Island city in South Florida. It is located on natural and manmade barrier islands between the Atlantic ocean and Biscayne Bay Biscayne Bay separates Miami beach from the mainland city of Miami. Though, the Island is connected to the mainland by the Venetian Causeway bridge, the wide and beautiful white beaches span from North shore open space park, past the Palm line Lumis park to South point park lining the shimmering turquoise colored waters of the Atlantic.

Miami beach is known as an LGBT Mecca with pride events drawing over 13,000 visitors annually in January of 2010, Miami beach pastor revised human rights ordinance that strengthened existing laws and added additional protections for transgender people, making Miami beaches, human rights laws, some of the most progressive in the state on the far Southern end South beach or Sobe as it's known has its own distinct personality.

From the art deco historic district with pastel colored mansions to its hundreds of nightclubs, restaurants, hotels, and boutiques. South beach is also infamous for the murder of Gianni Versace, who was shot to death on the front steps of his home on ocean drive in South beach in 1997. It is also the setting for several movies like Scarface and the bird cage and the 1980s show Miami vice.

The town of Miami beach was chartered in 1915 and became a city in 1917. By the 1920s, it had become a Haven for wealthy snowbirds from the North and Midwest who built winter homes there that's when the building of the grand hotels really began with the Flamingo hotel, the Fleetwood and the Nautilus among them.

And by 1941, while the rest of America was recovering from the great depression. It remained a retreat for the rich and famous with even the Duke and Duchess of Windsor vacationing there after his scandalous, advocation of the throne. That's the year that Ben Novak and his wife, Bella moved to Miami beach, then Novak was from New York and had helped run his family's hotel in the Catskills.

He had liquidated a clothing store. He and his wife had owned, which was failing in the depression era economy. And set his sights on the ultimate Babylon as Miami beach had been dubbed by a New York Tribune columnist. He sunk everything. He had into an

11 room hotel on 30th street with his wife working as a chambermaid.

It was rough going for a while until the second world war broke out, which as author John Glatt wrote, made Ben Novak rich beyond his wildest dreams. The army took over Miami beach in February of 1942, taking advantage of the ideal weather conditions for basic training, 100,000 soldiers from the army air Corps, and the Navy took over Miami beach and the U S government paid hotel owners.

Well, for the accommodations, the government paid up to $10 a night per room to house the soldiers, not including food. That's about $150 today. Within five years, Ben Novak sr had bought up five other hotels. Ben, no vaccine. Yer was a bit of a dandy. He was handsome. If a compact man who loved to dress Flamboyan currently, he was also a womanizer, often cheating on Bella.

But when he met a 21 year old model named Bernice Stimple in a nightclub in Manhattan, he was determined to marry her. Bernice was gorgeous with red hair, blue eyes and an enviable figure, though. It was love at first sight for Ben. It wasn't for Bernice. He was 38 years old, married wear a hearing aid and was too flashy.

Bernice was also married and her husband was still fighting in Europe, but Ben wasn't giving up. He asked her out repeatedly, tried to get her number from friends and eventually set up a fake photo shoot in Havana to lure her. She showed up with another model from her agency and was surprised to see Ben Novak there.

But Bernice was impressed. His romantic subterfuge had worked and it kicked off a stormy four year relationship before the two finally married in 1952 in New York city, though, Bernice by then had great success as a model. She was even the face of Coca Cola. She had agreed to give up her career and move to Miami beach with Ben.

Ben had promptly divorced Bella and abandoned their two year old son. They had adopted named Ronald when Bernice accepted his proposal. Bernice had come from a strained home life. Her parents divorced when she was still a child in the 1930s. And though her father waged a bitter custody battle with her mother, he did not spend time with her or her sister Maxine.

The girls were even sent to an orphanage while their father continued to deny their mother any contact with him. I think Bernice is isolated childhood influenced her later as a mother. She had difficulty connecting with her young son. The later in life, the two would be very close that closeness would lead to their death.

Newly married Bernice Novak came to Miami beach. And lived in the San Suchi hotel with her husband. Ben owned it with his partner, Harry Mufson. It was the first luxury hotel that Novak built, but he still had bigger dreams. He wanted to buy up an old crumbling estate that boasted 950 feet of unadulterated ocean front views.

He wanted to build the largest hotel in Miami beach in 1951, Ben and his partner, Harry Mufson managed to buy the estate for two point $3 million. That would be about 23 million. Today. They planned a 550 room grand hotel costing $10 million to build 100 million in $2,019. But Mufson and found out that Ben Novak had cheated him out of $15,000 on the send Suchi.

And then that Novak had only had his name put on the new deed. Muffs and backed out and got a lawyer leaving. No, that 24 hours to come up with partners to finish the deal. He managed to do it. One of the partners who put up the most money was none other than infamous mafia, boss, Sam Giancana and he would not remain a silent partner.

Once the deal went through Ben Novak hired a young architect named Morris Lapidus. No, that kid wanted a name and Morris Lapidus was trying to make a name for himself. He agreed to take on the project for a paltry 80 grand with the condition that he had complete design control. He even wanted to pick out the bell uniforms, even though he was given the impossible deadline of one year until opening Lapidus took the gig and moved his wife and kids to Miami beach.

He immediately set out to design a building uniquely different from other hotels, Lapidus sketched out a curved building, something he had done before in his New York department stores. A sweeping curved building as what I wanted, he would later say reportedly when he showed the plans to his client, Ben know that tore up the drawings in a rage and threw them in the trash saying he would dream up his own shape.

Just a few days later, he called Lapidus and said that he had his own brilliant idea. Why not have a curved building? He said, no one had ever designed a curved building. This kicked off a battle that would go on for decades. Even after both men were dead. Lapidus insisted. He came up with the design first and Novak said he came up with the idea on the toilet, a claim Bernice Novak would back up until her death, Morris Lapidus swallowed his pride.

He needed this job to propel him into the big leagues, but six months into the project in June of 1954, he had already gone through the $80,000 fee. He telled Novak. He was quitting unless he got 75,000 more. No that promised him the extra money upon completion. And laugh at us. Agreed, not wanting to ruin his reputation by walking away from the biggest project of his career, situated on ocean front Collins Avenue and the heart of what is now millionaire's row.

The fountain blue became the most majestic and impressive hotel on Miami beach. The iconic Crescent shaped building is unmatched and design and still holds an impressive place in Miami beach history. The grand opening was held on December 20th, 1954. But even the mayor of New York city being flown in for the ball that was held for 1600 celebrity guests, the guest of honor was the mayor of Fontainebleau France, Homer poncho.

You may have noticed that the hotel took on an Anglo saws pronunciation of its namesake, a commune in Paris. This was something that aggravated Bernice Novak, who often corrected friends who didn't use the French pronunciation, but it was done. The hotel would forever be the fountain blue to locals. I've heard it pronounced many different ways and Googling it.

French pronunciations made it even more confused. So from here on out, I'll refer to it as the fountain blue. That is the way Ben know that set it. And that's what became the norm. The lavish hotel was unlike any other luxury hotel with two nightclubs, several restaurants, a spa, several pools, including an Olympic size lap pool, and a freeform pool and elusive bow tie design that faced the ocean.

Even with millionaires and celebrities like Groucho Marx lining up to be seen at the blue, the hotel wasn't without its critics, some architects called it a monstrosity. If anything that only made been Novak prouder as he deemed his beloved film blue, the world's most pretentious hotel, the interior was elegantly styled with French influences, white marble floors, antiques, and statues.

And the hotel's main interior was the fame staircase to nowhere. That Morris Lapidus had copied from the Paris opera house while Novak certainly courted celebrities. It was the influence of mob boss, Sam Giancana that got Frank Sinatra to start playing the hotel in exchange for his own permanent penthouse.

Suite Sinatra began playing midnight shows and the Loronda room nightclub for 25 years. Sinatra would be a stalwart at the hotel, bringing in the rat pack and other celebrities with him. Judy Garland, Marlena Dietrich, Gary Cooper, and Joan Crawford. It's a who's who of movie stars in the fifties and Ben?

No, that meant for the fountain blue to feel exclusive during his ownership of the hotel, there was never a fountain blue sign in or outside the hotel. The iconic building spoke for itself. It didn't need a sign. Ben and Bernice moved into a duplex suite on the 17th floor. The four bedroom apartment had ocean views with a dining room, billiard room and a piano bar.

It was into this opulence that Ben know that jr was born in 1956. Bernice had long resigned herself to second. After the hotel in her husband's affections, he lived a and breathe the hotel and worked almost 24 seven. She told author Steven Gaines that the fountain blue was quote his baby, his wife, his mistress, all his dreams and ideas together.

Bernice spent her day shopping. Dressing herself in the latest designer clothes, the fitting a trophy wife to the famous hotelier, Ben jr, or Benji as he was called as a child, moved into the 17th floor with his parents. He had to live in wet nurse as a baby and a series of nannies throughout his childhood who took care of him.

Ben and Bernice were readily available for lavish birthday parties and photo shoots. But other than that, they were the epitome of the absentee parents. The year Benji was born. Ben Novak got into another fight with architect, Morris, Lapidus. He was designing the Eden rock hotel right across from the fountain blue on Collins Avenue.

Novak's secretly bought up parking space between the two hotels and soon began building a 17 story concrete wall designed to block the sunlight to the Eden rock swimming pool, suffice it to say Ben Novak was extremely petty and vindictive. He and Lapidus had maintained a strange relationship right through the opening of fountain blue.

When in front of investors, Lapidus asked for the rest of his fee, the agreed upon 75,000 when Novec acted like he didn't know what he was talking about. Lapidus became enraged and tried to attack him. It took several of the business partners to pull him off of Ben Novak, Novak insisted on an apology before he would pay.

The man has fee and thereafter, Lapidus not welcome. And the incredible hotel he had designed. Mader D's and managers had orders to throw him out on site. So he did have his own reasons for wanting to design a hotel next door to his masterpiece. He just somehow underestimated Novak's vindictiveness. The media called Novak's creation, the spite wall, and the two hotels wound up in court over it.

In 1959, the Florida district court of appeals rejected Eden Rock's claim to an easement allowing sunlight. And the new hotel was forced to build a second swimming pool for guests to have full access to the sun. From start to finish, the fountain blue would remain wrapped in one scandal after another, between Ben Novak,

Real Unsolved Case Files

seniors, many public feuds, the presence of mafia, bosses, and celebrities behaving badly.

The public swarmed to the hotel. Dying to see the rich and famous and be a part of history. It is said that Frank Sinatra set up Marilyn Monroe with John F. Kennedy and one of the fountain blue rooms. The FBI kept a tight watch on the hotel, as well as the IRS, the fountain blue was mobbed up as much as it was as a place that celebrities flocked to Sinatra and his friends often ended nights thrown cherry bombs off their balconies.

After calling downstairs to the poodle lounge for buckets of champagne, the prettiest girls to be sent up. And it was in this decadence that baby Benji grew up. He had a strict German nanny who forced the left-handed boy to write with his right hand. He developed a severe stutter under her strict toodling.

People notice that even when other kids were around, Benji had no interest in playing with him. He didn't know how to be a kid. He was always around adults and what's more, he became used to ordering them around. His tantrums were monumental. Benji'saunt Maxine, Bernice, his sister spoke with author, John Glatt extensively about Ben Jr's childhood quote.

When he wanted his parents, he couldn't just go down and call for them. They were with presidents, diplomats, Sinatra, and the rest. He was this little King, but this poor kid didn't get any love. The summer Benji was seven years old. A film crew took over the huge fountain blue swimming pool to film scenes for the new James Bond movie, Goldfinger.

He got to meet Sean Connery among many actors and celebrities. The little Prince of fountain blue, pretty much ran wild at the hotel. He befriended security guards and waiters who felt sorry for him making matters worse. The strain union between his parents was becoming more obvious ever. The womanizer Ben sr didn't stop his many affairs and Bernice and turn against several affairs with Latin musicians who played at the hotel.

But as with many womanizing tyrants, Ben know that senior

185

which sheet, but he wouldn't put up with it from his wife. He had one musician beaten and thrown out of the hotel. And by August of 1964 blind items were running a local gossip columns about a prominent hotelier and his wife having marital issues in October, Bernice filed for divorce charging Ben Novak, senior with cruelty and going for custody of Benji.

But she moved out of the house. I'm blue, leaving Benji with his absent father. And then Ben sr had a change of heart and did everything he could to win his wife back. Maybe he realized she was an asset. He couldn't afford to lose. Maybe he really loved her. There are many indications towards the end of both of their lives that they did indeed have deep love for each other, but Ben also needed Bernice.

She was in many ways, the glamorous face of the hotel by July of 1965, she dropped divorce proceedings and moved back into the hotel, but almost immediately. Bernice began an affair with a Latin drummer named George Rodriguez. Ben got suspicious and had her followed. And this time he filed for divorce himself.

Naturally, Bernice said that Ben was also having an affair this whole time, but it didn't matter. Ben sr filed for divorce on January 15th, 1966, just four days before Benji's 10th birthday. He charged infidelity mental anguish and said that Bernice had stolen from him and she was a bad mother. He sued for full custody of Benji.

Bernice countersuit saying that Ben sr was a verbally abusive alcoholic during their bitter divorce. Benji just ran wild. If he had been a spoiled handful before now, he was in cordial, but the hotel staff felt sorry for him. They knew they were his only friends that the fountain blue was his only family.

In January of 1966, the television show, Batman premiered and ten-year-old Ben Novak jr. Became obsessed as an adult. He would come to own the second largest Batman memorabilia collection in the world. He even commissioned his own Batmobile. You've got to one there. If he felt a connection to the lonely rich kid, Bruce Wayne, he also became enamored with police officers and detectives.

He had always been friendly with security at the fountain blue, but now he latched onto the mini police officers who were always hanging around the bars and restaurants in the hotel. Ben sr always let cops eat for free. Probably hoping they would look the other way in some of his dealings, but he wasn't degenerates to the Miami beach police.

But by then, the mafia had pretty much taken over the fountain blue. Author John Glatt reported that the mob paid Ben Novak senior $2 million a year to be their front man at fountain blue. Ironically, at the same time, sin city was burgeoning in the Nevada desert. Las Vegas had one thing, Miami beach couldn't offer gambling.

Ben sr spoke confidently to the press blowing off any concerns of company petition from Vegas or the Caribbean islands. Which were fast, becoming a popular tourist destination. Naturally the islands also allowed gambling, but when Ben sr applied for a permit to build a hotel on one of the Kat K islands, he was turned down by the Royal commission.

His reputation was catching up to him in January of 1967. The Miami Herald ran investigative articles by two reporters who had spent months examining the hotel's financial records. The front page articles went national with a headline screaming. The hotel was a front for gamblers and hoodlums specifically that Novak was connected to Meyer Lansky as well as Sam Giancana.

Of course, Ben Novak suited the Miami Herald and in response, the Herald subpoenaed Frank Sinatra to testify to the mafia's involvement in the fountain blue Sinatra lied under oath, denying everything. He canceled performances that February, but soon started up again until the Herald again, subpoenaed him that April, this time he left town to avoid testifying.

He could not be extradited back to Florida, but he would be arrested the minute he put a toe over the state line on April 20th, 1968, Ben Novak dropped his libel suit against the Miami Herald in exchange for a front page statement that he was the sole owner of the film blues operating company. But the paper didn't apologize or print a retraction of the mob accusations author.

John Glass said the rumors were that Sinatra strong arm Novak, and to dropping the suit. So he could return to Miami beach without risk of being jailed. Then suddenly on June 3rd, Bernice Novak agreed to settle their divorce out of court. She returned the items, been Novak, senior claims. She had stolen and she was no longer seeking custody of Benji.

It was, or that she got $25,000 a year in alimony. That would be almost $184,000 in 2019 money. And though she had taken a different suite at the fountain blue. She now moved out of her home for the last 14 years and bought a mansion in Fort Lauderdale, despite winning custody. Ben sr allowed Bingie to move in with his mother and the fall of 1968.

When he was 12 years old, he was enrolled in a private school that he was chauffer to daily. While at school he became interested in theater, specifically sound enlight, design. And he made a friend when he would keep until his death, the actor, Kelsey grammar, Kelsey's parents had divorced when he was young, but he was sent to private school just a few months after his father had been murdered in the Virgin islands.

The two lonely boys had a lot in common. Ben Junior's dad. Now 62 years old had remarried to a 22 year old model. He had little time for his son when he came to visit and teenaged Benji, who now prefer to be called Ben became even more of a tyrant at the hotel. Ben jr. Notoriously fired a chef who was busy, preparing the evening meal for a huge party for not stopping and making him a bowl of ice cream.

When the chef went to Ben senior about his son behavior, no, that told him to get the hell out. It would set a dangerous precedent. Ben jr. Had complete control and it was also teaching him to be a cold calculating businessmen.

As Ben jr was going through his teen years, awkward stuttering, and yet commanding his father was still trying to expand his empire in 1970. Ben sr bought the Sorento hotel. Just down the road from the fountain blue, during construction on a new wing, the entire building collapsed and Ben sr was liable for repairs, but after all the negative publicity of being associated with mobsters, he was unable to get outside financing.

He took $3 million from the fountain Blue's cash to finish the project a year after that, he bought more land with a new hotel in mind, but again, he could not get and investors with his ties to the mob. So he refinanced the fountain blue, taking out a $6 million mortgage. This was the beginning of the downfall for Ben senior, financially.

The golden days were over, but he did still have a few years left as King of the Felton blue in June of 1970. He put Ben jr. On the fountain blue payroll working security for $25 a day. It was six months before his 15th birthday. By the time he turned 15, he was going on regular patrols with the Miami beach police retired Miami beach, detective Joe Matthews spoke to author.

John Glatt explaining that this wasn't quote a privilege granted to the average kid, but Ben sr still held great influence and stay tight with the police, despite his reputation and connections to the mob. December of 1971 brought Ben sr, his third divorce. She had fallen in love with another rich successful man.

Ben sr would later say that none of his marriage has worked because he was married to the fountain blue. When Ben jr turned 16, he was handed the keys to a Lincoln town car at his birthday party by none other than Meyer Lansky. He got all kinds of extravagant gifts and money from his father's pals and movie stars.

And at 16 Ben jr. Wasn't just on the payroll as a figurehead, he was actually running all the sound equipment at the hotel, as well as working security for all the conventions held there. He was working hard and making great connections for his own future career. Ben jr was also still befriending police officers.

When he turned 17, he joined the Fort Lauderdale police department, youth auxiliary, not long after that. He graduated from the pine crest, private school and enrolled in the university of Miami as a mass comm major. But his real interest was in law enforcement. In September of 1974. He was accepted to the Southeast Florida Institute of criminal justice so that he could train as an auxiliary officer.

Ben jr. Went through the rigorous training required of all new cadets. And he graduated from the Academy in December. Now that he was certified, basically as a reserve officer, he had a uniform and a gun, but no power to arrest. He was to serve two 10 hour shifts a month and ride with a regular officer, but naturally the difficult young man wasn't popular.

Sometime around his 18th birthday, Ben jr. Was promoted to vice president of the fountain blue under his father, though. He was still studying at the university of Miami. He would angrily tell any staff that called him Bingy or Ben jr. That his name was Ben. He just wanted to be called Ben. He was now six foot, three inches tall with a full beard and it's understandable.

He wanted to be taken more seriously. And he was taking on a more important role at the hotel, right? When his father needed him to. Disneyworld in Orlando had opened three years earlier. And though Ben sr had always scoffed at the idea that it would pull money away. From my end, the beach, he was proven wrong by the Midland 1970s.

The fountain blue was getting by with convention business alone, which happened to be Ben Jr's forte, but then senior was in trouble. He was mortgaged up to his eyeballs, owing money everywhere, and was having cashflow issues at the fountain blue. By 1975, the IRS was investigating Ben Novak senior and late 1976.

The hotel started working with the black tuna gang smuggling, millions of dollars worth of marijuana from Columbia and to Miami gang leader. Robert Platt sworn and his autobiography would fully admit that the smuggling and distribution based for their operation was the fountain blue. During this time as author John Glatt points out, it is unknown.

If Ben jr was aware of the immense drug operation, going down in his father's hotel, he was extremely loyal to his father and the fountain blue and with his ties to Billy's, it is interesting to think about how much he really knew he would never have wanted a scandal to touch their beloved hotel, but I'm not sure he would go against his father's wishes either.

Now as a grown man, Ben was coming into his own. He never had steady girlfriends, but he frequented strip clubs in Miami beach and love to hang out with his cop buddies. He was characterized as a natural flirt and within a few years, he did have multiple girlfriends who he often referred to dr. Larry Robbins, a cosmetic surgeon and friend of his dad's Ben jr.

Had a morbid interest in watching breast augmentation surgery. His unusual sexual proclivities will come back to bite him later, but this was the beginning. In 1976, he was introduced to Jill Campion, tall and beautiful. She was an ex show girl and was looking for a new career. Ben became infatuated with her.

He actually pulled the same stunt his father had in order to get Bernice to go out with him. Ben junior set up a fake job interview for Jill at the fountain blue. When the interview was over, he told her he couldn't hire her because the fountain blue had a strict policy against dating employees. And he told her he intended to date her.

She later told author John glad that he completely swept her off her feet. She was soon taken aback at his rude behavior towards people though. He was still obnoxious, spoiled kid Bingy went around waiters security or bell hops, even at other hotels. Jill hated this and called him out on it. In June of 1976, the fountain blue owed 1.3 million in back taxes.

The walls were closing in on Ben sr. He tried desperately to raise the money to save the hotel. By November, Ben Novak senior had quit paying for his employees. Health insurance and paychecks were often late. One of his biggest creditors file to put the fountain blue in foreclosure. Franklin Sinatra stepped up and offered to buy the fountain blue outright, which insulted bin sr.

The two wound up in an Epic fistfight over the offer ending with Ben sr, throwing Sinatra out of the hotel. The singer would never perform there again. In January of 1977, right after evil Knievel pulled this stunt walking a tight rope between the fountain blue and Eden rock hotel. Ben sr was forced to file chapter 11, bankruptcy.

His mob ties stopped him from getting legitimate help and he had run off the one chance to save the fountain blue from bankruptcy by cutting ties with Sinatra. He was ordered by a circuit court judge to pay 3.2 million, which would be close to 14 million today. And he couldn't come up with the money.

The fountain blue was false for 27 million on the court steps to Steven mus and the Roland international corporation. That would be 116 million today. And Ben senior began moving his personal fortune to offshore accounts and his sister's name. Ben know that junior had to sit back and watch as his father lost his life's work.

What was supposed to be Ben Junior's inheritance. He was always surprised to get the keys to the kingdom one day, but it wasn't to be, but the smart young man had made many contacts in the convention industry while working at the fountain blue. Now he called up Amway and asked for a job, organizing their conventions.

They were delighted to hire him. He was very successful at Amway and traveled often for his job. He had a long engagement to Jill Campion. She was finding out that the two of them had little in common besides enjoying the nightlife and Ben could be controlling. He expected her to dress sexy and stay very slim.

She took diet pills, exercise, and tried to be the arm candy that Ben wanted, but he was constantly unfaithful to her. She told author John Glass, that he was just a liar. He would always lie to get what he wanted. She said, and though he had a good job at Amway. His mother Bernice still supported his lavish lifestyle.

Bernice was very sad. And when Ben senior lost the fountain blue, but she had made her own life in Fort Lauderdale. She and George Rodriguez were still a couple that she had always refused marriage because she didn't want to lose her alimony. And Jill was becoming disenchanted and alarm to see Ben jr.

Had started using cocaine, but she married him anyway in June of 1979 in an Orthodox Jewish ceremony, the Novaks were a Jewish family though. They had never been particularly religious right after the wedding. Ben jr. Admitted to his wife that he was five years younger than he had actually claimed. But he was really eight years younger as she would find out.

And she felt really foolish about it. She had always felt that Bernice Novak didn't like her and thought this was the reason, but I imagine Bernice had higher expectations for her son than an ex showgirl though. I'm sure the age difference didn't help. And Bernice still held the purse strings. Jill found out that Ben was stalling on buying a house because Bernice didn't want Jill's name on the deed.

Not long after that, she found out he had divorce papers drawn up. When he sheepishly told her he did it to show his mom so that he could bother house. Jill was done. They were divorced in March of 1981. After less than two years of marriage, Joel returned her engagement ring and received a $4,000 payoff.

That's almost $12,000 today, but still paltry in terms of the Novec fortune. Ben jr. Moved on quickly buying a new house on the beach, just down the road from his mother. Though they had a cold strained relationship when he was a child, they were extremely close. Now he still worked for Amway, but he was also devoting more time as a reserve officer volunteer for the Miami beach police department.

He wanted to make full detective, but his stutter stood in the way it was worse under stress, and he couldn't communicate fast enough in emergency situations. But he still went out partying with his cop friends. And in August of 1983, he met a stripper at a club and highly of Florida. She was young and blonde.

She went by the name Sylvia and was from Ecuador. Ben gave her his business card, but she didn't think much of him at first until she asked some of the other girls who he was Sylvia's real name was Narcissa Elise Pacheco. She went by Narcy. Unlike Ben jr. She had grown up very poor immigrating to America slowly with the rest of her siblings, staying close to her brother, Krista bell.

She claimed she had been born in 1956, but author John Glass said she has been accused of being older than she reported. She had a daughter named may of OD from a previous marriage. This didn't determine the two started a passionate affair. At one point Narcy threatened to burn down his house on Atlantic Boulevard because she thought he was cheating.

It did not bode well for how their relationship and eventual marriage would go. She was also into cocaine and the night life, and she was different from the women. Ben was used to seeing. Though he did see strippers and Showgirls, there was an unseemly quality to Narcy that everyone noticed though, many friends still thought she was very nice and that the two or in love naturally nice.

Couldn't stand her in November of 1983, Ben Novak senior held an auction for his personal collection of antiques furniture, art and other collectibles. He had kept from the fountain blue. Bernice came to the auction and outwardly showed no regret telling a reporter that you lose cinnamon for it. But privately, it was hard watching the last of the fountain blue being sold off.

Eventually many items wound up in Bernice, his private collection. She quietly bought it, many items herself and others were gifted after the auction, Ben sr, with a million dollars burning a hole in his pocket, decided to invest in a new nightclub. It was to be Alcatraz themed with waiters, wearing prison uniforms, and also accessible to the general public.

He had learned a lesson from Disney taking over and it was that he needed to cater to regular people, not just the Uber rich Ben jr. Was doing very well. He had begun his own convention business, calling it convention concepts unlimited. And like his father, his work ethic was exceptional. He was known to be tough exacting and an often rude businessmen.

He worked with hotels all over the world. And he demanded the very best and thought nothing of dressing down, anyone in the staff from hotel manager to bellhop, still behaving as the Prince of fountain blue. But later people would say for all his obnoxiousness, he always paid his bills. However, he had learned a valuable trick from his father.

He never signed a contract that required any payments upfront. That way he could walk away if he was unhappy, but that happened rarely. The hotels and vendors usually met his demands to avoid it. And like I said, just like Atlanta stir, he always paid his debts. Ben senior's venture into the nightclub business, failed miserably.

He was living with a 30 year old woman who had been miss Uruguay, but his ex wife came to see him regularly. Bernice wanted to be sure he took his medication and ate well. He was now 77 years old and had blood pressure issues. Bernice's sister Maxine told author. John glad that her sister had always carried a torch for her ex husband and had admitted late in life that she never should have divorced him.

You have to wonder if they had stayed married with Bernie, his influence. If things would've worked out yeah. Differently without Bernice has steadying hand, bill sr fell prey to all his worst impulses, maybe together they could have saved the fountain blue. In October of 1984, Ben sr signed over power of attorney to his son before being admitted into a nursing home after leg surgery.

Ben jr Promptly sued miss Uruguay for a hundred thousand dollar loan and some $15,000 in jewelry. She had kept, he also filed an injunction to stop her from seeing the frail old man Ben Novak senior died after a stroke than heart attack in April of 1985. While Ben jr was still in court with his ex girlfriend.

Miss Uruguay had countersued for 500,000 after Ben senior's death, but they reached a sudden undisclosed agreement. Two years later in April of 1987, Ben sr had taken care of his ex wife and son and his will as well as his sister, but his adopted son, Ronald from his first marriage whom he had turned his back on received $1.

This is so he could not contest bill senior's will. Bill Novak senior remained cruel towards his other ex wife and adopted son, even in death. After his father's death, Ben jr changed. He finally decided to inner speech therapy to correct his stutter and friends felt he took on personality, characteristics of his more cold-hearted father.

In the summer of 1987, he bought a luxury yacht worth over $500,000 with his inheritance. He docked her right outside of his beach house in Pompano. And he was still with Narcy at this point, taking her to dr. Larry Robbins for a boob job. And he loved having her pose on the boat and skimpy bikini's as he wrote up and down the intercoastal, his aunt Maxine reported that Bernice hated Narcy on first sight.

She told author John Glatt quote. This one was no beauty and Bernice hated her. She was so funny, educated and spoke with a thick Hispanic accent. But Bernice told her sister that if she wanted to see her son, she had to put up with Narcy. Now in her mid sixties, she was close to her son and was desperate to keep that relationship.

She regretted her early absentee mother years with Ben and wanted to make it up to him. Friends thought that Ben NRC were a love match. He seemed devoted to her and she was different from his other girlfriends. As his aunt pointed out. She wasn't beautiful. At least not in any conventional sense. She wasn't tall and statuesque has been, usually went for her dyed blonde hair and fake boobs gave her a definite era of cheapness.

But Ben was in love. He put Narcy to work for his convention company, working alongside him as he built his business. Narcy converted Judaism before they got married, hoping to win over Bernice. She agreed to sign a prenuptial agreement that meant if they divorced before 10 years of marriage, she would get nothing.

After 10 years, she would receive a $65,000 settlement that would be close to $130,000 today. But it was definitely paltry considering Ben's net worth was in the millions, the two married in December of 1990, despite Bernice has obvious misgivings. They took out a mortgage on a new luxury home almost immediately and began running his company together in earnest may abide.

Darcy's now 16 year old daughter had a baby boy in 1991 and another in 1993, she would visit her mother often, although they had a very strange relationship, may, would one day claim that her mother was very physically abusive to her as a child in John Glass book, the Prince of paradise, according to friends, Ben disliked his stepdaughter immensely.

But he still hired her to work in his office, along with his wife and mother Bernice, who didn't like me at first actually became close to the girl as they both hated Narcy. I think it's debatable how been really felt about may in the early years, but he didn't trust just anybody with his business. And in later years he seemed to care.

A great deal for her business was good, except that Ben know that jr was really gaining a reputation. He was blackballed by one big hotel chain for his obnoxious behavior. And it was here that Narcy took up the Slack. She sued vendors when she could. And she also helped him form partnerships with Latin American companies.

She was obviously fluent in Spanish by 1994, Ben and Narcy moved to Fort Lauderdale to be closer to Bernice. They found a six bedroom mansion on Del Mar place and took out a huge mortgage. Within two years. The Novaks bought the two adjoining lots on Del Mar renovating one, a large house and two new business offices.

Now Bernice just had a seven minute drive to work with her son. Friends couldn't understand why at her age, she still worked that much. Often six days a week. She made no bones about wanting to not only be around her son, but feeling the need to keep an eye on Narcy. She never trusted her daughter in law.

She had good reason, like a lot of people with new money Narcy went on extravagant spending sprees. She had an immense jewelry collection and over a hundred pairs of shoes. She also began lying about her past. She wanted to fit in and would tell friends that she came from a rich Ecuadorian family and then moved to New York to become a fashion designer.

She started dying her hair, a darker, less cheap looking color in many ways. It's hard to blame her for these lies about her past. She was trying to fit into the upper echelon of society. She was married to a multimillionaire now in his forties. Ben know that jr was a success. And in the late nineties, he really started showing it.

He bought an Island in The Bahamas and also part ownership and a private jet. However, he was so rude to the pilots that after a while they refused to fly him business associates say in the beginning, that Narcy was nice. She was the one who was approachable and reasonable, but she was becoming as ruthless as her husband.

And she was always suspicious of him. And she had calls too. The Ben jr. Carried on many affairs in Narcy made it her mission to catch him. They had horrendous fights, often physical with Narcy showing up with bruises, according to a neighbor, another friend. So they chased each other down the street and cars.

It was a stormy, passionate relationship to say the least and each giving as good as they got according to most friends in the summer of 1999, Bernice was convinced that Narcy was trying to poison her. She had a bottle of water in the office fridge. And after a while, when she took a drink, she thought it tasted strange.

By the time she got home, she said her throat was closing up. She had long suffered from asthma and as the event passed, that's what her doctor chalked it up too. But a friend of Ben's joke, Andy claimed Narcy had also poisoned Ben. He said he went to the hospital a few times after her cooking and Gandy himself had always refused to eat her food.

He insisted that she practiced voodoo and didn't trust her. He told author John Glass quote, it was a dangerous fucking situation. Ben stayed in his reserve status with the Miami beach police and close to many officers. His friend, Jim Scarbary became police chief in Hollywood, Florida in 1999. In 2002, he completed a 40 hour training program to stay in the reserves.

A cop friend noticed that Ben seemed depressed. He confided that he had found out Narcy had cheated on him. They were constantly fighting and becoming more violent, but they had passed the 10 year Mark in their relationship. And I guess North, he felt free to have her own affairs. Now that her settlement was secure, but we will find out that it would never be enough on Saturday, June 8th of 2002, Ben and Narcy went for dinner at a Mexican restaurant and they came home and went to bed at 1:00 AM.

Ben awoke to find three armed men in their bedroom. As he reached for his gun on his nightstand, in the dark. He distinctly heard, Narcy say, look out. He has a gun on his nightstand. The men pinned him to the bed and put a pillow over his face. As they handcuffed him with his own police handcuffs and blindfolded him.

They then tied Ben to a leather chair with ropes. As Narcy ran to disable the alarm system, she then allegedly told him she would cut off his penis and throw it into the canal. Allah, Raina, Bobbitt, as the men ransacked their home. Ben Novak was tied up for over 25 hours. They would allow him to urinate in a portable urinal.

On the side of his chair, Narcy took $370,000 in cash that Ben had stashed in a safe under the stairs. She took jewelry, antiques, family, heirlooms, guns, important business documents. And even some of his Batman collector's items. She cleaned out her side of the closet and her toiletries from the bathroom.

As she was doing this, Ben could hear her on the phone talking to an ex boyfriend from her old strip club who had just gotten out of jail. He also thought he heard the name of a major crime boss. He was terrified, but remained still and cooperative on Sunday evening, 18 hours into the ordeal. He heard Narcy call her yoga instructor named Radha.

She asked the woman to come help her pack up boxes. The woman came over and then heard them all loading boxes into trucks. After this Narcy finally removed his blindfold and told him, quote, if I can't have you, then no one will have you. The men that helped me we'll come back and finish the job I can have you killed anytime I want.

You're not dead now because I stopped them. And then she resealed his mouth with duct tape and left over seven hours later at two 30. Am she called Radha again to go there to the house, to move some furniture on the second floor. Narcy insisted she go, even though it was in the middle of the night. And so Radha did and found Ben Novak tied to the chair, eyes bulging.

She was horrified. She hadn't known. He was tied up in the house earlier as she untied him. He begged her not to call the police, but he did call Bernice who came over immediately after calling his mother, he then called his friend, a former Miami beach police officer who told him to call the police and get out of the house.

He admitted. He thought his wife was involved in the attack, but wasn't specific. He finally called the Fort Lauderdale police at close to 2:00 AM. Monday morning. They promised to send someone out. And then he called his old friend, Jim Scarbary, chief of Hollywood police though. He left out in Darcy's involvement.

When he talked, I told him what had happened. He was adamant that the police show up in unmarked cars and one of Scarbary to use his influence with Fort Lauderdale to make it happen. They all finally agreed to Ben making a statement over the phone. So he told his story to a Sergeant with the Miami beach police.

He also refused medical treatment though. He had some serious cuts and bruises, but without being able to investigate the scene, there was little, the police could do. Ben Novak was obviously terrified and they believed him. He had told the truth finally about

Darcy's involvement. But their hands were tied.

So all they could do was give him a case number for any future investigation by 8:00 AM on Monday, Ben was flexing his years as a reserve officer and wanted his wife found and arrested though. He was still resisting uniformed officers coming to his house. Finally, detective Steve Palazzo came to the Novak home in an unmarked car.

He noted Ben's obvious injuries and Ben showed him the reclining chair where he had been held. He also pointed to the safe and other places, things have been stolen, but that would be hard to prove what he did find interesting was how obvious it was that Narcy had moved out. All of her belongings ever bins protestations.

The detective did call in one forensic agent to process the scene. He noted that Ben stayed on the phone almost the entire time, still conducting business. While detectives were at her Fort Lauderdale home Narcy was in family court claiming she was a victim of domestic violence. She was staying at a motel and wanted her husband thrown out of their home so she could move back.

Now, the police had conflicting stories, but they had evidence of the attack and break in Tuesday morning. Ben did show up at police headquarters to make a formal statement. He repeated everything that happened and said that Narcy had orchestrated the whole thing. And then he left by Wednesday morning, Ben called another retired Miami beach detective named Pat Franklin for help.

Franklin was now a private investigator. After the two men agreed on a $3,000 retainer, Franklin came to his house when Franklin asked him what he wanted him to do. Ben said he wanted Narcy and his money back Franklin was flabbergasted, but he agreed to call Narcy and try to work things out that very afternoon, after getting a voicemail from Franklin Narcy marched into the Fort Lauderdale police station with several boxes and bags, she said it was things she had taken in the house.

And then with no prompting, she opened up an old Brown

accordion file and dumped the contents onto the table. It was pornographic photographs of women with artificial limbs. She then went on to tell detective about their kinky sex life. She said they were both into bondage. And that is what happened that night though.

She denied tying Ben to the chair. She claimed it had been a willing sexual encounter and that she didn't move her things until the following morning when Ben was working in his office, she refused to say, who helped her move though? But she also explained the picture she had thrown on the table. She said her husband had a strange fetish about amputees.

She also claimed that several years ago, Ben had hit her breaking her nose and that he took her to a plastic surgeon to have it fixed. And when she woke up, she also had new breast implants this year. He's Asian has never been proven and seems to be yet just another wild story of Narcissus, but the pictures were real.

And they scared the shit out of Ben Novak. When he found out the detective later said she was completely unbelievable. He said that she was so obviously lying, but her arrogance was what was so astounding. She truly seemed to believe she would tell her lies and get her away with this. No, what she knew was once Ben found out about the pictures, he would more than likely drop the case and he did.

They went back and forth for weeks with one agreement, being that she could keep the money, if she would waive all rights to any future claims, once they divorced. Pat Franklin was trying to broker these deals for Ben, as the police were ready to wash their hands of it. The whole sorted affair was becoming a nuisance.

They believed Ben Novak, but he interned acted so strangely and refused to cooperate. Detective Palazzo advised him to get an attorney and file for divorce and move on with his life. At one point, Pat Franklin met NRC at a coffee shop where she spewed hatred about her husband. He asked her to call been mainly so he could prove to his client that he had found her and was astonished when she got on the phone and started talking baby talk, crying, telling him she was sorry, and that she loved him.

She begged her husband not to send her to jail. Franklin took the phone back and told Ben that Narcy was now willing to cooperate when he hung up. He told author John Glass that Narcy wiped her tears and winked at him. She then gave him directions to a storage facility where all the stolen items were.

She met Franklin there, there, and unlock the building, showing him what was in boxes. Then she asked Franklin wants to know what kind of sick bastard your client is and showed him the folder with the amputee pornography. He said not all of it was porn. Some were just pictures of amputees being fitted for prosthetic limbs.

He said there were Polaroids going back to the sixties and seventies, men, women, and children, Ben would later sheepishly explained that after a group of MPT stayed at his father's hotel, when he was a child, his obsession began Franklin called Ben from the storage unit for his next instructions. And then asked if he had seen the pictures.

Ben told him he was no longer interested in recovering the property and that Narcy was blackmailing him. Franklin handed the phone to Narcy and they agreed that Ben would drop it all criminal proceedings against her and not file for divorce. Pat Franklin was again, astonished. Now he and the detectives knew that Ben was being blackmailed, but there was little they could do about it.

There was a little more back and forth with the police with Ben calling blue weeks later, demanding Narcy be arrested for threatening his life. But detective Palazzo had had enough of their antics. He again, told Ben there was nothing he could do and he should just hire a divorce attorney and be done with this bended Val for divorce.

And in the first hearing, they shocked the judge with their graphic and conflicting stories of abuse. Narcy claimed he beat her and made her have sex with other men. Ben told his story about being held hostage. It was insane, but by July 10th, they had come to a quote confirmation of understanding. The first line, read Ben a Narcy wished to do everything possible to reconcile their relationship and move forward with their lives together.

There were also certain financial agreements and most importantly privacy clauses, but the point was after all of this, the Novaks were reuniting. And despite what was obviously blackmail on Narcis part for the next seven years, they did appear to work on their marriage. Business was thriving. And though his mother and friends worried the Novaks appeared to be solid on Ben's 50th birthday, January 19th, 2006, he made out a new will leaving everything to Narcy.

He even had plans for them to be buried together. The only codicil was that if Ben's mother survived him, meaning if he died before she did Bernice would inherit $200,000 and half interest in the Del Mar place properties. The final note in the will was been stipulating that this new will, would automatically void their prenuptial agreement upon his death, whether he knew it or not.

He had now signed his death warrant and it probably never occurred to him that he was putting his mother in danger as well. Within three years, Ben and his mother Bernice would be brutally murdered and the trial and scandal would rock the nation.

Morris Lapidus, the architect who built the fable Fontainebleau hotel on Miami beach said if you create a stage and it is grand, everyone who enters will play their part.

Was the Prince, the lonely Prince growing up without love and affection without friends. Without boundaries, the Prince who preferred the company of strippers and prostitutes, and when his father lost his kingdom by the sea Ben Novak jr. Built his own empire, fortifying it with money. The only thing he could ever count on.

Growing up isolated and incapable of true intimacy and love. He chose for his wife, a stripper, a woman who loved money as much as he did. Narcy Novak was also bad at relationships. Her only true love in life what's money. After almost 20 years of marriage, she saw the Novak fortune slipping out of her hands.

So she brutally murdered her husband and mother-in-law so that she alone would hold the keys to the Novak kingdom.

Unless he died before his mother, Bernice would get $200,000 and half interest in the Del Mar place properties. And she was also named executor of his estate. There was another provision if Narcy died before him, Ben bequeathed $250,000 to each of her grandsons, Patrick and Marchello, and $100,000 to may abide his stepdaughter.

These are important cortisols to his will because the first, but the elderly Bernice Novak in Darcy's crosshairs. And the second regarding her daughter and grandsons will become very important. After murder. I told you had been abruptly decided to drop criminal proceedings against his wife after the home invasion.

And he also dropped the divorce. It was astonishing. Not just to the Fort Lauderdale police, who would invest a lot of man hours on the attack, but to friends, family, and even the private investigator Ben had hired. Everyone knew that Ben Novak jr was being blackmailed by his wife. Narcy Bernice Novak was very disturbed, not only by the attack on her son, but also the allegations made by Narcy about his sex life.

Her neighbor says she was so upset. She went to see a therapist for a while. She told her neighbor. There you go. Uh, knew what was going to happen. She only married my son for what he has and because she wants to control him, she understood intrinsically why her son stayed with Narcy. All she could do was stay close to him, be there for him.

And she was though, they hadn't had a close relationship. When Ben was a child, he was extremely dependent on his mother and his adult years. John Glatt reported in his book, the Prince of paradise that Ben called her late at night to talk. He also called her over to get in the middle of fights between him and Narcy to make peace.

She told one friend despondently I never thought my life would be like this. She became depressed. And her chronic asthma worsened, she slept with an oxygen machine beside her bed. She called Ben during these attacks, but often had to drive herself to the emergency room. Despite his mother's frail health.

Ben always called her when he needed something, even if it was just a rant on, for hours on the phone, but he wasn't always available when she needed him. During the same time Narcy Novak was reconnecting with her brothers, crystal ball and Carlos Valley's crystal ball, and his family came to visit every February.

Crystal ball's wife. Laura reported that Ben Novak was odd and quote, very picky. Guests only stay in the guest house. According to Laura, the no, that marriage was very strained. Other friends of the couple reported to author John, glad that they seemed very in love, ready to move on with their lives together.

It is certainly possible. They showed a different face to friends than family. Many people do. It's funny though. Bernice would talk about how horrible Narcy was and how she didn't trust her. And then Laura, on the other hand said that Ben was demanding and spoke abusively to his wife. She also claimed that they put crystal ball in the middle the same way they did with Bernice and who should we believe?

Maybe both. Bernice had good reason to feel the way she did about her daughter in law. And Ben Novak could definitely be salty with Northeast family. I think the point is intimate. Family members did not see a happy couple working things out. They saw a couple constantly at war. In the early spring of 2008 and insert an ad for a $300 an hour prostitute on a site called city vibe.com.

Her name was Rebecca bliss, and she was a former porn star who went by the name Mona love in 2007. She retired from porn and became a tattoo artist, but her boyfriend at the time shot her in the leg and hand ending that career down on her luck, unable or unwilling to go back to porn. She chose prostitution.

She said that her first visit with Ben was strictly business and he paid $600. She said they did talk quite a bit though. And he kept calling her. She told author John Glatt and the TV show 48 hours that they spoke every day on the phone. By June of 2008, Ben was in love with Rebecca and moved her into a luxury apartment in Fort Lauderdale, paying all of her living expenses.

So she no longer had to do sex work. He even named himself as husband on the lease. He signed for her that same summer Ben invited MakerBot and her sons to move into his guest house. She would continue working in his office slowly, taking on more responsibility and helping with conventions. His plan was so that Narcy could spend less time in the office, but he also told a hotel events coordinator at his last convention that he was grooming me to take over the whole business.

There has been a lot of back and forth over how Ben really felt about may Abad. And I think ultimately we may never really know, but if he had enough faith in her to talk about her taking over his business and moved her onto his property, I think he did care for his stepdaughter. In July of 2008, Bernice Novak made a new will an earlier will had left everything to Ben jr.

Except for $50,000 to her sister Maxine and 15,000 each to her nieces, Meredith and Lisa, of course, if Ben fell to survive her, that meant everything would go to Narcy. She told a close friend that she would do anything to make sure that Narcy didn't get her hands on her fortune or property. So in her new, will she left her entire estate to the Jewish Federation?

There is no mention of her sister or nieces. Ben know that jr was a millionaire in his own. Right. But when he found out his mother planned to change her, will he went ballistic. He complained that he and had two mortgages to pay off. I think this speaks to his character. He didn't need his mother's money.

He just felt entitled to it. And after he blew up at her, she left the will on her desk and never took it to her lawyer. So when she died, her estate pass to Ben jr. Meanwhile, by the end of the summer, Narcy became suspicious that Ben was cheating on her. She found receipts where he had bought furniture and finally figured out he was furnishing an apartment Narcy didn't know about.

May Abad later claim that she herself found the receipts and confronted her stepfather who told her about Rebecca bliss and that he planted a horse, her mother, she claims he promised he would still take care of her and her sons. She told many reporters that her mother was very jealous, but I think that's been made pretty clear several times.

Another friend have been said the affair was incidental, that things had gotten so bad at home. Ben was intending to file for divorce anyway. He was just trying to get his affairs in order. Surely Rebecca bliss said that he told her he was divorcing Narcy to Mary, her no disrespect to miss bliss, but that's generally what must cheating husband say?

Maybe he was head over heels for her. Hell Narcy was a stripper. When he met her, he did not have the snobbery or natural aversion to sex work that many people have. But we cannot know for sure. I think it's fair to say. He knew his marriage was over regardless of Rebecca bliss, though. When Narcy found out about the affair, she started trying to get Ben and Rebecca arrested.

She called the FBI to report an immigration fraud scheme. She said he would set up sham marriages and claimed Rebecca bliss was being put up in an apartment because she was set to marry a foreign convention guest. She also accused her husband of using cocaine and hinted at secret trips on a private airplane to and from Mexico in the early fall Narcy and Ben went to Puerto Vallarta.

Narcy called Mexican customs officials and claim that Ben was carrying $10,000 illegally and was also carrying a gun without a permit. So he was stopped before boarding a plane home. No money was found and they soon learned Ben was a retired police officer from his reserve days with the Miami beach police.

And he did indeed have a permit to carry a concealed weapon. When the FBI questioned her about the Mexico trip and her accusations, she denied it needless to say, even with her earlier claims about her husband, the FBI dismissed Narcy stories, finding that she was not credible. She had also taken to calling Rebecca bliss and supposedly at one point offered bliss, $10,000 to get out of Ben's life, which bliss refused.

She called bliss numerous times, shouting and rage. Rebecca bliss said Narcy screamed that they were not getting a divorce. And if she couldn't have him, no one could, obviously this isn't the first report of Narcy saying this exact thing. It's what she said to her husband after the home invasion, when she left him tied to the chair and she began stalking Rebecca bliss and earnest, she found out where her mother lived and bliss had a daughter.

She didn't have custody of, and Narcy even found her. Then in January of 2009, Narcy called the apartment complex where Rebecca lived and told them that her husband, Ben Novak jr. Had died and would no longer be paying the rent. The rental agent was confused by the call and told her to send a copy of his death certificate.

Narcy never did. But by now failing to get Rebecca bliss out of Ben's life and also failing to get him in trouble with the FBI or federal Raleigh's Narcisse plan, took a sinister turn. She had decided that Ben must die. And she also knew that Bernice being the executer of Ben's estate would be a problem.

She also merely wanted the old woman's portion of Ben's fortune. She wanted every last penny for herself. And so she started planning both murders with the help of her brother, crystal ball.

Narcissa bought a burner phone and kept in close contact with her brothers crystal ball and Carlos crystal ball was to set everything up for her. They were going to hire hitmen. Crystal ball spent his time networking and making contacts looking for just the right men. On Wednesday, February 11th, 2009, two hitmen hired by crystal ball made their first attempt on Bernice's life.

They were seen and chased off by a vigilant neighbor. One of them through an iron lawn ornament through Bernice's window.

As he ran off, Bernice was terrified by this and called Ben who told her everything was fine. And to just make sure the alarm system was on, but she still called the Fort Lauderdale police and made a report.

She was very shaken up crystal ball. The Lees was pissed that the first plan had failed and the men he hired now wanted nothing more to do with him. But a few weeks later he met a Nicaraguan immigrant named Ella hydro Garcia. Garcia was a crack addict with a long rap sheet who was in America, passed a six month work visa.

He was hungry for the money. And though his record was for petty crimes. He didn't seem phased by the plan to attack an 86 year old woman. Garcia would later say in court that quote, the plan was for me to give her a good beating and hit her in the teeth. Supposedly crystal ball told him that Bernice made been beaten RC every day as part of the Jewish religion.

He also said that Ben abused Narcy sexually that he forced anal sex and blowjobs on his wife. This might be a Hitman trying to justify his actions as not just motivated by money, but I wouldn't put anything past crystal ball or Narcy. Either way they all call it a lucky break. When on March 28th, Bernice Novak took a nasty spill outside the bank of America.

She had been inside putting her five carat diamond ring in a safety deposit box. She was still shaken up by the recent vandalism of her home. She tripped over a break in the sidewalk and landed face down on the pavement. The bank staff rushed out to help and offer to call an ambulance, but she refused.

She drove herself home and then called Ben to tell him what had happened. Ben was out of town, but the minute he got in, he went to see his mother and insisted she get checked out at the hospital. She was covered and cuts scrapes and bruises. But other than that, not seriously injured, but Ben was furious and wanted to Sue the bank of America for negligence, for the broken sidewalk.

Bernice had her neighbor take photos of her injuries. Her

neighbor recalled how awful Bernice looked being. 86 years old. Her skin was very thin and she was skinned up all over. The reason I say this was a lucky break is now Bernice Novak had a recorded and recent history of falls. This would very much work to Narcy and crystal balls advantage on Saturday, April 4th, Bernie still wasn't feeling great and had stayed home all day.

It was the 34th anniversary of Ben senior's death. And her son called to check on her. She told him that she missed his father terribly after this and another phone call with one of her friends, it was getting dark. So Bernice changed into her nightgown and poured herself a glass of Chardonnay. Ben would later question this detail, insisting his mother didn't drink wine, but her sister Maxine said she often had a glass at night to relax, though.

She insisted Bernice was not a heavy drinker. A little before 9:30 PM. Alejandro Garcia had a large monkey wrench in his pants and grabbed a bottle of rum and went to hide and Bernice, his bushes, he was waiting for her to come outside and move her car into the garage. A creature of habit. Bernice always moved her car into the garage at night.

Narcy knew this and the plan was always for her attacker to wait for her to come outside, which was very smart. No witnesses and no forced entry. Garcia is accomplished. A man named Melvin Madrano was waiting nearby and a getaway car Madrano was one of the men in the first plot to kill Bernice that had failed.

Now they stayed in touch by cell phone. Suddenly Bernice came outside just as expected. She opened her car remotely, then got inside and drove it a few feet into her garage. Garcia slipped into the garage behind her car. When she shut off the engine and opened the door to get out Alejandro Garcia, viciously swung the wrench.

He would later testify that she saw him first and screened. He hit her several times. And as she fell into the car, he reached in and grabbed the steering wheel with his left hand. As he beat her in the head with his right. He later said he couldn't remember how many times he hit her. Then he calmly wiped his fingerprints off the wrench and the steering wheel of the car and fled.

He said she was slumped across the driver's seat. The last time he saw her. He ran and got into the waiting car with Medrano and the two drove to Miami, but Bernice wasn't dead bleeding. And in shock, she pulled herself out of her car and made her way to the laundry room door, leading into her house. She left a trail of blood the entire way the blood trail led through her kitchen and living room.

And then into a half bathroom. Frail 86 year old Bernice Novak was aware of what was happening as she lost control of her bowels. There was evidence that she tried to clean herself up in the bathroom. Her underwear was found near the commode and blood and feces were mixed together all over the floor.

Author, glad posited in his book, the Prince of paradise that Bernice then realized that she had left her door open and her attacker could come back. So she staggered back to the laundry room and locked the door. She then tried to reach the panic button on her alarm system, but fell to the floor dying before she could glass recreation of the crime scene.

And Bernice's movements are extremely intuitive. He worked from crime scene photographs and the autopsy report. The first blow Bernie's received was to her face, fracturing her skull and knocking her glasses to the garage floor. The second blow broke her jaw, knocking out some of her teeth. There were at least three more blister I had with a wrench.

It was a vicious attack. Alejandro Garcia would later claim. He was only supposed to injure Bernice and put her in the hospital. He also later claimed he didn't even know she had died. That crystal told him she was in the hospital. Again, I call bullshit. You cannot bludgeon anyone much less an elderly woman that many times over the head with a heavy wrench and not have intent to kill the next morning at 5:30 AM.

Bernie says neighbor noticed her garage door open, but didn't want to call and wake her up. When she did call a couple of hours later, she didn't get an answer. So she went and knocked on the door. She had seen Bernice's car in the garage with a light still on and was getting uneasy. When Bernice didn't answer the door.

She went home and called the know that jr. Ben called the Fort Lauderdale police immediately to check on his mother. As he NRC jumped in the car, heading to Bernice's house, they got there before the police Ben found his mother and a pool of blood face down. He checked her pulse and found that she was already dead.

He called the police back this time to report her death. From the start, the Fort Lauderdale police did not suspect foul play. They thought she had fallen. There were no signs of forced entry and nothing had been stolen or ransacked. Her purse and jewelry were all out in plain sight. The detective on scene spoke with one of Ben's friends who told him of Bernice's recent fall.

And he noted this as well as the glass of wine in his notes. Bernice Novak's body was transported to the Brower County medical examiner for autopsy. The Emmy found multiple fractures, which caused internal bleeding in her brain fractures in her jaw. And one to her ring finger, despite the numerous grievous blunt force injuries, the Emmy ruled her death and accident caused by an unwitnessed fall at her home.

The assistant Emmy would later insist. He did not believe it was an accident saying I've never seen injuries like this from someone falling. He said he was overruled by the medical examiner. Dr. had visited the scene at Bernice his house to help make his rules. And he wasn't alone in his findings. The Fort Lauderdale police agreed even some old cop buddies have been who walked the scene at his insistence also felt there was nothing suggesting foul play with the absence of forced entry.

Every door in the house was locked and without any robbery, it did look like a tragic accident. The theory would be that she felt once in the garage and then kept falling as she made her way through the house. So a series of falls along with a few glasses of wine, cause the incredible injuries to Bernice Novak's skull and face that is difficult to accept.

And Ben, now that junior didn't, he and her sister Maxine would insist that Bernice Novak was not a drinker and the injuries were much more serious than she would have received an a fall, but their worries fell on deaf ears.

Even while Bernice's body still lay in the house. Ben Novak jr. Noticed that his mother's diamond ring was missing. The suddenly fueled has believed that it was indeed a robbery. He NRC would find the ring. A few days later when they checked her safe deposit boxes with Darcy's help, he moved his mother's jewelry and heirlooms to one of his safe deposit boxes.

The very night Bernice was found Narcy made arrangements for her body to be cremated as soon as possible within 24 hours before any of Bernice, his family or relatives could be formally notified. A Memorial service was planned for the following Friday. Her sister Maxine who lived out of state said she did not have time to make arrangements to get to her funeral.

She was very suspicious by how rushed at all was Bernice Novak's obituary appeared in the Miami Herald on Thursday, April 9th. Her age was incorrectly listed at her Memorial service. Ben Rose to give the eulogy and admitted he had not prepared a speech. George Rodriguez Bernice's longterm boyfriend was shocked by the eulogy where Ben revealed his mother's time in foster care, as well as her real age.

These were her two biggest secrets and she would have been mortified. He also compared his mother's death to the actress, Natasha Richardson, who had recently died from a head injury. She got while skiing, it was bizarre and had nothing to do with his mother. He then spoke about her strange relationship with Narcy saying that they had gotten along better in recent years.

I'm sure Ben's awkward and inappropriate eulogy was due to his being in shock, but it was hurtful to friends and family and attendance. As Bernice dimple Novak had led a truly remarkable life and deserves so much better. Making matters worse. The NAVEX hosted a reception at the Bonaventure country club in

Fort Lauderdale after the funeral.

It was a party featuring a country in Western band. Narcy even got up to sing while this might sound appropriate. For some funerals, it was not for Bernice Novak. Bernice didn't even like country music. And she was also the epitome of dignity and refinement. She would have been appalled at this tacky reception.

Narcy had also upset mourners at the Memorial because she had cut her hair and died at red and Bernice's style for the event. Walking around a tight, but expensive black dress, never removing her sunglasses. She greeted mourners as if she was at a convention also in the days and weeks after her death, Bernice's friends and relatives were angry at how her death was reported in the press.

They were angry at Bernice being portrayed as a drinker who simply had too much wine and fell and they were angry or still that the case was closed. So abruptly. Ben filed a wrongful death suit against the bank of America for Bernice's earlier fall insisting internal injuries led to the second fall that caused her death.

He was angry and lashing out, but he also had a history of being very litigious. Narcy not been cleaned up her niece's house, going through her possessions, keeping what she wanted and throwing out Bernice, his beloved book collection. Ben inherited his mother's estate per her original will, as she had never taken the new will to her lawyer, her sister Maxine received $50,000 and her niece has got small amounts as well.

Everything else went to Ben Novak jr. An estimated $2 million estate. And now Narcy and her brother crystal ball moved on to the next part of their plan to have been killed. They planned it for months deciding that it would be better if it didn't happen in Florida. Been a, Narcy had a convention plan for July at the Hilton and ride broken New York.

They plan to use Garcia and Medrano again for Ben's hit, but Madrona was arrested and deported back to Nicaragua on an unrelated charge. So Krista ball had Alejandro Garcia looking for a new partner. Crystal offered Garcia 15,000 for the head on Ben.

Joel Gonzalez. Ben stepped into the picture. Garcia offered him 3000 and Gonzalez agreed immediately.

Both men were supposedly told they were just supposed to injure Ben Novak to be more precise, cut off his balls either way Narcy wanted him unable to ever work again. Of course, this was a lie. Whether it is the lie of Garcia and Gonzalez minimizing their participation, or if they were truly lied to by Narcy and crystal ball is anyone's game.

Yes, on May 5th, 2009, that finally got the Batmobile. He had commissioned, it was $128,000 and he was delighted, but as fate would have it, he only got to drive at once and that was to get gas. Before he parked it in a secure garage towards the end of June, Ben NRC had dinner with Kelsey grammar and his wife.

They were pals from their private school days, grammar later reported to police that he felt something was wrong and that Narcy acted strange usually then on June 26th and know that jr hired a divorce attorney. But the attorney soon called Ben and told him he was dropping the case because he had received threats.

He did not elaborate, but he wanted nothing to do with the Novak divorce. But it's clear, not just from what family close friends and bins mistress said that Ben Novak was finally ready to pull the plug on his marriage, no matter what it costs him. At a convention over the 4th of July in Fort Lauderdale, Narcy made a point of telling two different business associates that Ben had.

A lot of enemies. One was a vendor trying to settle his bill and the other a long time friend who knew of Ben's callous manner in business. Neither men found the statements odd at the time, but they did after Ben's murder. Ben and Narcy arrived in New York on Thursday, July 9th. This would be just less than two weeks since Ben had first tried to hire a divorce attorney, it would appear that he planned a blindside Narcy with the divorce.

And in the meantime, keep business going as usual, considering how she reacted in the past. It seems smart on his part, but he had no idea what she was planning and how far she would go. On

Friday, the hit-man Alejandro Garcia and Joel Gonzalez scattered the Hilton and rye Brook, New York. They are caught on security camera footage a little before 3:00 PM, actually walking right past.

Been know that junior in the front lobby. The first night of the convention, when office planned and Ben Novak talked to the hotels event director for a while that night pointing out his stepdaughter may abide and expressing how proud he was of her. He told the woman, he looked forward to retiring and letting me handle the day to day work.

Again, I have discussed different perspectives on the relationship between Ben and his stepdaughter, but this event director was not a friend or family member. She had no reason to lie, but it does seem strange if he was about to divorce May's mother. But then again may had a terrible relationship with Narcy.

Ben knew that. And it's quite possible that may Abad was the only person he felt he had left in his life whom he could trust. Maybe he did have section for his stepdaughter Saturday. They, July 11th also went well at the convention with staffers locking a total of $110,000 in registration fees in their hotel room safety afterwards, around yeah.

Night Ben and Narcy retired to their room using the hotel key at 12:07 AM. Narcy had also offered to help with the departing breakfast the next morning, something she had never done before she went to bed, but Ben stayed up late working on his laptop. As he often did studying spreadsheets, answering email and searching eBay for more Batman collectibles.

When the hitmen showed up at the Hilton hotel at five, 10:00 AM, the light was still on and Ben in Darcy's room, Ben was still up working. They called crystal ball who told them to wait for his call. Ben funnily turned off the light and went to bed at 6:30 AM. Narcy called crystal ball at six 39 at 6:54 AM.

The hotel events director called Ben's phone because attendees were already lining up for breakfast, but none have been staff was there to register them. Remember Narcy had told her she would be there to help, but she wasn't there. She may not have anticipated her husband staying up so late. Ben did answer the phone and then called me to take care of it and went back to sleep.

It was 7:00 AM. When the Hitman arrived in the Novak suite, Narcy was waiting in the doorway to let them in. She put a finger to her lips to make sure they were quiet and then pointed to the bedroom where Ben was sleeping. She then led them into the kitchen where they removed their dress shirts and shoes.

They had shopped for appropriate clothing beforehand, so they wouldn't stick out at the hotel. They put on gloves and then pulled dumbbells out of a gym bag. Garcia's weapon of choice. This time they got on either side of the bed and Garcia counted to three, and then the men pounced, Ben Novak, junior cloud, and just boxers and his blocks Sox, awoke, and began screaming and fighting back.

Alejandro testified later that they just hit him everywhere has had chest ribs and abdomen as been struggled. He knocked the sunglasses off of Garcia's face breaking off a piece of the glasses, ironically, considering what was coming. Alejandro Garcia was blind in one eye and couldn't stand the light.

Gonzalez said he became scared and walked into the kitchen, but Narcy told him to go back. She walked in with him and handed him a pillow to muffle her husband's screams. Gonzalez walked off again. As Garcia kept pummeling bin. He testified that when he walked back in again with NRC screaming at him, Ben was now on the floor beside the bed, and Garcia was hitting him with the dumbbell.

Gonzalez said been was no longer moving, but was moaning in pain. Then the men use duct tape to tie Ben's legs together. And his hands behind his back Gonzalez said at this point, Ben wasn't fighting, but was breathing hard and had a lot of blood coming out of his mouth Gonzalez. Again, walked back to the kitchen where Narcy was pacing.

Alejandro Garcia now pulled out a utility knife and grabbed Ben by his hair. He plunged the blade into Ben's left eye and turned it.

He did the same thing to his right eye as been moaned and agony. He then went to CNRC who asked him if he had cut Ben's eyes, he assured her that he did, and that Ben would never see again, but offered to cut his eyes more.

She wanted, she said no. Then she ordered Garcia to quote, finish him off. As Ben was still making weak noises, clinging to life, despite the brutal attack. Garcia went back to the bedroom and wrapped duct tape around Ben Novak's head and mouth tightly. Ben know that jr. Then choked to death on his own vomit.

Narcy handed the killer's towels to clean up at the sink. As they redressed, she went and took a bracelet off of Ben's wrist. It was gold and spelled Ben out and diamonds He loved the bracelet. She handed it to Garcia who put it in his bag. Originally the plan was to tie in RC up and leave her in the room.

So it would look like a robbery, but Narcy had changed her mind. Instead they all left the suite together with the killers, taking a nearby stairwell. As Narcy walked down the hall, the hitmen were caught on surveillance footage in the lobby at 7:11 AM. It had taken less than 10 minutes to torture and murder.

Ben Novak. Narcy had purposely walked down the hallway scene on a security camera at 7:09 AM pulling a small suitcase for 18 minutes. She stood in one place appearing to make phone calls on her cell. She called me a bot a seven 19, and then Ben's phone at seven 31. She was setting up an alibi investigators believe that she knew exactly where the security cameras were.

When she finally came down to the convention for breakfast may notice she wasn't wearing any makeup. Her mother always wore makeup. She also said she was even more snappish than usual and acting strangely Narcy. Then went back upstairs to her suite and use the key card to get in a 7:45 AM. She immediately came out of the room, screaming, Shaleen against the wall in the hallway, screaming, help me help my husband.

A nearby guest, went into the suite and saw Ben's body. And as one does start at snapping photographs of the gruesome scene with his cell phone. When he came back out, a crowd was gathering around the hysterical Narcy he said she then ran back into the room and climbed on top of her dead husband straddling him though.

He was lying face down hogtied. He said she began beating him in the shoulders with her fist. By seven 50, the Hilton hotel security was called and the guard was told a man was having a heart attack. He ran to the fourth floor suite and found Narcy screaming on top of her husband's body. He said, she screamed, why me?

Why is this happening? His first instinct was to preserve evidence. So he lifted Narcy up and put her on a chair. He had to continue to sit and hold her back. As other security arrived and secured the scene. At seven 56 EMS arrived expecting a heart attack. They checked for a pulse and found none. They even hooked him up to a heart monitor and it was flatlined.

He was already blue. The EMS attendant pronounced been know that jr. Dead at 7:59 AM, may Abad soon entered the suite. And one of the EMS attendants heard her ask Narcy where the money was. Narcy then told another employee to go collect the bags with a $110,000. They had collected the night before and put it in the hotels main safe.

It doesn't look good that may was asking about the money, but I also think she could have been subtly accusing her mother of taking it by all accounts. She was dedicated to Ben's company and was a responsible employee. The chief of security said he overheard me in the hallway telling her mother to pull herself together.

He said Mae told her mother to shut up and stop it. Or she was going to throw up seemingly upset at Narcy Systerix at 8:30 AM. Crystal ball met the hitmen at a Dunkin donuts and pay them in $100 bills. He gave Garcia 7,000 and Gonzalez 3000, presumably. Garcia would receive his final payment back in Florida.

Bribery New York is about 20 miles North of New York city. It's an affluent small town, but not equipped to handle a murder investigation of this magnitude. Other police departments from Westchester County were called in to help with the investigation. The first detectives on scene immediately noted that there were no signs of a break in, or even really a struggle other than Ben Novak's bloodied corpse.

He had obviously been attacked as he slept with a lot of blood on the bed, sheets and floor beside it in the sheets, they found bins gold Rolex that had fallen off in the attack covered in blood. They also found a piece from a pair of knockoff felon. Tina sunglasses, Alejandro Garcia had forgotten to go back for that bit of evidence.

Ben's laptop sat on the desk with a bank bag with $15,000 cash inside, out in the open, not in the room safe. They did find droplets of blood in the sink where the Hitman had cleaned up. But other than that, the room had not been ransacked and nothing appeared to be stolen. Narcy readily answered any questions the detectives had for her, including when they asked if Ben had any enemies

And she said many, even some within the Miami beach police department. By five 30 Ben's body was taken to the medical examiners office. Police stayed with Narcy at seven 30, a senior investigator came to question Narcy. He had just spent several hours talking to Maya bod and now had new questions. Narcy again, went over the list of bins, enemies, including a comic book dealer he had recently argued with the dealer would later say it was a negotiation, not an argument.

The detective showed. Narcy the piece of sunglasses they found, and she immediately claimed it was hers. She said she broke her pear on the flight to New York. And Ben was probably trying to fix them. He liked to fix things she claimed, but when asked where the rest of the sunglasses were, if Ben was trying to fix them, Narcy looked puzzled.

She paused and then said she had lost them on the plane. When the detective pointed out that this didn't make sense, I've been, was trying to fix the glasses. Just said, I don't know. Around midnight, may Abad went to the hotel, safe to get money, to pay the convention concepts, unlimited staff for that weekend.

She also took enough money to pay for an event the following week. I think this explains May's question about the money that was overheard by EMS. She knew her stepfather always paid his bills. She felt responsible for the staff and intended to keep business going as usual. It is probably what Ben would have wanted.

Ben know that Junior's autopsy took place around 10:00 AM on Monday morning, along with the numerous blunt force injuries to his head, the gruesome injuries to both eyes. When they opened him up, they found more than 20 fractures to his ribs. The pathologist said they were so smashed. They resembled chicken bones while Ben Novak did asphyxiate on his own vomit.

The medical examiner noted that any of the hemorrhages on his brain or lungs could have killed him. Meanwhile hotel management was concerned about the remaining $105,000 in their safe. It was too much money to be responsible for nor sea immediately said she would take it with her to Fort Lauderdale, but a detective said that was not safe and she should deposit it in a local bank.

So he drove her to a bank and then watched as a teller handed. Narcy a stack of money from the deposit she was making. It was $5,000 that Narcy pocketed right there in front of the detective. By 11:30 AM. That day Ben's death was made. Public investigators would not say much except that they felt it was not a random attack, but someone with a connection to Ben Novak jr.

By 6:00 PM, that same evening investigators were prepared to formally interview Narcy Novak on camera. They were already fairly certain. She was involved with a murder. Narcy had made a huge mistake by letting the killers into the room. Investigators now knew from hotel security that the card was only used to enter the suite at 12:07 AM after the convention and at 7:45 AM.

When Narcy came back upstairs and found Ben's body, there was no other way in or out of the fourth floor suite. She had to have let them in and they didn't buy her bullshit story about the sunglasses either. She should have feigned ignorance completely, instead of trying to make up a story. Either way they had also now received a tip from someone in Fort Lauderdale about the 2002 home invasion that Narcy orchestrated.

And had already quite willingly told investigators about her husband's preference for kinky sex, specifically that he liked to be tied up in the manner that he was found. It didn't feel like a coincidence to investigators. So for the next eight hours, they grilled Narcy Novak. She remained composed, but several hours into the interview, the gloves came off.

She was confronted about the home invasion. She denied it happened and assisting Ben made it all up, that he was into rough sex and pointed. Now that they got back together after the incident. She also denied robbing the house indignantly saying that she only moved her own things out as was her. Right.

She also claimed her husband was a pedophile along with his fetish for amputees changing tactics. One detective asked Narcy if anyone pressured her into letting them into the suite that morning. Narcy acted confused, evil. The detective point blank said you opened that door for them. She adamantly denied the accusation and then asked if she was a suspect.

She offered to take a hundred lie detector tests to prove she was innocent. She probably thought she could beat the machine. So the detectives called her bluff and set her up for a polygraph examination with the New York state police, which she failed several times. When Narcy was being shown the negative results may bod burst into the room and try to attack her may now was sure her mother had killed her stepfather, but as we know, polygraph tests are not admissible and Narcy Novak had held up well under questioning.

They had nothing more than circumstantial evidence and even that was weak. So Tuesday afternoon, Narcy flew back to Fort Lauderdale. The Robert police called the Florida department of law enforcement to put her under surveillance. Narcy immediately hired armed guards for her home and went to her local bank, asking to withdraw the hundred thousand dollars in cash that she had deposited in New York.

When the bank teller told her they didn't keep that much cash on hand. She settled for half in cash and the rest into cashier's checks. She also decided to kick Mae Abad out of the guest house where she had been living. She came after her daughter with a crowbar it's caught on her own camera security footage.

Narcy strikes may who threw her arm up to protect her head, getting a nasty bruise on her bicep may filed a complaint with Fort Lauderdale police against Narcy for aggravated battery. They claim to have investigated the complaint, but took no action, which is strange as the incident was caught on camera.

Meanwhile, Narcy flew back to New York and gave one cashier's check to her brother, Carlos, presumably for him to give to crystal ball and the other cashier's check to an attorney named Howard Tanner for legal services. She was anticipating being charged in New York, but also under federal law. She had just laundered that money on July 16th, the Florida department of law enforcement served a seven page warrant on the Del Mar place house.

On the same day, reporter Julie Brown with the Miami Herald dug up Ben Novak Jr's original divorce petition from 2000. This was incredibly damaging for Narcy. As it outlined bins fears that she would kill him and included the quote. If I can't have you, no one will. The men who helped me we'll come back and finish the job that one day the Miami Herald as the Brower County medical examiner for Bernice Novak's autopsy report.

Reporter Julie Brown was dogged in her attempt to show that Narcy was also responsible for Bernice's murder. That hadn't actually been investigated as a murder. The Fort Lauderdale police still insisted they would not reopen Bernice Novak's case. After the 2002 home invasion, the Fort Lauderdale police department had seemingly wanted to wash their hands of the Novak family.

They had obstinately refused to investigate. Bernice has death, despite pleas from Ben and many other friends and family. But on

July 21st, an anonymous letter was sent to the Miami Springs police department. It was five pages, handwritten and broken English. The writer accused narcing Novak and her brother crystal ball, the, of orchestrating the murders of Bernice and Ben Novak jr.

The letter writer knew enough details like about Bernice has previous fall, that the letter was deemed genuine. Police felt it was written by an older religious woman, as there were many lines. Like I write out of respect for God. She wrote that Narcy Novak would stop at nothing to get her hands on the Novak

Millions police took the letter very seriously. But it would take three years to identify the author who was indeed Darcy's older sister, Leticia, Toronto, who was very religious and was horrified at what her siblings had done. Meanwhile, the news stories weren't limited to Miami or New York, the associated press had picked up the story and it was now a salacious national scandal during all of this.

No one had claimed been now that Junior's body from the New York morgue. His aunt Maxine, Phil was shocked and told the press quote, here is the Prince of fountain blue and he's being treated no better than a homeless. No one could claim Ben's body except Narcy who was his legal next of kin actor, Kelsey grammar even spoke up offering to pay for Ben's funeral, but Narcy refused.

Narcy was more than willing to let Ben sit on ice. She worked moving money and removing valuable items like Bernice's jewelry collection from Ben safe deposit boxes. Her name was not on the boxes, but she calmed a bank employee into giving her access. The employee was not aware of Ben's murder. And Narcy promised he would be by that afternoon to add her name.

She also moved all of his Batman collection out of the warehouses, where it was stored into new warehouses. It was the second largest collection in the world and worth millions. She had, again, conned to the warehouse men and to believing Ben was alive and aware of them. Yes, July 29th, nor see petition Broward County circuit court to be named as executor to Ben's estate.

She also requested to have her husband cremated. The court refused the second request as it was specified and Ben's will that he was to be buried in his family's mausoleum and Queens, New York on August 7th may abide filed her own petition, objecting to her mother being named executor of Ben's estate.

This would kick off years of legal battles ever been. No that Junior's fortune. By August 14th may persuaded a circuit court judge to freeze Ben know that Junior's assets as well as remove, nor see as executor of his estate while his murder investigation was still underway. Broward County hired probate attorney Douglas Hoffman to act as curator of Ben's estate.

And his first action was to arrange for Ben Novak's burial. But after numerous hearings with Hoffman trying to recover money and items that Narcy had already taken, she did finally agree to add here to his will and let him be buried. Ben, now that jr was laid to rest on September 2nd, 2009, his aunt Maxine, Phil spoke to the press and said she felt at peace, but quote, she let him lay there for 52 days.

And then she said, she heard that Kelsey grammar had indeed paid for the funeral. During these weeks, police were starting to uncover holes in Narcy story. They questioned crystal ball. And while at his house noticed Western union payments to two men, one was Alejandro Garcia on August 31st crystal ball, aware that he was about to be implicated called a New York investigator and said he had overheard another man arranging to give money to Alejandro Garcia at a Miami gas station.

The morning after the meeting. By September 10th, may Abad took the gloves off and outright accused her mother of murdering her stepfather in probate court. Now crystal ball, and Narcy wanted may abide dead. They had already tried to plan to get her arrested weeks before when she first petitioned the court, the plan was to plant drugs in her car and tip off the police, but it never happened.

Crystal ball called up Ella hundred Garcia and told him he had another job for him. Despite much pressure from rye Brook detectives, Fort Lauderdale police announced in mid-October that they had no intention of reopening Bernice Novak's case. But now the FBI had stepped into the investigation. November investigators were ready to arrest Ella hundre Garcia for Ben know that Junior's murder Gonzalez were identified on hotel security footage after crystal balls tip.

The police still believed that Narcy and her brother hired the Hitman, but they needed the killers to roll on them. First. They arrested Alejandro Garcia and then Joel Gonzalez, but they took their time. They wanted the case against Narcy and crystal ball to be airtight in March. The FBI seized assets from Ben Novak, Junior's estate and Barden RC from taking the title of the Batmobile and other antique cars, boats, and other expensive items.

The Miami Herald pointed out that there stilled warrants meant that the FBI violent crimes task force was gathering evidence to prove that Narcy Novak had been involved in a criminal conspiracy for financial gain. Investigators now realized that with Alejandro Garcia cooperating with the government, that mayabroad's life was in danger, but witness protection paperwork takes months.

And so they incredibly told her just to be careful and protect herself. A detective from Westchester County who had investigated Ben's murder. Alison Carpentier loaned may have bought $5,000 to relocate herself and her children. The detective would lose her job for this kindness once Narcy and crystal ball went to trial, and it was revealed finally on July 8th, almost a year to the day of Ben's murder.

The FBI arrested Narcy Novak at 6:00 AM. While her brother crystal ball valleys was arrested in New York at the exact same time. Both Alejandro Garcia and Joel Gonzales had sang light canaries. The indictment charged them with conspiracy to commit interstate domestic violence and stalking because according to author, John Glatt, there was no federal murder statute they could use at the time.

Interestingly, this law was instituted in 1994 after the murder of Nicole Brown Simpson, and it meant life and present for Narcy and crystal ball. If they were convicted. Finally after the federal charges and arrests, the Fort Lauderdale police agreed to reopen Bernice Novak's case examiner read Alejandro Garcia statement.

He realized it matched Bernice, his injuries. Exactly. And now changed her death ruling to homicide from his jail cell. Crystal ball tried to have Ella Hondros Garcia killed before he could testify. He wanted Joel Gonzalez to Shiv him in prison. But Gonzalez refuse and then turned him in on April 5th, an 11 count superseding indictment filed in federal court on Narcy Novak and crystal ball Felice for orchestrating Bernice Novak's death, racketeering, attempting to murder Alejandro Garcia, and Narcy was also charged with money laundering for the money she moved from the bank right after Ben's murder.

Finally on September 20th, more superseding indictments were filed against Narcea and Cristobal. The six felony counts included murder and aid of racketeering. The charge carried a mandatory life sentence without parole. The trial of Narcy Novak and crystal began on April 23rd, 2010, and would last for a dramatic nine weeks.

Alejandro Garcia made an excellent witness with total recall. He told it in a measured matter of fact, way of how he brutally murdered the elderly Bernice Novak, as well as Ben Novak, jr. Joel Gonzales was also an excellent witness explaining how Narcy handed him the pillow to try and smother her husband and that she did give the order to kill him.

Gonzalez also revealed that crystal ball valleys had offered him $150,000 to implicate may Abad rather than Narcy Novak cell phone evidence from Northeast burner phone to crystal ball. And then the two hit men only added more credibility to the Hitman's testimony. There were literally hundreds of calls between the siblings and the months leading up to the murders Narcy know that declined to testify in her own defense.

That crystal ball stupidly took the stand and the prosecution handily countered every lie with video surveillance, bank statements, phone records, and many other pieces of evidence by the end of the trial, 60 witnesses had testified and some 300 pieces of evidence were entered into the record. During the prosecution's closing argument, crystal ball stood up and again, accused may abide and was sternly admonished by the judge.

He also tried to change his plea in the 11th hour and wanted to testify again, claiming he would tell the truth. This time the judge refused the trial was over Narcy Novak now declined to be in the courtroom. As the verdicts were read, she had spent the entire trial stoically silent insisting on wearing her prison.

Orange jumpsuit when even may have bought, had offered to bring her clothes to wear. On July 20th, the jurors found both Novak and valleys guilty on all counts, except one, which was the violent crime in aid of racketeering. This was because the government had never found Ben's gold bracelet and as nothing else was taken from the hotel room that morning, they could not prove it was a robbery.

So they were technically found not guilty of the felony murder of Ben Novak jr. But Narcy Novak was found guilty of 12 of the federal counts and crystal ball. The Lees was found guilty of 14 at their sentencing. The lead prosecutor characterize the siblings as pathological liars and dangerous psychopaths.

The judge agreed sentencing them both to life in prison without parole. In following years, the two would try to turn on each other to cut new deals, but it didn't work. And now they're the criminal proceedings were over the battle in probate court for Ben Novak jr. His estate was just getting started.

The daughters of his aunt Maxine, Phil, who had since passed away Meredith and Lisa, Phil sued trying to extend Florida Slayer statute to Narcisse daughter and grandchildren in Florida. As in many States, one cannot profit from a crime, meaning you cannot kill someone and still inherit their estate. The field stance was that may have bought and her children could still deposit money into narcissist prison account.

And the Slayer statute should apply to them as well. The fields also sought to have been know that junior second, well revoked the will, where he had left everything to Narcy except for caudal souls for his mother may abide and her children, they charged that Ben Novak jr. Was under duress with threat of physical harm when he signed the second will.

The case went all the way to the Florida district court of appeals who ruled on July 29th, 2015, that the Slayer statute did not apply to Narcis daughter or grandchildren though. Many legal experts feel the statute should be amended as it has been in other States, the Florida court held to the letter of the current law and granted may Abott and her children been know that Jr's entire estate.

However, they did remand for further proceedings on the second charge that Ben know that juniors will, should be revoked because it was made while he was under the threat of physical harm or duress.

I did, however, hear back from Douglas Hoffman, the attorney for Ben know that Junior's a state that the will was not revoked. Litigation was concluded and the estate was closed. As there is no public record of this. And mr. Hoffman did not elaborate. I believe a private settlement was reached between Maya bod and the fields in your sense, Ben know that Junior's relatives have not made any public comments that may abide has been available for any and every interview and print or television.

It still makes me wonder about all of her motivations. She had nothing to do with the murder of her stepfather, but she fought like a cat to maintain control of his estate. And she continues to profit by granting so many television appearances. But despite the ugly battle for the Novec fortune, there is only one true villain in this entire family saga.

And that is Narcissa Elise Novak Narcissa is a named arrived from the Greek God Narcissus, which as we know is the root word for narcissism. Narcy Novak is the ultimate narcissist only caring for herself and her own greed with NOLA, for anyone not even her own daughter. It was characterized as a psychopath in court, which as she has shown no empathy or remorse for her actions seems fair.

ANOTHER VOLUME IS IN PROGRESS

Thank you for reading this book. Hope you've enjoyed reading these interesting true crime cases.

Another volume of Real Unsolved Case Files is in progress.

ABOUT THE AUTHOR

Being a big fan of true crime, Rachel always looking to figure out something mysterious happening around the world.

Every good story contains an element of mystery. It's in our human DNA to ask why—to solve the puzzle, to discover the secret. It's what pushes humanity forward. Everyone wants to be the first to figure it out.

Real Unsolved Case Files

CPSIA information can be obtained
at www.ICGtesting.com
Printed in the USA
LVHW022301070522
718181LV00016B/1344